1000 DIFFICULT BIBLE Q[illegible] ANSW[illegible]

By

George H. Sandison
and Staff

BAKER BOOK HOUSE
Grand Rapids, Michigan

From the edition printed by
The World Syndicate Company
Paperback edition issued 1976
by Baker Book House
ISBN: 0-8010-8071-1

PRINTED BY DICKINSON BROTHERS, INC.
GRAND RAPIDS, MICHIGAN
1976

FOREWORD

THIS volume is the outcome of Biblical research covering a period of almost a quarter of a century, and represents the combined labors of careful and painstaking scholars, pastors, professors and theologians of all denominations. Their investigations have been conducted along the lines followed by the ablest orthodox expositors of the present day. To the average student and Bible reader, it will be found a valuable means of reference, and a source of constant edification, enlightenment and education.

In the domain of practical everyday Christian living, and particularly in dealing with problems that are constantly arising for consideration, it will be found especially helpful. Many of the questions with which it deals are such as are familiar to the average man or woman, and they will find in it material aid toward their solution.

In view of the steadily growing interest in all forms of Bible study, and with a sincere desire to be of service to the multitudes who yearn to know more of God's Word, and to place at their disposal a means of real help which we are led to hope will be welcomed and appreciated, the present volume is respectfully submitted by the compiler.

Difficult Bible Questions

FACTS ABOUT THE BIBLE

1. Who Wrote the Various Books in the Bible?

Genesis, Exodus, Leviticus, Numbers, Deuteronomy —Moses (scholarly opinions differ here, but so far no thoroughly convincing arguments have been advanced to disprove the Mosaic authorship of large portions of these books); Joshua—Joshua (also ascribed to Phineas, Eleazar, Samuel and Jeremiah); Judges—ascribed by Jewish tradition to Samuel; Ruth—unknown; I and II Samuel—unknown (probably the work of Samuel, Nathan and others); I and II Kings —unknown; I and II Chronicles—probably Ezra; Ezra—probably Ezra; Nehemiah—Nehemiah; Esther —probably Mordecai, or Ezra; Job—uncertain (has been attributed to Moses, or Job); the Psalms—David, Moses, and others; Proverbs—Solomon and others; Ecclesiastes—formerly ascribed to Solomon, now thought by many to belong to a later period; Song of Solomon—Solomon; Isaiah—Isaiah; Jeremiah—Jeremiah; Lamentations—Jeremiah; the remaining books of the Old Testament were written by the prophets whose names they bear, with the probable exception of Jonah; Matthew—Matthew; Mark—Mark; Luke—Luke; John—John; Acts—Luke; Romans to Philemon—Paul; Hebrews—unknown (has been ascribed to Paul, Luke, Apollos, Barnabas); James—James; I and II Peter—Peter; I, II and III John—John; Revelation—John.

2. Inspiration of the Bible.

The question is asked, "How can I know that the Bible is inspired?" Even in this late day, when the number of Christians has multiplied from a mere handful to four hundred and seventy millions, or fully one-fourth of the entire population of the globe, there are people who doubt the inspiration of the Bible. At different times during the last twenty centuries assaults have been made against the Sacred Book, which Gladstone termed the "Impregnable Rock of Holy Scripture," but without avail. It has a firmer hold on the hearts of men than in any previous age. Mr. Moody, the greatest of American evangelists, was once asked whether he regarded the Bible as inspired, and his answer was brief and to the point: "I know the Bible is inspired," he said, "because it inspires me!" There are countless thousands who will echo this answer and whose lives have been transformed by the same inspiration. Not only the great religious scholars, but the masters of secular literature regard the Bible as unapproachable in its high standard of expression, its magnificent imagery, the transcendent nobility of its rhetoric, the authority with which it appeals to the hearts of men, the universality of its application and the power it exercises over the souls of men. It bears within itself the evidence of inspiration, and wherever it is known and read and its precepts followed, its influence is uplifting and inspiring. The theory of inspiration does not exclude, but rather implies, human agency, however. "Holy men of God spake as they were moved by the Holy Spirit." (II Peter 1:21).

3. What Is Higher Criticism?

The ordinary study or criticism is directed to finding out the meaning of the passages, their correct translation and their significance and bearing on doctrines. The higher critics go above and back of all that, applying to the books of the Bible the same tests and methods of examination as are applied to other ancient books. They try to find out who were really the authors of the books and when they were written and whether any changes have been made in them since they were written. This latter question they try to solve by a close examination of the text. When they find, for example, such an expression as "There was no king in Israel in those days" (Judges 17:6), they conclude that that sentence was inserted as explanatory, by some one who edited the book after the contemporaneous historian had finished it. Or to take an example of a different kind: There is a statement in Psalm 51:16 that God desires not sacrifice, while in the nineteenth verse it is said that he will be pleased with sacrifice. The explanation the higher critics give is that probably the latter verse was added later, by some priest who did not wish the people to cease bringing sacrifices. The best scholars of the present day believe that many of the conclusions reached by the higher critics are erroneous, and that others are mere guesses for which there is not sufficient evidence.

4. What Are the Proofs of Bible Authenticity?

"Can we prove the authenticity of the Bible by outside evidence?" is a frequent question. The authenticity of the Bible is being proved by the old records on monuments, by tablets recently deciphered, and by discoveries in Bible lands. That is if by authenticity you mean its historical truth. As to inspiration, the best evidence is its effects. The man who loves the Bible and tries to conduct his life according to its precepts is a better man for the effort. The Bible-reading nation advances in the best line of civilization, caring for its poor and afflicted, and becoming in all ways better. Another evidence of its being inspired is the revelation it gives a man of himself, holding a mirror to his gaze by which he recognizes himself. Another evidence is its survival. No book was ever more violently attacked, no book was ever more misused, yet it has outlived the attacks of foes and the faults of friends and is read today more widely than ever. These are a few of the reasons for believing it came from God.

5. Can We Find Any Reference to Christ in Contemporaneous Secular Writers?

Yes. There are references to Christ in connection with Christians, by several historians. Tacitus, who was prætor under Domitian in A. D. 88, only fifty-eight years after the Crucifixion, refers to Christ (Annal XV:44). Pliny the younger, who was tribune in Syria about the same time, also refers to him (Epistle X:97). There are also references in Lucian, who lived about the middle of the second century. He states explicitly the fact of Christ having been crucified. Suetonius and Eusebius also refer to Christ. Besides these evidences, there was the persecution of the Christians under Nero, which is recorded by all historians. Nero died A. D. 68, only thirty-eight years after the Crucifixion. It is therefore clear that there were many Christians before that time. How could the sect have come into existence without a founder? If you saw an oak growing in a place where there was no tree fifty years before, you would suspect that some one had planted an acorn there, and if four men told you how, when and by whom it was planted, you would be prepared to believe them. So there is good reason for believing the Gospel narratives, when you read in secular history of the existence of the Christian Church fifty years after the Crucifixion. Their stories are a credible explanation of a well-established fact.

6. Does the Bible Teach Science?

It is not a scientific textbook, nor was it written to teach science, but religion. The discrepancies between the story of creation as given in the Bible and that given by the scientists are very much such as we should find in two descriptions of a great battle, if one of them was written by a clergyman who knew nothing of military tactics, and the other by a military expert who knew nothing of religion. The important fact for us—the fact that is of more momentous interest than all the discoveries of science—is that God made the universe. For this knowledge we are not indebted to science, which has not yet attained it, but we do get it from the Bible. A person who wants to know the latest discoveries of science as to geology and astronomy, should study the recent books of science;

but if he wants to know the way to God and eternal happiness, he should go to the Bible. Each has its own sphere.

7. Why Should We Believe the Scriptures?

Some people answer this query by saying that the reason is found in the fact that the Bible is the only book handed down to us through the ages. That is not the best answer. Some ancient writings, like the Vedas, for instance, are almost as ancient as the Bible. And many tablets and monuments are in existence containing words written as long ago as the writings of the Scriptures. There are many powerful arguments for the Bible, but the greatest is that every person who will really study it finds that it does tell the truth about the human soul. When a man reads in an arithmetic that two and two make four, he does not stop to ask himself why he should believe the arithmetic. He knows instinctively and intuitively that the arithmetic is telling him the truth. So when an honest man studies the Bible he finds it full of truths about himself. The Bible tells him he is a sinner, and he knows that is true. The Bible tells him about God, and he finds in his heart a deep conviction that just such a God exists. The Bible offers forgiveness, and the man knows he needs it. Step by step, and point by point, the Bible shows the man what he is and what he needs and points the way to finding the fulfillment of his needs and desires. People find in the Bible help for bearing their trials, power to resist temptation, assurance of immortality and friendship with God. A man who never saw the Bible before, when he reads of God in it, realizes that he always needed and longed for God, but did not know how to find him till the Bible showed him the way. Particularly does it show him how to find God in Christ. That, after all, is the supreme mission of the Bible—to lead men to Christ. But, again, taking the Bible as literature, we find that it hangs together, that it bears within itself the evidence that it is true. Start with the writings of Paul. Here is a level-headed, highly educated, practical man who has left to the world's literature certain letters to groups of friends. These letters tell about Paul's personal knowledge of Christ, his personal friendship for him, his personal endeavors to forward the work of Christ which he had formerly antagonized until Christ himself appeared to him and set him right. Paul tells of becoming acquainted later with men who had known Christ in the flesh—Peter, James, John and others. We find that these men also wrote about Jesus, John writing three letters and a narrative of his life; Peter writing two letters, and apparently giving much of the information to his nephew Mark, who wrote another version of the life of Jesus. Luke, another friend of Paul, and probably also a personal friend of Jesus, wrote another version of his life and wrote the history of what his apostles did through his power after he had risen from the dead and gone back to the heavenly world. These were all good, honest, intelligent men. We may believe what they wrote about Christ and his salvation, just as we believe what Cæsar wrote about the Gallic Wars. Further, we find that Christ came from a people whose history is recorded in the books of the Bible and whose prophets uttered messages from God. Peter connects the messages of the prophets with those of himself and the other apostles in II Peter 3:2: "That ye may be mindful of the words which were spoken before by the holy prophets, and of the commandment of us the apostles of our Lord and Saviour." The Bible holds together about the person of Christ as the great divine-human document which reveals him to the world.

8. Has Bible History Been Substantiated?

Yes, to a very notable extent by investigations in Bible lands. Excavations of ancient Babylonian tablets have corroborated the Biblical story of the Flood. The discovery of Assyrian inscriptions has proved the identity of Sargon, one of the greatest of the kings of that nation (see Isa. 20:1-4); identification of the site of Nineveh and of the Tower of Babel or "Birs Nimrud." Many facts concerning kings, nations, cities and events have been brought to light in these ancient records of brick, stone or papyrus, confirming Scripture history.

9. Were the Gospels Written by the Men Whose Names They Bear?

Presumption based on internal evidence is in favor of that theory. There has been no serious question as to the authorship of Matthew. Mark is supposed to have derived his knowledge of the events he recorded from Peter. Our knowledge of Peter's character leads us to believe that if he undertook to write a Gospel it would be such an one as the Gospel according to Mark. Such an expression as that in Mark 14:72, "When he thought thereon he wept," implies an intimate knowledge of him such as would be written by Peter himself, or by a close associate. The introduction to Luke's Gospel shows that many Gospels were in existence when Luke wrote, and as he knew of them, he may have availed himself of the material they contained. His remark about writing "in order" suggests compilation. The authorship of the fourth Gospel has been hotly disputed, chiefly because some critics held that the writer of Revelation could not have written the elegant and cultured Greek of the Gospel. The majority of the commentators now, however, are in favor of the belief that John wrote it.

10. When Were the Gospels Written?

The genuineness of the four Gospels rests upon better authority than that of any other ancient writings. It is the general conclusion of the most eminent scholars that all four were written during the latter half of the first century. Before the end of the second century they were in general use and acceptance as one collection. They are mentioned by Tertullian, in a book written about A. D. 208, as being the work of two apostles and two disciples of apostles. Marcion also mentions their apostolic origin. Origen (who lived A. D. 185-253) refers to them as "the four elements of the church's faith." Theophilus, Bishop of Antioch (A. D. 168), also mentions the Gospels in his writings, and Jerome tells us that Theophilus arranged the four into one work. Tatian (who died about A. D. 170) compiled a Harmony of the Gospels. Justin Martyr (A. D. 99-165) gives many quotations from the Gospels. Many other witnesses might be cited to the same purpose. None of the original manuscripts are now in existence.

11. Curiosities of the Scriptures.

In the Bible the word "Lord" is found 1,853 times. The word "Jehovah" 6,855 times.

The word "Reverend" but once, and that in the 9th verse of Psalm 111.

The 8th verse of the 97th Psalm is the middle verse of the Bible.

The 9th verse of the 8th chapter of Esther is the longest.

The 35th verse of the 11th chapter of St. John is the shortest.

In the 107th Psalm four verses are alike: The 8th, 15th, 21st and 31st.

Ezra 7:21 contains all the letters of the alphabet except J.

Each verse of the 136th Psalm ends alike.

No names or words of more than six syllables are found in the Bible.

The 37th chapter of Isaiah and 19th chapter of II Kings are alike.

The word "girl" occurs but twice in the Bible, and that in the 3d verse of the 3d chapter of Joel and Zechariah 8:5.

There are found in both books of the Bible 3,538,-483 letters, 773,693 words, 31,373 verses, 1,189 chapters and 66 books.

The 26th chapter of the Acts of the Apostles is the finest chapter to read.

The most beautiful chapter is the 23d Psalm.

The four most inspiring promises are John 14:2-6, 37; Matthew 11:28; Psalm 37:4.

The 1st verse of the 51st chapter of Isaiah is the one for the new convert.

All who flatter themselves with vain boasting should read the 6th chapter of Matthew.

All humanity should learn the 6th chapter of St. Luke from the 20th verse to its ending.

12. Symbols of Christ and Christianity

"What symbols are used for both Christ and his people?" is a frequent question. There are six symbols used for both Christ and his people.

1. A BRANCH. *For Christ,* in Is. 11:1-4, "A branch out of his roots shall bear fruit," and "with the breath of his lips shall he slay the wicked;" in Zech. 6:12, 13, Heb. 3:1-4, Is. 4:2, Zech. 3:8, Jer. 23:5, 33:15, 16. *For his People.* John 15:5, "Ye are the branches;" Is. 60:21, "The people also shall be all righteous, the branch of my planting;" also, Rom. 11:16, Ps. 80:11, 15.

2. LIGHT. *For Christ.* In John 8:12, Jesus spake, "I am the light of the world;" also, in John 9:5, Luke 2:32, and I John 1:5, "God is light." *For his People.* Phil. 2:15, "Among whom ye are seen as lights in the world," Matt. 5:14, Eph. 5:8, Acts 13:47, Is. 42:6, Prov. 4:18.

3. A STONE. *For Christ* in I Pet. 2:4, 6, 7, 8, "A living stone," "A chief corner-stone," "the stone which the builders rejected," "a stone of stumbling;" also, Ps. 118:22, Eph. 2:20, Matt. 21:42. *For his People.* I Pet. 2:5, "Ye also as living stones are built up a spiritual house;" also, Eph. 2:21, 22.

4. A TEMPLE. Used *for Christ* in Rev. 21:22, "And I saw no temple therein for the Lord God the Almighty and the Lamb are the temple thereof;" also, John 2:19, 21. *For his People.* I Cor. 3:16, 17, "For

the temple of God is holy which temple ye are," and I Cor. 6:19, II Cor. 6:16.

5. A SUN. *For Christ.* Ps. 84:11, "For the Lord God is a sun and shield;" also, Mal. 4:2, Rev. 21:23, 22:5. *For his People.* Judges 5:31, "Let them that love thee be as the sun;" also, Matt. 13:43.

6. A STAR. *For Christ.* Rev. 22:16, "I am the bright and morning star," II Pet. 1:19, "Until the day dawn and the day-star arise in your hearts;" also, Num. 24:17. *For his People.* Dan. 12:1-3, "And they that be wise shall shine," "and they that turn many to righteousness as the stars for ever and ever."

13. What Are the Sacred or Symbolical Numbers?

There are certain numbers employed in Scripture that are known as sacred or symbolical numbers. Among these are *seven* (perfection), as the triune symbol of deity and the four quarters of the earth; *forty,* a "round number," signifying duration, distance, quantity; *ten* (completeness); *five,* as used in offerings etc.; *four,* related to the quarters of the globe, the shape of the holy of holies in the temple, etc.; *three,* symbol of supreme divinity; *twelve,* which derives its significance from the twelve tribes and which has been called the "square number," the "zodiacal number," the "apostolic number." 12x12 means, symbolically, fixity and completeness, and taken a thousand-fold, it gives the grand multiple of 144,000 (otherwise a countless multitude), one thousand symbolizing the world wholly pervaded by the divine—a world redeemed!

14. Why Is Seven Used More than Any Other Number?

The symbolism of "seven" should be traced back to the symbolism of its component elements, "three" and "four," which represent divinity and humanity. Hence, "seven" represents the union between God and man. Among the Persians, the Greeks, the ancient Indians, the Romans, and all nations where seven days in the week were recognized, the influence of the number seven prevailed. It was called by Cicero "the knot and cement of all things," because in "seven" the spiritual and natural world were comprehended in one idea. Some writers claim that the Hebrews borrowed it from their heathen neighbors. The Sabbath, being the seventh day, suggested seven as the appointment for all sacred periods. The seventh month was ushered in by the Feast of Trumpets; seven weeks was the interval between the Passover and the Pentecost, and so on, recognizing seven as the symbol of all connected with the Divinity.

15. What Significance Attaches to the Frequent Use of Forty?

It is not merely an arbitrary period or a "round number," but is chosen to convey the sense of fullness. Some of its prominent Scriptural uses are: Moses was forty days on the mount (Ex. 24:18, etc.); Elijah, strengthened by angel food, fasted for forty days (I Kings 19:8); the rain of the flood fell for forty days (Gen. 7:12); Noah opened the window of the ark after forty days (Gen. 8:6); the spies spent forty days in searching Canaan (Num. 13:25); Moses twice fasted and prayed for forty days (Deu. 9:18-25); Ezekiel bore the iniquities of Judah forty days (Eze. 4:6); Nineveh was allowed forty days to repent (Jonah 3:4); the Israelites wandered forty years in the wilderness (Num. 34:33); Goliath defied Saul's army for forty days (I Sam. 17:16); forty days was the period of embalming (Gen. 50:3); the Lord fasted for forty days (Matt. 4:2, etc.); the arisen Lord was seen for forty days (Acts 1:3); the Jews were forbidden to inflict more than forty stripes (Deu. 25:3). It is noteworthy that Jerusalem was destroyed forty years after Christ's ascension, and tradition says Jesus was forty hours in the tomb. Lent lasts for forty days, as does also quarantine. St. Swithin betokens forty days' rain, while many ancient laws concerning physicians, knights, husbands, wives, widows, sanctuary privileges, fines, etc., all cluster about this number.

16. Who Compiled the Old Testament?

It is claimed that the books of the Old Testament were collected and arranged under the supervision of Ezra, though modern scholarship disputes the claim. The epistles of Paul to the various churches were collected and incorporated with the other epistles and the Gospels and Revelation into one book during the first half of the second century, and as we learn from Eusebius, were in general use soon after the year 300 A. D.

17. What Are the Omitted Books of the Bible?

The excluded books are known as "Apocrypha," and are as follows: I Esdras, II Esdras, Tobit, Judith, several chapters of Esther which are found neither in the Hebrew nor the Chaldee, The Wisdom of Solomon, The Wisdom of Jesus, son of Sirach, or Ecclesiasticus, Baruch, The Song of the Three Holy Children, The History of Susanna, The History of the Destruction of Bel and the Dragon, The Prayer of Manasseh, I Maccabees, II Maccabees. They were excluded by the early Christian Church on the ground that they were of doubtful authority and not tending to spiritual edification. This decision has never been reversed, although in some periods of the Church's history a number of the apocryphal writings were published in smaller type after the regular books in the Bible. At one time the volume of apocryphal writings was even larger than the genuine, but very many of them, being rejected, quickly perished.

18. What Are the Famous Songs of the Bible?

The great songs of the Old Testament, besides the Psalms and certain metrical passages in Job, are: Lamech's Sword Song, Gen. 4:23, 24; Noah's Song, Gen. 9:25-27; Moses' and Miriam's Song, Ex. 15:1-19, 21; War Songs, etc., Num. 21:14, 15, 17, 18, 27-30; Moses' Prophetic Song, Deut. 32:1-43; Song of Deborah and Barak, Judg. 5:2-21; Samson's Riddle Song, Judg. 15:16; Hannah's Magnificat, I Sam. 2:1-10; David's Song of the Bow, II Sam. 1:19-27; David's Song over Abner, II Sam. 3:33, 34; David's Thanksgiving, I Chron. 16:8-36; Hezekiah's Song, Isa. 38:10-20; Jonah's Prayer Song, Jonah 2:2-9; Habakkuk's Prayer Song, Hab. 3:2-19; and the four original songs in the New Testament: Luke 1:46-55; Luke 1:68-80; Luke 2:14; Luke 2:20-33.

19. Who Was the Author of Revelation?

"Was the Book of Revelation written by the same John who wrote the Gospel and the Epistle?" This question has been long disputed by scholars. Dionysius, in A. D. 240, was one of the earliest to express a doubt. It was attributed to John Mark, the companion of Paul and Barnabas and the author of the Gospel of Mark; to John the Presbyter, to Cerinthus, and others. The majority of German scholars agree with Luther in denying that Revelation was written by the apostle. On the other hand, there is internal evidence of John's authorship. His description of himself is in the manner of John. The apostle was the only man of prominence of that name who was banished to Patmos. The addresses to the seven churches of Asia show a knowledge of them consistent with the fact that the apostle was their overseer. On the whole, therefore, there seems good reason to believe that it was written by the Apostle John. The differences in the style of the Gospel and the Revelation, which are very marked, doubtless first gave rise to the doubt of the apostolic authorship. These are accounted for by the age of the author and by his perturbation of mind under the excitement of the visions.

OLD TESTAMENT PERSONS AND THINGS

20. What Were the Meaning and Result of Abraham's Sacrifice?

The story of Abraham will ever be an important one, and particularly that part of it dealing with the memorable doings at the place he named "Jehovah-jireh," where, as related in Genesis 22, he showed his wonderful obedience to God. Whatever may be conjectured to the contrary, the record in Genesis is clear and unmistakable. It was a test of Abraham's faith in God. Some critics want to know why, if God is all knowing, he should have said to Abraham: "For now I know that thou fearest God" (Gen. 22:12). The problem of foreknowledge is an extremely difficult one, and discussion about it is usually fruitless. God in this case speaks of the test of Abraham as though it had been an experiment. He proved him and found him firm in faith and perfect in obedience. It was in obedience to the Lord's command that he stood ready to offer up his son Isaac, and not because he himself had chosen such a sacrifice, in order to be like his idolatrous neighbors, who offered up their children to Moloch. Genesis 22:2 dismisses this latter suggestion altogether.

The immediate effect of Abraham's successful test was the great blessing which God bestowed on him (verse 16), which, together with God's covenant, made

Abraham the most important Biblical character and his name better known than that of any other human being on earth. All the promises to Abraham have been fulfilled, except the return of his descendants to the promised land. His seed is past all reckoning. Not only have all the Jews been his offspring, but Christians as well are in a sense his spiritual children. Their faith in Christ brings them into his family and makes them heirs of the promises made to him. The land of Canaan was promised to his seed forever. Since they are not in possession of it now we must believe they will return, as many other prophecies also declare. The promise was, however, not made to Abraham alone, but to him and his seed, which includes Christ—to the literal Israel and also to the spiritual Israel. The complete fulfillment of the covenant awaited the coming of Christ, "the seed," concerning whom it was made. See Galatians 3:16.

21. Did Abraham See God in One of the Three Men Who Visited Him?

There is doubtless difficulty in reconciling the passage in Genesis 18 with the statement in John 1:18, that "No man hath seen God at any time." Authorities regarded the Genesis passage as relating to one of the "theophanies" of the Old Testament; that is, a real appearance of God to man. It is believed, however, that these appearances were of Christ the Son, rather than God the Father. The New Testament teaches that Christ existed co-eternally with the Father, and it is not inconceivable that he would at times take the appearance of humanity when he wished especially to make himself known to men. This explanation reconciles all these occurrences with the statement of John that no one has seen God; that is, God the Father. Christ is the personal manifestation of God to man.

22. How Are We to Interpret the Miracle at Ajalon?

The passage in Joshua, 10th chapter, describing the miracle of the sun and moon at the time of the battle in the vale of Ajalon, has been much discussed. Some commentators hold that it is a passage in which the inspired historian departs from his narrative to introduce a highly poetic quotation, in other words, a poetical figure of speech, not to be interpreted literally—as though one might say that "God and all nature fought on the side of Joshua." Again, the reference to the poetical book of Jasher as the source of this passage lends color to this explanation (see verse 13). Others prefer the literal view, regarding it as a miracle in which the hours when sun and moon were both visible (the sun on the heights of Gibeon at noon and the moon in the valley) were extended into a whole day, or twelve hours of light (see Macdonald's *Principia and the Bible*), the continued radiance of both orbs lighting the battleground. Still another interpretation is that the sun and moon were heavily obscured by storm clouds (see verse 11), and that Joshua's prayer was that they should withhold their light and that the gloom or semi-darkness of the storm might last until the battle was fought, giving the Israelites the advantage of a surprise with smaller numbers, the strength of which the enemy could not properly estimate.

23. Did Adam and Eve Actually Eat Fruit, or Is the Saying a Parable?

The only source of information is the Bible narrative and it contains no intimation that it is to be understood otherwise than literally. Theologians who have preferred to regard the narrative as a parable or allegory have usually been led to do so by the suggestion that the eating of fruit which was "good for food," and "pleasant to the eyes," and was moreover within reach, was an offense too venial to have been justly visited with a punishment so severe and far-reaching. The objection, however, is not well founded, because it ignores the main point involved. The gravity of the offense consisted, not in the act itself, but in the fact that Adam and Eve in committing it were consciously and wilfully violating God's explicit and emphatic command. They were punished for disobedience. Even if we should hold that it took some other form than the actual and literal eating of fruit, the principle is the same. There is no valid reason for rejecting the Bible narrative or putting any other construction on the words than is there implied.

24. Was Adam a Red Man?

Adam means "red" and so also does the word Edom, both having relation to the ruddiness of flesh and the color of the clayey soil. (See Gen. 2:7.) Some commentators hold that Adam, the first man, was probably of the complexion of the Arabs, or Edomites, ruddy though dark, while others take a different view. No definite theory can be formed on this subject.

25. What Language Did Adam and Eve Speak?

There are many mundane things beyond the reach of present human knowledge and the site of Eden and the language of our first parents are among the number. Some philologists have ventured the conjecture that the primeval language must have been a simple vocabulary whose formation is indicated in Gen. 2:19, and which was strictly limited to the natural requirements of our first progenitors; in other words, signs and sounds apprehensible by the senses. All agree that speech, or the power of expressing emotions, or desires, was coeval with the creation of man. The earliest monuments and inscriptions yet discovered do not reach as far back into antiquity as the confusion of tongues at Babel (about B. C. 2200), previous to which (Gen. 2:1), the Biblical record states that "the whole earth was of one language and one speech," although probably there were many variations and dialects, each containing some element of the original tongue. Man's first utterances were probably what philologists term a "physical language," limited to the expression of simple needs and afterwards expanded to meet man's growing experience with his own nature and the world around him.

26. What Became of Aaron's Rod?

It was preserved in the tabernacle and, according to Paul (see Heb. 9:4), it was kept in the Ark, beside the two tablets of stone and the pot of manna. There is no mention of any other receptacle. The statement in I Kings 8:9 implies that by Solomon's time these relics had disappeared. It is possible, however, for a different interpretation to be placed on Deut. 31:26, which may mean that the rod was kept beside the Ark, and not within it.

27. What Was the Name of Cain's Wife?

The name of Cain's wife is nowhere mentioned in the Bible. Arab traditions are preserved in one of which she is called *Azura,* in another *Save,* but these are not seriously regarded by scholars.

28. Who Was David's Mother?

Her name is not given in Scripture. The reference to Abigail, one of the members of Jesse's family, in II Sam. 17:25, is frequently misunderstood. The Nahash there mentioned is either another name for Jesse or it refers to Nahash, king of Ammon, one of whose wives afterward became the wife of Jesse, as stated in the chronicles of the Jewish church.

29. Who Named Eve?

Adam bestowed upon his companion the name of "Eve" (Gen. 3:20).

30. Egypt—Date of Great Famine in:

Began approximately 1875 B. C.

31. Egypt—When Did Joseph Come to?

Believed to be about 1895 B.C.

32. Ham: The First Negro.

Ham, one of the sons of Noah, was the progenitor of the negro race (see Gen. 9:18-27).

33. Jacob—Date of His Journey to Egypt:

About 1874 B. C. Date of his death, 1857 B. C.

34. How Many Walls Had Jerusalem?

There were three walls about Jerusalem. The first was built by David and Solomon; the second, enclosing one of the northern sections of the city, was built by Uzziah, Jotham and Manasseh, and restored by Nehemiah; the third was built by Herod Agrippa, and was intended to enclose the hitherto unprotected suburbs which had grown out from the northern part of the city. According to Josephus, who is not always thoroughly reliable, the circumference of the city, evidently including all the sections enclosed by the three walls he describes, was thirty-three stadia, a little less than four English miles.

35. What Is the Origin of the Name "Jew"?

The appellation "Jew" is derived from the patriarch Judah, and was originally applied to all members of that tribe and also to subjects of the separate kingdom of Judah, in contradistinction to the seceding ten tribes, who retained the name of Israelites. During the captivity and ever since, the term "Jew" seems to have been applied indiscriminately to the whole race.

36. Who Were the Kings of Judah in Succession?

The names of the kings of Judah in their canonical order are: Rehoboam, Abijah, Asa, Jehoshaphat, Jehoram, Ahaziah, Athaliah (queen), Joash, Amaziah, Uzziah, Jotham, Ahaz, Hezekiah, Manasseh, Amon, Josiah, Jehoahaz, Jehoiakim, Jehoiachin, Zedekiah.

37. What Was Manna?

It is supposed that the manna of the Israelites was a saccharine exudation of a species of tamarisk, the sap of which was set flowing by an insect. Several trees yield manna, as the flowering ash of Sicily and the eucalyptus of Australia. In India a sweet exudation comes from the bamboo, and a similar substance is obtained from the sugar-pine and common reed of our own country.

38. What Is the Meaning of "Mizpah"?

Mizpah, or Mizpeh, was the name of several localities in Old Testament history. The word means "a watch-tower," and in literature the whole of the beautiful remark made by Laban to Jacob (Gen. 31:49) has been included in its meaning: "The Lord watch between me and thee when we are absent one from the other."

39. Who Was Moses' Ethiopian Wife?

Commentators hold that the Ethiopian (or Cushite) woman mentioned in Num. 12 as the wife of Moses, against whom Aaron and Miriam complained, was Zipporah. Their opposition is believed to have been caused by jealousy of her relatives and their influence.

40. What Became of Moses' Rod?

There is nothing to show what became of Moses' rod. Aaron's rod, however, is said (in Heb. 9:4) to have been preserved in the sacred Ark of the Jews along with the tables of the law and the pot of manna.

41. What Was the Name of Potiphar's Wife?

Her name is not given in the Bible, although it has been preserved in tradition. The Koran gives her name as Zuleika, and certain Arab writers call her Raïl.

42. What Two Bible Chapters Are Alike?

The two chapters in the Bible that are alike are II Kings 19 and Isa. 37. Both are regarded as the work of Isaiah, relating a series of events which in one book are placed in their proper historical setting and in the other find their true place among the prophecies.

43. Was Sarai a Relative of Abram?

In Gen. 20:12 Abram speaks of Sarai as his half-sister, the daughter of the same father, but not the same mother. The common Jewish tradition referred to by Josephus (*Antiquities* 1, 6, 6) and also by Jerome, is that Sarai was identical with Iscah (see Gen. 11:29), daughter of Haran and sister of Lot, who is called Abraham's "brother."

44. What Is the Meaning of "Selah"?

The word "Selah," which occurs a number of times in the Psalms, was a musical or liturgical sign, whose meaning is unknown. Some regard it as a pause in the music, to mark a transition in the theme or composition. It seems to have no grammatical connection with the sentence after which it appears, and has therefore nothing to do with the meaning of the passage. It was a note to the singers of the psalm, or to those who were accompanying the singing with instruments.

45. What Was the Fate of Amalek?

The Amalekites were a wicked, oppressive, war-like and cruel people. They were powerful and influential and possessed cities in the south of Canaan. (See I Sam. 15:18; Judg. 10:12; Num. 24:7.) They were the first to oppose Israel (Exo. 17:8); Saul overcame them (I Sam. 14:48); David invaded their land (I Sam. 30:1-2), and what was left of them was completely destroyed during the reign of Hezekiah (I Chron. 4:41-43).

46. Who Were Called "The Children of Lot"?

The Ammonites were so called (Deu. 2:19). They were a cruel, covetous, proud, reproachful, vindictive, superstitious and idolatrous nation (see Amos 1:13; Zep. 2:10; Eze. 25:3, 6; Judg. 10:6; Jer. 27:3). Their chief city was Rabbah (II Sam. 12:26-27), where they were governed by hereditary kings (II Sam. 2:20-21). They had various encounters with Israel. With the Philistines they oppressed Israel for eighteen years (Judg. 10:6-9). Saul suceeded against them as did David, and Joab overcame them (I Sam. 11:11; II Sam. 10:7-14). Solomon intermarried with them and introduced their idols into Israel (I Kin. 11:1-5).

47. Who Were the Amorites?

They were one of the seven nations of Canaan and were governed by many independent kings (Josh. 5:1; Josh. 9:10). They originally inhabited a mountain district in the south (Num. 13:29), but later acquired an extensive tract from Moab, east of Jordan (Num. 21:26, 30). They had many strong cities (Num. 32:17, 33). They were profane, wicked and idolatrous (Gen. 15:16; Josh. 24:15). They interfered with Israel (Num. 21:21) at times, again were peaceful, but were finally brought into bondage by Solomon (I Kin. 9:20-21).

48. Where Was the First Altar Built?

In Genesis 8:20 we find the first reference to an altar, namely that one on which Noah offered his sacrifice to God for deliverance from the danger of the Flood. Armenian tradition says it was built on Mount Ararat.

49. What Language Was Spoken at Babel?

The tower of Babel is always an interesting subject for discussion. Philologists are divided concerning the language spoken before the "Confusion of Tongues" at Babel. What little we know of it is learned at second-hand from the testimonies of classical authorities. The Babylonians called the locality of Babel "Barsip" (the Tower of Tongues). A French expedition to Mesopotamia found a clay cake or tablet, which showed that the language at some indefinitely remote period was written in the form of signs and hieroglyphics; but even this was probably long after the dispersion at Babel. What universal language was spoken by prehistoric man thousands of years ago will probably never be definitely known. It may have been Babylonian or Arabic in character, but this is mere conjecture. Supplementary to the Bible record, there are many traditions preserved concerning the Tower and its fate, and these mostly claim for it a Babylonian origin, holding that Babylonia was the cradle of the human race. The site of the tower, according to modern opinion, is identified as *Birs Nimrud*, a huge mound covering gigantic ruins and situated at Felujiah in Mesopotamia; but this identification is by no means certain.

50. What Was the Cause of the Babylonian Captivity?

The political cause of the captivity was the repeated revolt of Judah against the power of Babylon. Relying on the help of Egypt, the king broke his promise of fidelity and refused to pay the tribute he had promised to pay. The prophets uttered many warnings against this suicidal course, and still more against the idolatry and accompanying immorality which prevailed. They assured the nation that, beset as Judah was by dangers from her powerful neighbors, she would be safe, if only she would be faithful to God. But the king and people were continually forsaking him and turning to evil courses, until at last God gave them up to their enemies. This was the spiritual cause of the captivity. The neglect of the Sabbatic years, mentioned II Chronicles 36:21, was only one of many provocations. The writer mentions it incidentally, to show that what the people would not do voluntarily, was done when they were carried away and the land rested seventy years.

51. Why Was God Angry With Balaam?

You need to read the entire story in Numbers 22 to get a complete idea of the situation. Balaam was in the first instance forbidden to go. That answer should have been sufficient for Balaam, but when the princes came with alluring offers of gifts and office and honors, he bade them remain to see whether there might be any fresh instructions. He obviously hoped that permission would be given. He showed his ignorance of God's ways in supposing that Barak's gifts and promises could make any difference to God's decision. His answers to the men also showed that he would like to comply if God would let him. Probably, too, God read in his mind an intention to pronounce the curse for which Barak was willing to pay. Hence the warning by the way, which would brace up his wavering resolution to utter the word of the Lord even if it was disagreeable to Barak.

52. In What Language Was the Message on the Wall to Belshazzar Written?

The words, as they are found in Daniel, are pure Chaldee, and if they appeared in the Chaldean characters on the wall, might have been read by any person present who understood the alphabet of the Babylonian language. Authorities differ as to the language in which the famous *Mene, Mene, Tekel, Upharsin* appeared. Dr. Hales suggests that it may have been in primitive Hebrew; Josephus implies that it was in Greek. Another explanation is that while the observers may have been familiar with the language, its meaning or signification may have been hidden from them, until explained by the prophet.

53. What Are the Essential Facts About Cain?

The Genesis narrative tells us that the Lord had no respect for Cain's offering, as he had that of Abel, his brother's. The reason for this must have been a wrong spirit in Cain (Gen. 4:3-7). Verse 7 states: "If thou doest well, shalt thou not be accepted? And if thou doest not well sin lieth at the door." There have been many interpretations suggested for the last part of this verse; but whatever translation may be given the specific words, the whole narrative implies that the trouble with Cain was with his motive. He did not come humbly, worshipfully, as Abel did, and probably his offering was less costly, less of a real sacrifice. Again, it has been thought that in the acceptance of the animal sacrifice and the rejection of the fruit sacrifice there was a suggestion of the fact that sin requires death for an atonement. Abel's was the first of the long line of offerings for sin in which blood was shed, culminating in the sacrifice of Christ's body on the cross.

The mark upon Cain has been a fertile subject of conjecture among Biblical scholars. Some hold that it was probably a sign given to Cain as assurance that no man should kill him, but the nature of the sign, and whether it was something perceptible to others, are left in uncertainty. One commentator suggests that it may have been an aspect of such ferocity that he became an object of horror and avoidance.

Lastly, the question is asked about the land of Nod, to which Cain was banished after the murder of Abel and where he found his wife. The land of Nod means simply "land of exile." We may gather from Gen. 4:14-15 that at the time referred to, the human family had multiplied considerably. Cain's wife was doubtless some blood relative, probably a sister. An ancient Arab tradition states that her name was Azura. From the account in Genesis, we may conjecture that although only four persons are mentioned in the sacred narrative up to this point, the human race had increased rapidly (Josephus says that the Jews held a tradition that Adam had thirty-three sons and twenty-three daughters). Cain's fear of punishment may therefore have been directed toward his own relatives.

54. How Many of the Children of Israel Entered Canaan?

The number of adults over twenty years of age who left Egypt is stated in Exodus 12:37, at about six hundred thousand. Allowing the normal proportion of children to such a host we may infer that the total number was probably between one and two millions. Three or four months later, when they were at Sinai, a more careful count was made and the number of adults is then given (Ex. 38:26) at 603,550. Two years later another census was taken and the number is stated (Num. 2:32) at exactly the same figure, but as the Levites were not included and there were 22,000 of them, we may assume that by that time the adults numbered about 625,000. Thirty-eight years later, immediately after a pestilence had swept away large numbers and just before entering Canaan, another census was taken. The figures are given (Numbers 26:21) at 601,730, which shows a slight decrease. Of these only two—Joshua and Caleb—were left of the adults who crossed the Red Sea. With these exceptions, the entire adult generation died in the wilderness.

55. What Was the Sin of the Canaanites?

The Canaanites were descendants of Ham (Gen. 10:6) and comprised seven distinct nations (Deu.

7:1). Though great and mighty (Num. 73:28) they were idolatrous, superstitious, profane and wicked (Deu. 29:17, Deu. 18:9-11, Lev. 18:21). They had many strong cities (Num. 13:28). Israel was warned against making league or intermarrying with them or following their idols or customs (Deu. 7:2; Jos. 23:12; Ex. 23:24; Lev. 18:26, 27). They were partially subdued by Israel (Josh. 10, Josh. 11, Judg. 1). Some of their descendants were still found in the time of Jesus (Matt. 15:22; Mark 7:26).

56. Is It Possible to Approximate the Date of the Creation?

An ever fruitful topic is the date of Creation. The chronology which one finds in the marginal columns of many of the older Bibles, notably in the Authorized Version of King James, is not a part of the Bible itself by any means. It is the work of Archbishop Ussher, an illustrious prelate of the Irish Church, who lived 1580-1656. His chronological labors were directed towards affording an idea of the time that elasped between certain events in recorded history. For this purpose he took the year 1 A. D.—the beginning of the Christian era—as his starting point, and reckoned backwards as far as reliable recorded history afforded good working ground. He reckoned as far back as 4,000 years before Christ, and then finding no more available material in the form of history, either written or inscribed, he had necessarily to stop. He did not by any means imply, however, nor are his figures interpreted by Biblical scholars to mean, that he had reached the point of Creation. On the contrary, he had simply gone as far as recorded history enabled him to go. The Mosaic books in the Old Testament did not claim, in any sense, that the world was created in 4000 B. C. The first line, first verse, and first chapter of Genesis distinctly tells us that "in the beginning" God created the heaven and the earth. Moses was educated at the court of Egypt and imbibed all that was worth learning of the Egyptian civilization, which was old even at that date. But before Egypt there had been still older kingdoms and civilizations. Any one looking up the history in any good encyclopedia of Babylonia, Phoenicia, Chaldea and other ancient nations will form some idea of the great antiquity of that portion of the world's history which has not yet been definitely written. In the last century, the world has yielded up many of its secrets to excavators, and consecrated scholarship has made unquestioned discoveries, which are accepted by all the churches, showing that recorded time must now be pushed back to a period at least 2,000 years earlier than Ussher's computation. How far beyond this we have to travel to get at the date of Creation is as much a conjecture as ever. Science tells us that countless ages may have passed in the early stages of the world's geological development; and even before man appeared on the scene. It is true that scientists differ in this as they do in many other things, but the essential fact remains that the world is far older by many thousands of years than our forefathers supposed. We have better light on the subject than they had, and yet in no vital sense does that light conflict with the words of Scripture "in the beginning." In the New Testament also the same identical language is used at the opening of John's Gospel, chapter 1, verse 1, "In the beginning was the

Word." Thus we see in both dispensations, the old and the new, a recognition of the fact that the date of the world's creation is far beyond man's computation.

57. What Time Was Consumed in the Work of Creation?

Many have asked: "How long did it take God to create the world and what was the order in which the various beings and things were brought forth?" There are many theories propounded concerning Creation. Some interpreters contend that the Bible account should be taken as meaning literal days, while others, remembering that a day is as a thousand years in God's sight, interpret them as meaning periods of indefinite duration. This problem has been a theme of endless discussion and science is powerless to decide it. The first three days of Creation comprise the inorganic era and the last three days the organic era. The first two chapters of Genesis are repetitive of the story of Creation, the first seven verses of chapter 2 reciting more briefly what was already stated in the first chapter in a somewhat different literary form. As to the order in which Creation proceeded, we have nothing else to guide us than Genesis and the order there given is: first day, light (general); second day, earth and water divided; third day, land and water outlined and vegetation created; fourth day, light (direct); fifth day, lower animals created; sixth day, mammals and man created; seventh day, rest.

As to the length of time between the Creation of Adam and of Eve, that is one of the disputed points on which no one can speak conclusively. Theorizing is futile and traditions (such as some found in Jewish literature) do not avail.

58. Was David Justified in Ordering Solomon to Have Joab and Shimei Executed?

Dean Stanley, strange to say, avers that in the order given to Solomon (I Kings 2:5-9) King David "bequeathed a dark legacy of long cherished vengeance." Dr. Terry's view seems more probable, that "this dying charge was not the offspring of personal revenge, but a measure of administrative wisdom." "David," says Wordsworth, "does not mention among Joab's sins that which caused him personally the most poignant grief, the murder of Absalom." He dwells on the fact that Joab had treacherously slain Abner and had also assassinated Amasa, shedding the blood of war in peace. Shimei had blasphemously insulted the royal majesty of Israel. David, it is true, had sworn to spare Shimei, but this oath was not binding on Solomon. David seems to feel that he had been too lax in punishing crime. His own guilt, though repented of, may have made him feel that the son of Zeruiah, in particular, was too strong for him. Hence this charge to Solomon as keeper of God's law and guardian of the kingdom's safety. In one sense, the execution of these men may be looked upon as an act of retributive justice (they being the enemies of the king), yet in the view of some commentators, the personal vindictiveness that David cherished in the matter, and the absence of a disinterested purpose to secure justice and the welfare and security of Israel, his kingdom, call for condemnation of David in his instructions to his son.

59. Were Daniel's Companions in the Lions' Den His Brothers?

In Dan. 1:6 the companions and Daniel are spoken of as the children of Judah. This means of the tribe of Judah. There is no evidence that they were brothers in the sense of blood relationship. Shadrach was the Chaldee name of Hananiah, the chief of the "three children," or young men of the tribe of Judah, who were Daniel's companions. He was taken captive with Daniel and a number of others at the first invasion of Judah by Nebuchadnezzar about B. C. 606. All four were young men of kingly bearing of the royal tribe of Judah and of superior understanding or education. Meshach was the Chaldee name given by the Babylonian court to Mishael, and Abednego was the name similarly bestowed on Azariah.

60. Who Were King David's Wives?

He had a number of wives, but those that are known chiefly to history are Abigail of Carmel (I Chron. 3:1); Michal, the daughter of Saul (II Sam. 3:13); and Bathsheba (I Chron. 3:5).

61. Why Was David "A Man After God's Own Heart"?

This question has often been asked, both by scoffers and the serious. David, it is true, had fallen into deep sin many times; but his struggles, his remorse, his repentance, his efforts at reparation—these also must be considered. He lived in a rude and warlike age. His whole life, as one biographer says, was "the faithful struggle of an earnest human soul toward what was good and best—a struggle often baffled, yet never ended." This was the character of the man who was illustrious as soldier, shepherd, poet, king, prophet; who kindled patriotism, united Israel, and made it a great nation, and who drove out the worship of strange gods in the land. In view of all the blessings that came to the Hebrew race through David's reign; in view also of "the oath sworn unto David," and of the many evidences of his repentance and his trust in God, as expressed in the Psalms, his career must be regarded as a whole rather than judged of by specific acts, if we would try to find out how David in any degree merited the commendation which the sacred historians accord him.

62. From Whom Were the Edomites Descended?

They were descendants of Esau. They inhabited a fertile and rich country specially given to them (Deu. 2:5; Gen. 27:39). Their country was traversed by roads though it was mountainous and rocky (Num. 20:17; Jer. 49:16). They were governed by dukes and later by kings (Gen. 36:15-30; Num. 20:14). In character they are said to have been wise, proud and self-confident, strong and cruel, vindictive, idolatrous and superstitious (Jer. 49:7, 16, 19; Eze. 25:12; II Chron. 25:14, 20; Jer. 27:3). They inhabited the cities of Avith, Pau, Bozrah, Teman and others. Though they were implacable enemies of Israel, it was forbidden to hate them (Deu. 23:7) or to spoil, and they might be received into the congregation in the third generation (Deu. 23:8). Saul made war against them and David conquered them (I Sam. 14:47; II Sam. 8:14). They took refuge in Egypt and returned after David's death (I King 11:17-22) when they confederated with Israel's enemies only to again be overthrown (2 Chron. 20:10) but finally aided Babylon against Judah (Psa. 137:7, Oba. 11).

63. What Became of Elijah's Body?

The bodies of Elijah and Enoch were doubtless changed or transformed as Paul describes in I Cor. 15:51, 52—the verses immediately following the well-known passage, that flesh cannot inherit the kingdom. They were changed into spiritualized bodies like in some degree that with which Christ rose from the dead. His resurrection body seemed to be made of flesh, but it was clearly different from that which he possessed before his death. All the redeemed, the saints who have died before Christ's coming and those who are alive when he comes, are promised these new "celestial" bodies for the heavenly life. These are the views of commentators who have discussed the subject.

64. Was There Rain Before the Flood?

Read Genesis 2:4-6. This, according to some geologists, indicates that the earth, being then in a cooling condition, had no rain; and they also affirm that there may have been none until the great precipitation at the Flood cleared the atmosphere, and established new conditions. (See chapters 8 and 9.) Of course, these are merely scientific speculations or conjectures, but they are not opposed to Scripture.

65. What Was the Population of Earth Before and After the Flood?

All the information we have in Scripture concerning the population of the earth before the Flood is contained in Genesis chapters 4, 5 and 6. It is made clear in Gen. 5:4 that Adam had a numerous progeny. Jewish tradition says he had thirty-three sons and twenty-three daughters. Chapter 5:1 tells of the increased population. There must have been intermarriages. This is the view generally accepted by commentators, as the only reasonable explanation, where no other light can be had on the subject. The only record we have of the repopulation of the world after the Flood is that found in Genesis, ninth, tenth and eleventh chapters.

66. Was the Rainbow Visible before the Flood?

There is no recorded evidence that a rainbow was visible from the earth before the Flood. Some commentators hold that the conditions described in Genesis 2:6, "But there went up a mist from the earth," etc., lasted until the atmospheric change wrought by the Flood and that the rainbow was a natural consequence of such change. This, however, despite the fact that scientific support is claimed for such view, is merely conjecture. The Bible (Gen. 9:13-17) is very clear to the effect that God established the rainbow at that time as "the token of the covenant" between Him and mankind and hence we need no conjecture.

67. How Soon After Adam's Fall Did Idolatry Begin?

Adam and some of his descendants as late as the time of the Flood, are believed to have lived under a revealed system, in which, through their patriarchs and otherwise, they had a knowledge of God sufficient for their condition. Afterwards there arose the nature-worship, called *Fetishism*, consisting of the setting up and worshipping of animals, trees and stones, etc.—an idolatry invented by those who for their sins had been forsaken of God (Romans 1:28). There is no distinct mention in the Bible of any idols prior to the time of the Flood, but it is reasonable to suppose that idolatry was one of the abominations for which that terrible punishment was visited on the earth. The first positive indications of idolatry which appear in history are found in the worship of *Set* or *Sitekh* (equivalent to the Hebrew Patriarch, *Seth*), to whom divine honors were paid by the Egyptians. Some Jewish writers interpret Genesis 4:26 to mean that *Enos,* the son of *Seth,* was the originator of idolatry in that he paid divine honors to the host of heaven instead of to God alone.

68. What Is Known of the Hittites?

They were descendants of Canaan's son Heth. One of the seven Canaanitish nations, they dwelt in Hebron and were governed by kings (Deu. 7:1; Gen. 23:2, 3, 19; I Kin. 10:29). Their land was promised to Israel and it was commanded to destroy them; but Israel did not destroy them entirely (Deu. 7:1, 2, 24; Josh. 14:13; Judg. 3:5). Among their prominent personages were Ephron, Ahimelech and Uriah (Gen. 49:30; I Sam. 26:6; II Sam. 11:6, 21). Esau, Solomon and many other Israelites intermarried with the Hittites. They were a warlike people and made many conquests.

69. What Is Known of the Hivites?

They formed one of the seven nations of Canaan, descended from Canaan (Gen. 10:15, 17). They dwelt near Lebanon. The Shechemites and Gibeonites were affiliated with them (Judg. 3:3; Gen. 34:2; Josh. 9:3-7). Esau intermarried with them. Their land was promised to Israel and it was commanded to destroy them (Deu. 7:1, 2, 24). In the reign of Solomon, a remnant of the Hivites was made tributary to Israel (I Kin. 9:20, 21).

70. Who Were the Ishmaelites?

They were descendants of Ishmael, Abraham's son, and were divided into twelve tribes (Gen. 25:16; Gen. 16:15, 16). They were also called Hagarites, Hagarenes and Arabians (I Chron. 5:10; Psa. 83:6; Isa. 13:20). They were governed by kings, were rich in cattle and dwelt in tents (Jer. 25:24; Isa. 13:20; I Chron. 5:21). Though they were the merchants of the East and traveled around in large caravans (Gen. 37:25; Job 6:19), they were frequently lawless and would waylay and plunder travelers (Jer. 3:2). After harassing Israel, they were overcome by Gideon (Judg. 8:10-24; II Chron. 5:10; II Chron. 26:7). It would seem that later they became more peacefully inclined, as they sent presents to Kings Solomon and Jehoshaphat (I Kin. 10:15; II Chron. 17:11).

71. When Did the Change in Jacob's Spiritual Nature Occur?

It began at Bethel but the change there was extremely slight. Jacob regarded his vision there very much as a business arrangement. If God would help him and give him bread to eat and bring him back safe, then God should be his God and he would give him a tenth of all. At Jabbok the crisis was much more far-reaching. He realized there his danger and his need of a blessing. He no longer bargained with God, he saw that his own strength was futile, he was a humble suppliant for God's favor. From that night on he was a different man, by no means perfect, but far better than before.

72. Did Jephthah Really Offer Up His Daughter As a Sacrifice?

Both the Authorized and Revised Versions leave the question in doubt, and commentators have been divided in opinion as to whether she was sacrified or doomed to live the life of a recluse. Human sacrifices are an abomination unto the Lord. A new reading or translation which several notable scholars have urged as the correct one is: "It shall surely be the Lord's *or* I will offer up to him a burnt offering." Hebrew scholars declare this to be the more accurate rendering. (See Judges 11:30, 31, 39.) It changes the aspect of the case and makes Jephthah to say practically that if the first living thing that came forth from his house to meet him was one that would be unacceptable, then a burnt offering of an acceptable character would be substituted. This would lead to the conclusion that the daughter was not sacrificed, but condemned to a life of perpetual virginity and a burnt offering offered up in her stead. Several eminent writers, including Joseph Kinchi, Ben Gerson and Bechai (Jewish authorities) and a number of Christian authors, held that instead of being sacrificed she was shut up in a house specially prepared by her father and visited there by the daughters of Israel four days in a year as long as she lived. In support of this theory it is pointed out that the Hebrew term employed to express Jephthah's vow is the word *neder,* which means a "consecration" and not *che-rem,* which means "destruction."

73. Why Do the Jews Face the East When Praying?

In Jerusalem, the Jews always turned their faces toward the "holy hill" of the temple while praying (see Dan. 6:10; II Chron. 6:34). The Samaritans, on the contrary, faced Mt. Gerizim. In the court of the temple, the Jews in prayer faced the temple itself (see I Kings 8:38) to the Holy of Holies (see Ps. 5:8). Daniel, while praying in exile, opened his window toward Jerusalem (see Dan. 6:10). Modern Jews in Europe and America customarily face the East in prayer. It was a custom among the early Christians to face the East but that has long been discontinued. Mohammedans face in the direction of Mecca.

74. Will the Jews Be Restored to Palestine at Christ's Second Coming?

Students of prophecy are not agreed on the subject. The majority infer, from various passages, that they will be restored before the coming of Christ in the second stage of that coming. The first stage is thought to be in the air to summon those Christians who are looking for him, to meet him (see I Thess. 4:16, 17). The second stage is after the great tribulation when he comes to reign.

75. How Often Was Jerusalem Destroyed?

The Holy City has been captured and recaptured many times by contending forces. In several of the sieges it has been partially ruined, but in at least four it has been practically destroyed, the first about 1400 B. C., when captured by the tribes of Judah and Simeon; the second in 586 by Nebuchadnezzar; the third in 170 B. C. by Antiochus Epiphanes; the fourth, and doubtless most terrible, in 70 A. D., by Titus. The city was restored by Hadrian in 135 A. D., and since then has changed hands many times. It now belongs to Turkey, and has about 60,000 inhabitants.

76. Why Was the Temple Built in Jerusalem?

In II Sam. 24:16-25 we learn how the threshing floor of Araunah came to be chosen for the site of an altar of commemoration and sacrifice. Moreover, Scripture and Jewish tradition unite in pointing to that threshing floor as the spot upon which Abraham prepared to offer Isaac (although some eminent authorities have disputed this). Read also the account of the purchase of the site from Ornan (Araunah) in I Chron. 21:26-28; and in the next chapter (I Chron. 22:1, 9, 10) which shows how David had a divine revelation that his son should build the temple there.

77. Who Was Job?

According to leading commentators, Job was a personage of distinction, wealth and influence who lived in the north of Arabia Deserta, near the Euphrates, some 1800 B. C. His life was patriarchal, his language the Hebrew of that early day, when it was interspersed with Syriac and Arabic. He lived before Moses. His book is probably the oldest book in the world. It is now interpreted as a public debate in poetic form, dealing with the Divine government. It abounds in figurative language. The "day" mentioned in Job 2:1 was one appointed for the angels to give an account of their ministry to God. Evil is personified in Satan, who also comes to make report. The question to Satan and his response are simply a dramatic or poetic form of opening the great controversy which follows.

78. Did God Give Job into the Hands of Satan to Be Tempted?

"Tempted" is scarcely the word to use in that case. Job was tried or tested. The question was what his motive was in serving God. Satan with his natural doubt about any one having pure motives, asserted that Job served God only for what he gained by it, and that if his property was taken away from him, he would curse God. So Job was put to the proof, to see what he would do under trial, and whether he was really as disinterested as God believed him to be. The object of the author appears to have been to correct a false view of adversity, which view was prevalent in his time. People had the idea that severe calamities were punishments dealt out by God because of sin. When a man of good moral character, therefore, was in trouble, people suspected that he had sinned secretly, and that God was punishing him for it. It was often a cruel and unjust suspicion. In writing this description, the author evidently was trying to eradicate it. After reading such a book, a man who saw another in trouble, instead of despising him as a sinner, might say, "Perhaps he is being tried as Job was," and so might sympathize instead of blaming him. Our concern should be to learn the lesson the book was designed to teach, rather than to discuss the question whether it is history or parable, for that question cannot now be authoritatively answered.

79. Did God "Blot Out" the Day on Which Job Was Born?

This question is doubtless prompted by the ancient tradition or superstition that we have less days in February than any other month, as Job was born in February. This of course is a fallacy. There was no February in the time of Job, 1520 B. C. The months, or divisions of time, were not as we have them now. The year of the Jews consisted of twelve lunar months of twenty-nine and thirty days alternately, a thirteenth being from time to time introduced to accommodate it to the sun and seasons. Let it be noted that while Job cursed his birthday, he did not curse his Maker, so why should the Lord drop a day on account of a little weakness in his servant, who, despite his great sufferings, never uttered any reproach against the Author of his being? Our months as at present, we have from the Romans. With those people February had originally twenty-nine days in an ordinary year, but when the Roman Senate decreed that the eighth month should bear the name of Augustus, a day was taken from February and given to August, which had then only thirty, that it might not be inferior to July, named in honor of Julius Cæsar.

80. Are the Speeches of Job's Friends to Be Regarded as Inspired?

This question is answered authoritatively in the book itself (see Job 42:7), where God is represented as saying, "My wrath is kindled against thee and thy two friends; for ye have not spoken of me the thing that is right." One gets a clearer idea of the book by regarding it as a symposium on the problem of suffering, each speaker being a representative of a school of thought. Each speaker keeps to the same aspect of the subject but all agree in regarding unusual suffering as an evidence of unusual sin. They imply that in Job's case, he being outwardly so good a man, his sin was aggravated by hypocrisy. This was unjust, because, as we learn by the first chapter, it was precisely because he was so good a man that his affliction came upon him. The author of the book evidently wished to administer a warning to the people of his time against being uncharitable in their inferences.

81. Is the Book of Job a Real History or a Dramatic Allegory?

Job is believed to have been a real personage—a type of the earliest patriarchs, a man of high intelligence and great faith. The story is cast in dramatic form. Professor S. S. Curry, of Yale and Harvard Divinity Schools, thus outlines it: the place, a hill outside the city; a rising storm, flashing lightning, rolling thunder and a rainbow; the speakers, God, the patriarch Job, his friends, and Satan; the theme, the mystery of human suffering, and human existence." To which may be added, a sublime faith in the divine wisdom, righteousness and justice. The book of Job is regarded by the highest Bible scholarship as a spiritual allegory. The name Job is derived from an Arabic word signifying "repentance," although Job himself is held to be a real personage. (See Ezek. 14:14 and James 5:11.)

82. Why Did the Wicked Kings of Judah Let Their Sons Pass through Fire?

It was a heathen form of worship to Molech, Milcom or Chemosh, which the Israelites had borrowed or adapted from the Moabites and Amnonites. Human sacrifices were made in high places to Molech. The chief interpreters Jarchi, Kimchi and Maimonides wrote that in the worship of Molech, the children were not burned, but were made to pass before two burning pyres as a purificatory rite. It is quite clear, however, that in many cases lives were actually sacrificed (see Psalm 106:37, 38; Jer. 7:31). It was assumed that by this rite the victims were purged from dross of the body and attained union with the deity.

83. Who Were the "Lost Tribes"?

The "lost tribes," so-called, were the Jews carried into captivity by Shalmaneser (II Kings 17:6), and chiefly belonging to Israel or the ten tribes. Many theories as to their location and their descendants have been ventilated, and they have been successively located (by ingenious investigators) in Hindustan, Tartary, China, Africa, Great Britain and among the aborigines of North America. More reasonable conjectures hold that while some returned after the exile, and others were left in Samaria, many remained in Assyria and afterward joined with the Jews in forming colonies throughout the East, so that, in a certain sense, they shared the ultimate history of their brethren of Judah.

84. What Secular Evidence Have We of the Fate of Lot's Wife?

The pillar which is mentioned in the story concerning the fate of Lot's wife, in Genesis 19, is referred to by a number of writers. Josephus (in *Antiquities* I, 11, 4) wrote that it still remained in his day, and he had seen it—*i. e.*, the peculiar formation of crumbling, crystalline rock associated by tradition with the event. Clemens Romanus, Irenæus and Benjamin of Tudela also wrote of the strange formation as visible in their day, but later writers stated that it had ceased to exist. It is related that, by a singular coincidence, Lieutenant Lynch, who led an American exploring party around the Dead Sea, found on the southwestern shore, at a place called by the Arabs Usdum, a pillar some forty feet high, composed of salt crystals, capped with carbonate of lime, which he assumed to have been detached by the action of the winter rains upon the rock-salt hills. Professor Palmer claims in one of his books to have seen this same formation, which the Arabs, in their usual manner, had connected with the Bible story, although it is not at all certain that the locality is identical with that indicated in Genesis. Several commentators hold that the geological character of the rocks and the prevalence of salt crystals justify the conclusion that the Bible passage might be interpreted to mean "*like* a pillar of salt," and that the body of Lot's wife "had become fixed for a time to the soil by saline or bituminous incrustations."

85. Who and What Was Melchisedec?

It is in the fourteenth chapter of Genesis that Melchisedec is historically presented to us. The incident and its record, although so brief, and standing in such singular isolation from the thread of the history which it interrupts, is not only in itself most striking and interesting, but also in its typical teaching profoundly instructive. How suddenly and altogether unexpectedly does Melchisedec here appear before us—a most kingly and majestic form, yet clad in priestly robes, and with the mystic emblems of eucharistic offering—bread and wine—in his hands. We see those priestly hands raised in blessing; we observe the great patriarch, Abraham—the father of the faithful and the Friend of God—bowing before the mysterious priest-king, and presenting to him the tithes of all his spoil; and then, as abruptly as it appeared, the vision passes away, and for nearly a thousand years the voice of inspiration utters not again the name of Mechisedec. Then, however, in an ecstatic Psalm of a most distinctly Messianic character, and descriptive of our Lord's exaltation in the day of his power, we meet with it once more in the solemn declaration: "The Lord hath sworn and will not repent, thou art a priest forever, after the order of Melchisedec (Ps. 110:4). Again, something like a thousand years pass away, and then, once more, the writer of the Epistle to the Hebrews take up the subject of this mysterious personage, who, "Without father, without mother, without genealogy, having neither beginning of days, or end of life; but made like unto the Son of God; abideth a priest continually" (Heb. 7:3); and on the two brief references to him, above given, which are all that the Scriptures contain, founds an argument to show the superiority of Christ's priesthood, as being "after the order of Melchisedec," to that of Aaron, or Levi, which it had superseded.

Who was Melchisedec? Much labor has been wasted in attempts to answer the question. Later Jewish tradition identified him with Shem; and it is certain that

that patriarch was not only alive in the days of Abraham, but even continued to live till Jacob was fifty years old. (Compare Gen. 11:11 with verses 12:26, 21:5, 25:7-26.) According to others he belonged to the family of Ham, or of Japheth; and it has been said that this is necessarily implied by the language of the Apostle when drawing a parallel between Melchisedec and Christ, he says that our Lord belonged to "a tribe of which no man gave attendance at the altar." Some, again, have suggested that he was an incarnate angel, or other superhuman creature, who lived for a time among men. Others have held that he was an early manifestation of the Son of God; and a sect, called the Melchisedecians, asserted that he was "an incarnation of the Holy Ghost." But, in all these conjectures, the fact has been strangely overlooked that the reticence of Scripture on the point is typical and significant, for, could it be determined who Melchisedec really was, it could no longer be said that he was "without father, without mother, without genealogy"; which statement is to be understood, not as implying that he was not a natural descendant of Adam, but that he designedly appears and disappears in the sacred narrative without mention either of his parentage or death.

There can, however, be no question that, whoever Melchisedec may have been, he was an eminent type of Christ. This is placed beyond doubt, not only by the language of the 110th Psalm—the Messianic character of which has ever been recognized by Jews and Christians alike—but especially by the argument of the Apostle, in the seventh chapter of the Epistle to the Hebrews, in the course of which there occurs the explicit declaration that he was—in the various respects mentioned—"made like unto the Son of God."

86. Who Were the Moabites?

They were the descendants of Lot and were neighbors of the Amorites on the opposite side of the River Arnon (Num. 21:13). They were governed by kings and possessed many great cities (Num. 21:28-30; Is. 15:1; Num. 23:7). They were proud, arrogant, idolatrous, superstitious, rich, confident and prosperous. They were mighty men of war (Is. 16:6; I Kin. 11:7; Jer. 27:3; Jer. 48:7, 11, 14). The Amorites deprived them of a large part of their territory (Num. 21:26). The Moabites refused to let Israel pass through their country and were so greatly impressed and alarmed by the multitude of the Israelitish host that, with Midian, they sent Balaam to curse it (Num. 22 to 24). Subsequently, Israel was enticed into their idolatry and even intermarried with them. They were always hostile to Israel until Saul subdued them (I Sam. 14:47) and were later made tributary to David and the Jewish kings (II Sam. 8:2-12; II Kin. 3:4), but finally joined Babylon against Judah (II Kin. 24:2).

87. Why Did Moses Strike the Rock?

The account in Num. 20 very clearly shows that Moses disobeyed the divine command in striking the rock as he did. For the moment he apparently lost his faith, and his temper as well. He had been explicitly instructed to "speak unto the rock" (verse 8) instead of which he addressed the people in hasty and passionate words and smote the rock twice. (See Ps. 106:32, 33.) His whole attitude betrayed his doubt not of God's power, but of his will to help a people who had been rebellious. Further, Moses was irreverent (see verse 12) in that his language and bearing detracted from the sanctity of the occasion and was therefore displeasing to God. He had been entrusted with a great enterprise and his perfect obedience to and implicit faith in God were indispensable. As the result showed, his failure involved serious consequences for the whole nation.

88. What Was the Dispute Over Moses' Body Between Michael and Satan?

The passage in Jude 1:9 referring to the dispute between Michael and Satan over the body of Moses, is regarded by Vitringa, Lardner, McKnight and other distinguished commentators as symbolical, "the body of Moses" being intended to represent the Mosaic law and institutions (see Zech. 3:1), in the same manner in which modern Christians call the Church "the body of Christ." According to others, it has reference to a Jewish legend connected with the secret burial of the great lawgiver (Deu. 34:6). The *Targum* of Jonathan attributes the burial of Moses to the hands of angels, led by Michael as the guardian of Israel. Other views set forth in the Hebrew books are that Satan disputed the burial, claiming the body because of the blood of the Egyptian whom Moses slew, and because of the leader's sin at Meribah. Having "the power of death," he opposes the raising of Moses' body again for these reasons, but the latter's visible presence with Enoch and Elijah at the Transfiguration gave evidence of Michael's triumph, and was also a pledge of the coming resurrection. Josephus, the Jewish historian (in *Anti-*

quities 4:8), states that God hid the body of Moses, lest it should be worshiped by the people.

89. Did Nebuchadnezzar Literally Eat Grass?

We do not know any more on the subject than is related in the Bible. The natural inference from the narrative is that the king was temporarily deprived of his reason, and insane people often do things as unnatural as eating grass. There is nothing improbable in the Biblical statement. On the other hand, some authorities suggest that the narrative means nothing more than that the king left his palace and the cares of state and lived the life of a peasant for seven years; or, as we might say, vegetated in rural seclusion; but the plain statement of the text is that generally accepted. Daniel 4:35-37 indicates that he became, at least outwardly, a believer in the true God.

90. What Were the Dimensions and Material of Noah's Ark?

According to the directions in Genesis 6:15, the Ark was 300 cubits long, 50 cubits broad and 30 cubits high. Bible students have been greatly puzzled over the length of the cubit, which seems to have varied greatly in ancient times. It is evident, however (from Deu. 3:11), that it was taken as a measure from the human body, and may have been either from the wrist to the end of the third figure, or the entire length of the lower or forearm, from the elbow to the wrist, or even from the elbow to the finger-point. One authority, Celsus, says the cubit was identified with the *ulna,* or under and larger of the two bones of the arm. The Egyptian cubit, which the Hebrews may have taken, measured six hand-breadths and the Jewish rabbins (as the *Mishna* states) assigned six hand-breadths to the Mosaic cubit, while Josephus says a cubit was equal to two spans, the span being equal to three hand-breadths. Ezek. 40:5, 43:13 speaks of the cubit "which was a cubit and a hand-breadth" which was the Babylonian cubit. It would thus seem that the Ark, though its size cannot be confidently stated, was a very spacious vessel, probably exceeding 500 feet in length, fully 85 feet broad and over 52 feet high. In 1609 Peter Jansen of Horn, in Holland, built a vessel of these proportions and found that it would stow fully a third more cargo than ships of its size built in the ordinary manner. It had 3,600,000 cubic feet of space, and after nine-tenths had been assigned for food storage there was still room for 7,000 pairs of animals, each with 50 cubic feet of space. It was, in fact, a huge floating storehouse, rather than a ship.

As to the materials of which the Ark was built, we find in Genesis 6:14 that Noah is told to make an ark of "gopher" wood. There are various conjectures as to what kind of wood this was. Bunsen holds that it was a wood found only in Egypt; Dietrich believes it was a heavy reed-like growth; Gesenius affirms that it was pine, fir or cedar, and Bochart says cypress. Chaldee translators declare it to have been the *sissu,* a dark-colored wood of Arabian growth and highly valued. A majority hold to the opinion that cypress was meant, on account of its enduring qualities.

As to the time occupied in building it, much has been said but little of real worth. The only Bible passage supposably referable to this question is Genesis

6:3. This passage is variously interpreted. By some it is held to refer to a shortening of human life; by others it is interpreted as meaning that the period stated would be further granted as a respite—an opportunity for repentance—failing which the divine presence (the Shecinah, which had hitherto continued at the gate of Eden) would be withdrawn from the world on account of its wickedness. The best answer is that nowhere is it stated in the Bible how long Noah was engaged in building the Ark. The Lord had offered a respite of 120 years, after the warning to the human race (see I Peter 3:20; II Peter 2:5), and it was during this period that Noah, who was a "preacher of righteousness," not only labored in the work of awakening the people to the enormity of their sin and of urging them to repentance, but also used a portion of that period in preparing the Ark for the emergency that would arise, if the people did not listen to his cry for repentance.

91. What Were the "Bitter Herbs" Used at the Passover?

Since endive, chicory, wild lettuce, or nettles, were important articles of food to the ancient Egyptians, it is likely that these were the bitter herbs of the Passover feast, more especially so, as they are at the present time eaten by the Jews in the East.

92. Were the Patriarchs Really As Old As the Bible Record States?

Some of the "higher critics" claim that the ancient calendar of the antediluvians made the year really a month, or lunar period. Others, with somewhat more reason, assert that a year was a season of growth equal to three of our months. Hensler and Hufeland, two German authorities, claim that the patriarchal year was three months till Abraham's time, eight months till Joseph's time, and thereafter twelve months. One eminent Bible scholar has pointed out that if we accept the monthly year theory, Mahalaleel's sixty-five years before the birth of his son Jared would make him a parent at five years and three months of our reckoning; Enoch would be the same age when his son Methuselah was born, and the ages of the other patriarchs at the birth of their children would be equally preposterous. Of course, such conclusions absolutely condemn the monthly year theory. Conditions among the antediluvians were totally different from those after the Flood. There had been no rain, and the sun and planets were not visible; in the moist atmosphere, growth was greatly stimulated and all natural conditions tended to animal and vegetable longevity, precisely as the Bible indicates. Besides, as that period produced animal types of giant proportions, created for strength and endurance, the analogy of nature would seem to demand that man should bear some harmonious proportion to his surroundings. Genesis 6:4 (first clause) clearly implies this. Age and stature, not only human but otherwise, became greatly diminished after the Flood.

93. Was Pharaoh Drowned in the Red Sea?

All the evidence is against the theory that he was drowned in the Red Sea. Some very interesting information, furnishing striking confirmation of the Bible narrative, has recently been obtained, by deciphering the inscriptions on ancient Egyptian monuments. From these it appears that the Pharaoh who "refused to let the people go" was named Menephthah. He was the youngest son of the great Pharaoh, Rameses II, the Pharaoh who oppressed the Hebrews and ordered the killing of the male infants, and whose death is mentioned in Exodus 2:23. Menephthah was an old man, at least sixty, when he came to the throne, and was constitutionally timid and feeble. He joined with him in the government his brilliant son Seti, a young man resembling in person and character his grandfather, the great Rameses. Seti was virtually king though his father, Menephthah, was king in name. The Bible alludes to Seti as "the firstborn of Pharaoh who *sat on the throne*" (Ex. 12:29). This young man's tomb has been found, and a record of his achievements, showing him to have been a great general and administrator. But his name does not appear in the list of the Pharaohs and the inscription on his tomb shows that he never became king, but died suddenly, while still only a prince. The Bible tells us how he died. It was on the night when the angel slew the firstborn. Menephthah, as we know by the Bible narrative, pursued the Hebrews. He had no son now to take command as on former occasions. He was then an old man eighty-two years of age. What more likely than that, when he saw the Israelites descend into the Red Sea, he should send on his army and stay behind himself, not caring at his age, and at night, to undertake so perilous a journey. The Egyptian records state that once before, on the eve of battle, when he should have led his army, the old man had a convenient vision, ordering him not to enter the battle but to give the command to his son. He doubtless excused himself on this occasion and so saved his life. A parallel case of a father and son reigning simultaneously is found in Belshazzar, who, though exercising kingly functions, does not appear on the list of kings. He was associated in government with his father, Nabonnidus, and, like Seti in Egypt, died before his father.

94. What Is Meant by "I Will Harden Pharaoh's Heart"?

This expression in Exodus 7:3 has been a stumbling-block to many. There is a point reached by those who have long persisted in wicked courses which is known as judicial blindness, a point at which—God's restraining spirit being withdrawn—they become unable to distinguish right from wrong or good from evil. They grow hardened and morally incorrigible. (See Mark 3:5; Rom. 11:25; II Cor. 3:14; Eph. 4:18.) Under such circumstances, the offender turns even blessings into sin by abusing them, and unless overtaken by some great adversity, continues in his course, blind to consequences. This was doubtless the case with Pharaoh. Egypt had sinned deeply, and so long as its rulers were unchecked by some stronger power, they would continue to sin. Pharaoh, long accustomed to the abuse of power, steeled himself against all sense of justice and mercy, and this the "permissive act of providence" allowed, in order that the culminating punishment should be the more severe. In other words, Pharaoh was permitted to go on in his sin, in order that his fate might be made an awful example to the whole world.

95. If God "Hardened" Pharaoh's Heart, Was It Possible for Him to do Otherwise than He Did?

The true interpretation is that the divine message of warning and the plagues which followed were the occasion of Pharaoh's heart being hardened. Thus the expression which has been translated as "hardened," is, in Hebrew, "strong," implying that the influence of the events had been to make the king's heart stubborn or rebellious. (See Ex. 7:13, 14, 8:19, and 9:35.) Elsewhere in the same narrative the Hebrew expression is capable of being translated "made heavy" (as in Ex. 7:14 and 8:15 and 32, also Ex. 9:34). The passage in Exodus 7:23, which may be rendered as in the Authorized Version, and also as "he (Pharaoh) set his heart even to this," expresses the condition of Egypt's ruler, who had set his face like a flint against Jehovah, and was alternately depressed and defiant, but not repentant.

96. Who Were the Philistines?

Their origin is nowhere expressly stated in the Bible; but since the prophets describe them as "the Philistines from Caphtor" (Amos 9:7), and "the remnant of the maritime district of Caphtor" (Jer. 47:4), it is probable that they were the "Caphtorim which came out of Caphtor," and who expelled the Avim from their lands and occupied them (Deu. 2:23), and that they were the Caphtorim mentioned in the Mosaic genealogical table among the descendants of Mizraim. There is equal authority for believing Caphtor to have been the island of Cyprus, or a land somewhere between Egypt and Ethiopia, or a part of Northern

Egypt. Some have claimed that Caphtor and the modern island of Crete are identical; but the best authorities do not agree with this conclusion.

97. Who Wrote the Book of Proverbs?

Some ancient authorities, rabbins and others attribute the book to Solomon; others hold that it has a composite origin and is the work of a number of writers. The ablest modern critics hold the latter opinion. It is probable that Solomon was the author of the portion beginning with the first verse of the tenth chapter and ending with the sixteenth verse of the twenty-second chapter. As we learn from the first verse of the twenty-fifth chapter, the collection of proverbs extending to the end of the twenty-ninth chapter was also attributed to him, but was not compiled until 250 years after his death. The remainder of the book appears to be composed of six portions by different hands at different periods. One of these is the introduction, which occupies the first nine chapters. This was probably written by the man who compiled the whole book, but whose name is unknown.

97A. Who Composed the Psalms?

The Book of Psalms (which is the Psalter of the Hebrews) has many authors, the principal one being David. Some are attributed to Hezekiah, Josiah, and Zerubbabel, two (the 72d and 127th) to Solomon, several to the Levites and the Asaphites, one, at least, to Jeduthun, eleven to the sons of Korah, one to Ethan (Psalm 89), while many are of uncertain authorship. Moses is given by tradition as the author of Psalm 90, being the only contribution of which his authorship is reasonably certain. The Psalms cover a period of a thousand years. They were composed at different remote periods, by various poets; David, the most prolific contributor, being indicated as the author of seventy-three Psalms in the Hebrew text and eleven in the Septuagint.

98. What Figure Is Conveyed by the Words "Rachel Weeping for Her Children"?

The passage in Matthew 2:18 relates to the Babylonian captivity. Rachel, the wife of Jacob, and mother of Joseph and Benjamin, is figuratively represented as rising from the tomb and lamenting over the loss of her children. Ramah in Benjamin was a scene of pillage and massacre in Jeremiah's time (see Jer. 31:15), and hence is chosen by the prophet in his figurative scene of lamentation.

99. What Was the Width of the Red Sea at the Point Where Israel Crossed?

It is generally held by a majority of writers and travelers that the passage was made at Ras Atakah Point, about six miles south of Suez, and opposite the southern end of Jebel Atakah. At Ras Atakah, the land runs out in the form of a promontory for fully a mile into the sea beyond the regular shore line. Beyond this, there is a shoal for nearly a mile more, over which the water at low tide is usually about fourteen feet deep. Beyond this, and before the true channel or center is reached, there are two other comparative shoals; the channel itself is somewhere about fifty feet deep and three-quarters of a mile wide. There is another succession of shoals on the eastern shore.

The distance from shore to shore is about five and a half miles.

100. Whence Came the Queen of Sheba?

It is supposed by well-informed authorities that she came from Yemen, in Arabia Felix. In Matthew 12:42 she is referred to as the "Queen of the South," who came from "the uttermost parts of the earth," a term applied by the ancients to southern Arabia. Not improbably she was a lineal descendant of Abraham by Keturah, whose grandson, Sheba, peopled that part of the then known world. The Arabic account of this queen gives her the name of Bilkis or Yelkamah, a monarch of the Himyerites; but their account is probably more legendary than accurate as to detail.

101. What Problems Did the Queen of Sheba Put to Prove the Wisdom of Solomon?

The Bible here gives us no clue but tradition has preserved some of the questions which she is said to have put to Solomon to test his wisdom. These, we believe, are principally found in the Talmudical writings. It is said she introduced a party of children all dressed alike, and asked the king to tell which were boys and which girls. King Solomon ordered vessels to be brought that the children might wash their hands. The girls rolled up their sleeves, but the boys plunged their hands into the water at once, and were easily detected by the king. The queen next ordered her attendants to set before Solomon a number of beautiful bouquets and asked him to indicate which were the real flowers and which the false. Solomon ordered the keeper of his gardens to bring in a hive of bees, and they almost instantly settled upon the natural flowers and began to extract the sweets from them, leaving the artificial flowers untouched. Other traditions illustrative of Solomon's wisdom are told by the ancient writers.

102. What Was the Sin of Saul—1. Sam. 13: 13, 14?

His chief sin was disobedience. Samuel, the recognized representative of God in the nation, had commanded him to wait till he arrived in Gilgal, saying he would come in seven days. Saul did not wait till the end of the seventh day, thereby showing an impatient and disobedient spirit. God demands that men obey Him implicitly. "To obey is better than sacrifice," Samuel said to Saul on another occasion of his disobedience. Probably, also, Saul had no right to conduct the ritual of sacrifice. As to Samuel's doing so, he may simply have ordered it done, directing Eleazar the priest to conduct the ceremony; or his office of prophet may have given him the authority to act also as priest. Furthermore, though not a descendant of Aaron, he belonged to the priestly tribe of Levi.

103. Why Were "Shepherds" an Abomination to the Egyptians?

The reason of the Egyptian hatred of the shepherds is a historic one. The Hyksos or Shepherd Kings, hundreds of years before Joseph's time, had invaded and conquered Lower Egypt and ruled the Delta, although they never occupied the whole country. They came from the East and were probably Arabians, and are represented as having been a cruel and arrogant race, who subjected the Egyptians to great hardships. (See Gen. 46:34.) They were finally driven out of the country by a coalition of forces under several kings. They were probably called Shepherds because of the simplicity of their life, which was largely pastoral and semi-barbaric. Manetho, the Egyptian historian, says that they were the builders of Jerusalem, but his reference is probably to the Canaanites rather than the Jews. Some writers suggest that they were the progenitors of the Bedouins, and that the Amalekites, Midianites, and other hostile nations who opposed the Israelites after the Exodus were also descended from the stock of the expelled Shepherds. It is not improbable that the Philistines may also have been a branch of the same Shepherd family.

104. Who Were the Sidonians?

These people were descendants of Sidoa, a son of Canaan, and were formerly a part of the Phœnician nation (Matt. 15:21, 22; Mark 7:24, 26). They dwelt on the sea-coast in the cities of Zidon and Zarephath (Josh. 11:8; I Kin. 17:9; Luke 4:26), and were governed by kings. In character they were careless, idolatrous, superstitious, wicked and unpenitent (Judg. 18:7; I Kin. 11:5; Jer. 27:3-9; Matt. 11:21, 22). Their business was commerce and of course they were skillful sailors (Is. 23:2; Eze. 27:8). They supplied the Jews with timber, who in turn supplied them with provisions (I Chron. 22:4; Acts 12:20; Eze. 27:17). Although they were hostile and oppressive to God's people, Solomon and Abijah intermarried with them, and Israel followed the Sidonian idolatry (Judg. 10:12; Eze. 28:22-24; I Kin. 11:1, 16:31).

105. What Is Known of Sodom Outside the Bible?

Comparatively little. Sodom was a small but populous country, and according to Josephus (*Antiquities,* chapter 9, book I) was rich and flourishing, with five kings controlling its affairs and with a certain degree of ancient civilization. Doubtless they were idolaters, but they had an opportunity, through the presence of Lot and his household, of knowing the true God. In chapter 11, book I of the *Antiquities* the historian tells of their great wealth and pride, their injustice toward men, their impiety and peculiar vices. So persistent were they in wickedness that the overthrow of their chief city and the destruction of the people came upon them as a punishment.

106. Can Any Spiritual Lesson Be Drawn from Solomon's Song?

Undoubtedly, as from every other part of the Bible. The difficulties in regard to it arise from the various views as to its plan and purpose. No less than sixteen of these have been advanced by expositors. Three only, however, have commended themselves to any large number of Bible students. One of them regards it as the yearning of God's people, when separated from the Temple and the ordinances of the Jewish service. A second view is that it represents, under the image of an intense love, the relation of Christ and his people. Paul uses the same symbol in Eph. 5:22-23. This was evidently the view taken by the men who put the headings to the chapters in the King James Version of the Bible, which headings have been discarded in the Revised Version. The third view is the literal, which is taken by modern scholars and is growing in favor. It is that the poem celebrates the trials and triumph of a country maiden, who when carried away from her humble home and her rustic lover to become an inmate of the king's harem, rejects with scorn the magnificence and luxury offered her and remains faithful to her lover, with whom she returns. The lesson is obvious. It is the lesson of a fidelity to truth and righteousness which no offer of wealth and luxury can disturb.

107. Where Was the Twelfth Tribe at the Time of the Jewish Kings?

Rehoboam reigned over one and Jeroboam over ten. (I Kings 11:31-35, 12:21.) The tribe of Levi was not counted because it had no land possessions (Num. 18:20-24), except cities for dwellings, with their outlying fields for pasturage (Num. 35:1-8). The tribe of Joseph was divided into two parts, Ephraim and Manasseh, which are usually spoken of as two distinct tribes. But in this division Joseph seems to have been counted as but one tribe, making Jeroboam's ten. Although Rehoboam at first retained only Judah, most of the tribe of Benjamin soon joined his kingdom. Simeon and Dan also became part of the kingdom of Judah.

108. What Was the Real Sin of Uzzah?

The sin of Uzzah (I Chron. 13:9, 10) and its sudden punishment have been a subject of much discussion. None but priests of Aaron's family (that is, of the priest's household) were permitted to touch the Ark. Uzzah was of a Levitical family. In the house of his father, Abinadab, the Ark had rested for twenty years. When Uzzah put forth his hand to prevent the Ark from falling he was smitten, Josephus explains, because he touched it, "not being a priest." Others, however, have taken the view that Uzzah's sin was not that of laying unordained and unconsecrated hands upon the Ark in a moment of excitement, but rather—if the real reason lay in this direction at all—because he recklessly and sacrilegiously appropriated to himself powers and privileges which he well knew belonged to higher persons. One commentator writes: "The whole proceeding was disorderly and contrary to the distinct and significant regulations of the law which prescribed that the Ark should be carried on the shoulders of the Levites (Ex. 25:14), whereas it was here conveyed in a cart drawn by oxen. Besides, it should have been covered. There seems to have been no priest in charge, and it would appear that the sacred vessel was brought forth naked to the common gaze." Uzzah as a Levite should have observed and remedied these things, but his growing familiarity with the mysteries of the Jewish religion had made him careless, and the punishment came upon him at a time when it would most effectually check the evils among the people. That it had this effect is evident from I Chron. 15:2-13.

109. Did the Witch at Endor Really Raise the Spirit of Samuel?

Much has been written on the question whether, in the scene at Endor, an imposture or a real apparition appeared. Eustathius and a majority of the early Christian fathers held the former opinion, and represent it as a deception of the evil one; Origen held the latter view. It should be remembered that Saul, at the time was forsaken of God and that, rendered desperate by his sins, he had recourse to this woman, who in the Hebrew writings is described as "a mistress of Ob" or a necromancist (not a "witch") who obtained a living by pretending to have intercourse with spirits, while the Greek writers describe her as a ventriloquist. Josephus, the Jewish historian, describes her as one of a class of fortune-tellers who had been banished by the king. Saul's highly wrought nervous condition at the time, combined with the fact that he himself saw no vision or spirit, but simply listened to and accepted the necromancer's description of an aged man of godlike appearance, should be taken into consideration, and these facts doubtless influenced the early fathers in reaching the conclusion that the wretched king had been the victim of an imposition.

110. What Is the Real Meaning of the Visions Described by Zechariah?

The chapters containing the visions are chiefly concerned with the hope founded on the approaching end of the seventy years, which, as Jeremiah predicted, would be the period of the captivity in Babylon. These are the meaning of the visions, according to some interpreters: The flying roll, a huge book with wings, contained the record of sin and curse. The prophet sees it flying from the Holy Land, destroying on its way the houses of the thieves and perjurers. The woman in the ephah (5:5-11) represents the principle of evil and of temptation. She, too, like sin and the curse, must be removed from the land, and she is carried away to the land of Shinar, which the Jews regarded as the fit abode of wicked things. The chariots of the winds (6:1-8) are God's messengers commissioned to avenge Israel. The black horses go north, that is to punish Persia; the dappled, south, that is against Egypt; and the white, west, that is against Greece, then becoming formidable. The horses of the fourth chariot have a general commission for any part of the world in which enmity to Israel might develop.

NEW TESTAMENT PERSONS AND THINGS

111. How Was the Apostles' Creed Formulated?

According to one ancient writer who quotes from tradition, it was Peter who contributed the first sentence—"I believe in God the Father Almighty"; John added—"Maker of heaven and earth"; James—"And in Jesus Christ, his only Son our Lord"; Andrew—"Who was conceived by the Holy Ghost, born of the Virgin Mary"; Philip—"Suffered under Pontius Pilate; was crucified dead and buried"; Thomas—"He descended into hell; the third day he rose again from the dead"; Bartholomew—"He ascended into heaven and sitteth at the right hand of God the Father Almighty"; Matthew—"From whence he shall come to judge the quick and the dead." The other clauses were contributed by James (son of Alpheus), Simon Zelotes, Jude and Matthias. It should be remembered, however, that neither Luke nor any ecclesiastical writer before the fifth century makes mention of an assembly of the apostles to formulate a creed, and the early fathers never claimed that the apostles framed it. Its date and the circumstances of its origin are uncertain.

112. Did John Write the Last Chapter of His Gospel?

We know that it has been asserted by some critics that this chapter must have been added by another hand, because the evangelist concluded his work in the previous chapter. This, however, is not accepted by sound scholarship, for the reason that it is not unusual in the New Testament writings and in other good books, for authors to insert supplementary matter, to which class the chapter in question clearly belongs. There is no evidence that John's Gospel was ever known in the early Church without this chapter. John, it is true, refers to himself in the third person; but he did so also in chapter 19:35 in practically the same terms as in 21:24. The best commentators agree as to the genuineness on *prima facie* evidence.

113. What Were the Locusts That Became the Food of John the Baptist?

Some writers think it may have been the common locust or green grasshopper, which, when prepared and dried, tastes somewhat like a shrimp. Many ancient authors mention them as food. Diodorus Siculus refers to a people of Ethiopia, who were called *acridophaghi,* or locust eaters. Porphryius says that whole armies have been saved from starvation by eating locusts. Aristotle and Aristophanes assert that they were relished by the Greeks, and Layard, the discoverer, found evidence that they were eaten in a preserved state by the Assyrians. Later commentators, however have conjectured that the "locust" mentioned in Mark's Gospel as being the food of John the Baptist, was the carob, the fruit of a tree of the locust family, which is a sort of sweetish bean, in pods, much used by the poorer classes.

114. What Is Known of John's Birth and Early Training?

He was of the priestly race by both parents, his father, Zacharias, being a priest of the course of Abijah, and Elisabeth a descendant of Aaron. Of the first thirty years of his life, the only history we have is contained in a single verse, Luke 1:80. But it is a reasonable presumption that he received the Jewish ecclesiastical training of that period. He was the chosen forerunner of the Messiah (Luke 1:76). Dwelling alone in the desert region westward of the Dead Sea, he prepared himself for his work by discipline and constant prayer. One of his instructors, Banus (mentioned by Josephus, the Jewish historian), tells how he lived with John in the desert, eating the sparse food and bathing frequently by day and night. At last (about A. D. 25) John came forth from his hermit-like seclusion in the wild mountainous tract in Judea lying beyond the desert and the Dead Sea, and took up the work of his real office, preaching repentance and baptism, and attracting great multitudes.

115. Was John the Baptist Sentenced to Death Before the Dance of Salome?

While there is no record to prove it, the presumption is that Herod, in his mind, had already condemned John on political grounds as one whose existence endangered his position and authority, but his awakened conscience and the fear inspired by John's teachings restrained him. He had kept John in the prison of Machærus nearly a year when the Salome incident occurred, which gave Herodias her opportunity to be revenged upon the Baptist, who had rebuked both her and Herod for their sinful relations. It cannot be asserted that Herod would have executed John had not the king been caught by his pledge to Salome. On the contrary Mark 6:26 tells us that he "was exceeding sorrowful."

116. When Did John the Baptist Die?

The date is somewhat difficult to determine with any degree of reliability. The first Passover of Jesus' ministry is believed to have occurred in A. D. 27. His baptism at John's hands took place immediately before that time. John's imprisonment in the tower of Machærus in all probability began in A. D. 27 and in the first half of that year, but Herod's unwillingness to put him to death may have delayed the climax until the beginning of A. D. 28. Tradition says he was buried in Samaria.

117. Was John the Baptist Elijah?

The statement in the affirmative is made a number of times in the New Testament. (See Matt. 11:14, 17:10-12; Mark 9:12, 13. See also Mal. 4:5.) But some of the ablest commentators hold that we must interpret the connection figuratively, and that there is no reason for believing that this means any more than that he was the new Elijah of his time, a rugged prophet, like Elijah in temperament, habits and speech, unafraid even of kings. He himself said distinctly that he was not Elijah (John 1:21). The sense in which the expression was used is made clear in Luke 1:17: "He shall go before him in *the spirit and power* of Elijah." In the narrative of Elijah's appearance at the transfiguration there is no suggestion that he was John the

Baptist, whom all the men present had known and seen, and who had only recently died. One of the things that distinguishes the philosophy of the Bible from that of uninspired teachings is that it never confuses or obscures personal identity. Each soul has a distinct personality, which can never be merged or changed into another.

118. John the Baptist's Place in Prophecy.

"Who was the last prophet of the old dispensation?" John the Baptist came as the forerunner of Christ, and so may be considered the last prophet of the old dispensation. Christ said: "All the prophets and the law prophesied until John" (Matt. 11:13). Otherwise, if you regard him as belonging to an intermediate dispensation, the last would be the prophet called Malachi, the writer of the last book in the Old Testament. It is not certain that Malachi was his name, as the word may be translated, "My messenger."

119. Why Was Twelve the Number of the Apostles?

All of the twelve disciples were Jews. Their number was doubtless fixed upon after the analogy of the twelve tribes. They were mostly Galileans, taken from the common people, and some at least had been disciples of John the Baptist. (See Matt. 12:25; John 1:35; Matt. 19:28.)

120. Have We a Historical Record of the Deaths of the Apostles?

The records of their end are found in traditions preserved by the early Church. Matthew was martyred in Ethiopia; Mark in Alexandria, Egypt; Luke was hanged on an olive tree in Greece; John, after many perils, died a natural death in Ephesus; Peter was crucified in Rome, head downwards; James the Great beheaded at Jerusalem; James the Less beaten to death with a fuller's club in the temple grounds; Philip hanged at Hieropolis; Bartholomew flayed alive; Thomas slain with a lance at Coromandel; Jude killed with arrows; Simeon crucified in Persia; Andrew crucified; Matthias stoned and beheaded; Barnabas stoned to death by Jews at Salamis; Paul beheaded at Rome under Nero.

121. If Paul Had Not Expected a Resurrection Would He Have Lived a Self-indulgent Life?

No, he was not that kind of man. In the passage in I Cor. 15:32 he is considering the attitude of an opponent, and is stating such an argument as might be made by one who believed there was no life beyond the grave. In effect he says: "A man who does not believe in immortality might naturally say, in considering such a life as mine, that it is folly. Instead of fighting with beasts as I did at Ephesus, and enduring all kinds of hardship and persecution, it would be better for me if I simply enjoyed the good things of life. Such a man could never be persuaded to become a Christian, if there was no prospect of a future life.

122. Is It Known Who Were Paul's Parents?

The name of Paul's parents are not given in the Scriptures. The only mention of his blood relations is in Acts 23:16 and Rom. 16:7, 11, but whether

Andronicus, Junia and Herodion were really relatives or simply friends is an open question.

123. What Are the Dates of the Pauline Epistles?

According to the best authorities the epistles of Paul were written at about the following times:

Romans ....58 A. D. at Corinth.
I Corinthians ....57 A. D. at Ephesus.
II Corinthians ......58 A. D. at Philippi.
I Thessalonians .....52 A. D. at Corinth.
II Thessalonians ....52 or 53 A. D. at Corinth.
Philippians ....61 A. D. at Rome.
Colossians ....63 A. D. at Rome.
Ephesians ....63 A. D. at Rome.
Galatians ....58 A. D. at Corinth.
Philemon ....63 A. D. at Rome.
I Timothy ....65 A. D. in Macedonia.
II Timothy ....67 A. D. in Rome.
Titus ....66 A. D. in Macedonia.

124. What Do We Know of Paul's Personal Appearance?

All we know of it, from his own writings, is found in II Cor. 10:10, which indicates that he did not possess the advantage of a distinguished or imposing presence. His stature was somewhat diminutive, his eyesight weak (see Acts 23:5 and Gal. 4:15) nor did he regard his address as impressive. Much of this personal criticism, however, may have been the outcome of the apostle's desire to avoid magnifying himself or his own talents. A fourth century tablet represents him as venerable-looking and dignified, with a high, bald forehead, full-bearded, and with features indicating force of character. One ancient writer says Paul's nose was strongly aquiline. All the early pictures and mosaics, as well as some of the early writers (among them Malalus and Nicephorus) agree in describing the apostle as of short stature, with long face, prominent eyebrows, clear complexion and a winning expression, the whole aspect being that of power and dignity. The oldest known portrait is the Roman panel of the fourth century, already referred to above.

125. What Was the Cause of the Dispute Between Peter and Paul at Antioch?

"When Peter was come to Antioch, I withstood him to the face, because he was to be blamed," wrote Paul in Gal. 2:11. In view of this statement of Paul, some have questioned whether we may regard both Paul and Peter as having been acting under inspiration. The question of inspiration is not involved in the incident that took place at Antioch, when Paul rebuked Peter for his inconsistency. It is simply a question of human weakness. While under the influence of certain High Church Jewish-Christians, who came from James, Peter withdrew and separated himself from the Antioch Christians, "fearing them of the circumcision." The result was that Barnabas, and doubtless many others, were affected by his example, which became a scandal in the community. To save the Church from an apostasy, Paul took Peter to task for his conduct and rebuked him openly, as his conduct was an attack on Gospel liberty. The writings of Paul and Peter that have found their way into the New Testament Canon are, beyond doubt, inspired, but to say that every word they uttered during their Christian lives was inspired is what we do not believe. Paul and Peter had human weaknesses and limitations, like other men. But when they wrote authoritatively under the guidance of the Holy Ghost, they were kept free from errors and mistakes, and in this way were inspired.

126. Was Paul Familiar with the Scriptures?

It is made clear in Acts 27 that Paul was familiar with "all the learning of the Greeks." Tarsus, his native city, was a famous seat of learning and philosophical research, and he probably had the advantage of training in its schools. The son of a Pharisee and trained from boyhood to the pursuits of a doctor of Jewish law, he presumably was instructed in the elements of Rabbinical lore, including of course the Jewish Scriptures. These are the inferences of those writers who have studied his life career. This could not apply to the New Testament writings as we now know them, for they were only in the making, and must have been very incomplete; but it is a fair presumption that in his later career, as an apostle, he was not ignorant of such writings as may then have been in existence, dealing with the events of Jesus' life and ministry. There was no New Testament, in the modern meaning of the term, in Paul's day, and could not have been, for obvious reasons.

127. What Part Did Paul Have in the Stoning of Stephen?

Paul, at the time of Stephen's martyrdom, was more than a mere spectator; he was an active assistant.

There is nothing in the Scripture to show that before his miraculous conversion, he had shown or expressed regret at his participation in Stephen's death. On the contrary, he had become, and was, up to the moment when he was stricken down, one of the bitterest and most relentless persecutors of the Christians. (See Acts 26:10, 12.) What he may have thought, in his own heart at times, of his share in the tragedy, or what influence it may have had upon him, can only be a matter of surmise. There was nothing to outwardly reveal that he brooded over it or that he repented at all, before his own transformation.

128. Was Paul Ever Married?

There is no evidence in the New Testament to show that he was ever married, and commentators have held that various passages in which he urges celibacy, show him to have remained single by choice. But this is only an inference. Others take the opposite view, pointing out that at the age of thirty, he was a member of the Sanhedrin (Acts 26:10); as such he "gave his vote" against the followers of Jesus. Being the youngest of the judges, he was appointed "judicial witness" of the execution of Stephen. According to Maimonides, and the Jerusalem *Gemara,* it was required of all who were to be made members of that Council that they should be married, and fathers of families, because such were supposed to be more inclined to merciful judgment. (See *Life of St. Paul,* by Conybeare and Howson, volume 1, chapter 2.)

129. What Were the Dates of Paul's Missionary Journeys?

Paul's introduction by the sacred historian (when he was a witness of Stephen's martyrdom), is supposed to have been about A. D. 36. At that time he was probably between thirty and forty years of age. His conversion took place A. D. 37. He left Damascus A. D. 37. First missionary journey undertaken A. D. 44; his second, three years later, and his third, four years after the second.

130. When Did Paul Go to Rome and How Long Did He Stay?

According to the best available information, the shipwreck occurred in the year 56 A. D., and late in the autumn of that year Paul reached Rome as a prisoner. The length of his stay is uncertain. Acts 28:30 says two years, and the author probably knew. It is probable that Paul was then set at liberty and made another preaching tour, going farther west than before. He was afterwards again seized and taken back to Rome. How long a time elapsed between his second arrival and his execution there no one knows.

131. Did Paul Baptize?

He answers this question himself (I Cor. 1:17). He implies that he had something better to do. Christ sent him not to baptize but to preach the Gospel. The value of baptism in the case of the Corinthian converts was that it was a public profession of their faith—it placed them on record. This result would be attained whoever administered the rite, and, therefore, Paul relegated the duty to some other Christian. After he left, the Corinthians began to think there was some special significance about it, and for this Paul reproves them.

132. Did Peter Go to Rome?

There is nothing in the book of Romans to indicate Peter's presence in Rome at any time, but that is merely negative evidence. If he ever visited Rome, it was probably during the last year of his life, although Eusebius in the *Chronicon* says he visited it in A. D. 42. Jerome also mentions Peter's visit to Rome. Catholic writers assert that he was there for a number of years. There is no evidence of the fact in the New Testament books. It is generally accepted, however, that he was in Rome in his last year when he became a martyr as our Lord predicted (John 21:18, 19). Dionysus of Corinth writes that Peter and Paul suffered martyrdom in Italy together. Irenæus confirms his presence in Rome. Caius, Origen, Tertullian and others bear similar testimony.

133. Was Peter Converted Before His Denial of Christ?

Peter was a man of resolute character, bold and decisive. He was easily the leader of the twelve. Honest-hearted and warmly attached to Christ, he believed himself immovably loyal; yet in the hour of temptation he proved unstable and weak. Jesus knew his heart and warned him against over-confidence in his own loyalty. "I have been praying for thee," he said, "that thy faith fail not." He needed this divine strengthening. His faith had failed once before in a crisis (see Matt. 14:29), and what he needed to confirm him now was the "power from on high" which would come later. The tempter was to sift all the disciples, and Jesus foresaw Peter's weakness, but he was preserved from falling by this special intercession. His case shows, perhaps more completely than any other in the New Testament, the weakness of the natural and the strength of the spiritual man. Even at the moment of his denial of Christ, it needed but a glance from the eye of his Lord to make him instantly repentant. After the enduement with the Holy Ghost, he stood forth as the leader of the apostles, faithful unto death.

134. What Was Paul's "Thorn in the Flesh"?

It referred to some bodily affliction affecting him individually and physically, but not his work as an apostle. In Gal. 4:13, 14 he refers to it as an "infirmity of my flesh"—some form of bodily sickness which had detained him among the Galatians. It was probably something that caused him acute pain, and also some degree of shame, since it "buffeted" him (I Pet. 2:20). There have been many conjectures as to its real character. Some have imagined it to be blasphemous thoughts, and others, remorse for his former life; but the most probable view is that it was an affliction which caused him physical annoyance, possibly a disorder of the eyes, or some nervous ailment. At all events, we are assured that it was so persistent and recurrent that he speaks of it in terms of apology and mortification.

135. For What Purpose Was Judas Chosen as a Disciple?

He was attracted, as the others were, by the preaching of the Baptist or by his own Messianic hopes. It can be imagined, however, that baser motives may have mingled with his faith and zeal. He must have possessed some qualifications, probably plausibility being one, and he may even have excelled the rest of the twelve in business ability. Again, he may have joined the twelve in all sincerity, and yielded to temptation only when he found the handling of the money made him covetous. It was evident that Jesus knew from the beginning what Judas would do (John 6:64). Volumes have been written in the futile effort to explain why Judas was chosen.

136. In What Sense Was Judas a Devil?

Little is known of the life of Judas before his appearance among the apostles. He was probably drawn by the Baptist's preaching, or by his own ambitious hopes of the coming of a Messianic kingdom, in which he might play an important and lucrative part. He seems to have declared himself a disciple of Jesus, as the others did, and as he was intrusted with the finances of the little company, we may judge that he enjoyed a measure of confidence, although this seems to have been undeserved. (See John 12:6.) That Jesus himself knew the heart of Judas from the beginning is made clear from the text. (See also John 6:64-71.) Our Lord knew his inmost thoughts. He knew Judas to be deceitful and treacherous. He knew of his criminal confidences with the priests, which culminated in the betrayal. (See John 18:3-5.) The act of betrayal was not the outcome of a sudden impulse at the Last Supper, but was the closing scene in a long career of deceit and treachery. Judas was probably ambitious, and like several other apostles believed that Jesus would set up an earthly kingdom in which he himself might have an influential part. Of his early history before his name appears in the list of the apostles, nothing is known. The name "Iscariot" is variously explained, some writers holding that he was so called because he belonged to Kerioth in the tribe of Judah.

137. How Did Judas Die?

Several explanations of the apparent discrepancy between Matt. 27:3-10 and Acts 1:18, 19 have been offered. The first, with relation to the death of Judas, is that the word translated as "hanged" in Matt. 27:5 is capable of a different interpretation, *i. e.*, death by a sudden spasm of suffocation, which might have been accompanied by a fall before the spasm spent itself. Another suggestion, which has been made by some eminent scholars, is that the work of suicide was but half accomplished when, the halter parting, Judas fell with the result stated in Acts 1:18.

138. Was It Repentance or Remorse That Drove Judas to Suicide?

All we know is what the Scripture tells us. It may have been remorse, or chagrin over the failure of his plans, but it could hardly have been repentance. It was suggested by DeQuincey, with some plausibility, that in betraying Christ, he was seeking to precipitate a crisis, out of which he expected to see Christ emerge triumphant. He thought Christ would use his miraculous power to save himself, and when in danger of death, would declare himself King, and would set up his kingdom, in which the disciples would hold high office. When he found that Christ intended to submit, he perceived that his scheme to force his hand had failed, and he was overwhelmed by the catastrophe he had precipitated. The suggestion is not sustained by the conception we gain of him in the Gospels, but it is possible to imagine an ambitious and avaricious man acting in that way; if, as is possible, he was impatient with Christ, who had powers so great and yet was so slow to use them to advance his own interests and those of the men who had left all to follow him, he may have tried this scheme. The suggestion, however, is pure conjecture. No one has been able to analyze satisfactorily the character of Judas.

139. Were the Apostles Converted Before the Day of Pentecost?

Jesus had said many things to and about His disciples before his death, which indicated that they were converted men: "Rejoice, because your names are written in heaven," Luke 10:20; "Now ye are clean through the word that I have spoken unto you," John 15:3; "Ye know him" (the Spirit of truth), "for he dwelleth with you, and shall be in you." In the last verse he distinguishes them from "the world." The world, he said, cannot receive the Spirit; but the Spirit was already with the disciples, and was to come into their hearts in greater fullness, as he did on the day of Pentecost. In the high-priestly prayer Jesus said: "I pray not for the world, but for them which thou hast given me; for they are thine;" "They are not of the world, even as I am not of the world;" "Thine they were, and thou gavest them me; and they have kept thy word," John 17:9, 14, 16, 6. Although Peter was a converted man, he fell into sin and denied his Master. It is the common experience of justified Christians that, while they do not habitually sin, they slip occasionally into transgression. But after the fullness of the Spirit had been received on the day of Pentecost, Peter and the other apostles stood firm. This also has been the experience of many Christians since the apostles' time, who have found, in a larger blessing, sanctifying and keeping grace. Jacob's experience was the same. Before his blessing at Jabbok, he had met God at Bethel and received the promise: "I will not leave thee" (Gen. 28:15); God had spoken to him again, while he dwelt with Laban (Gen. 31:3-11); the angels of God met him at Mahanaim (Gen. 32:2). But after the experience at Jabbok, or Peniel, he lived to the end of his days a purer, higher spiritual life.

140. Was the Gift of Tongues Retained by the Apostles Until Their Death?

The endowment of the "gift of tongues" was apparently continued to the Christians during the apostolic age. Jesus before his ascension breathed upon his disciples and said "Receive ye the Holy Ghost." Fifty days after the crucifixion, the disciples received special power, when the Holy Ghost came upon them. It was to be a sign—to belong to only a few—the apostles and evangelists—and with this gift they went forth to preach to the nations. Later, Paul wrote that he "spake with tongues more than all." In I Cor. 13:8, however, we see that "tongues" were already ceasing, as belonging to the past. Many times since then the question has arisen whether the gift of tongues was continued to succeeding generations. The attitude of the early Church, neither to quench nor forbid them (see I Thess. 5:19), yet not to invite or excite them, was a safe one. If they were of God, the fact would make itself apparent; if they were simply hysterical jargon, they would quickly subside. Throughout Church history, there were many spurious instances. Irenæus wrote of some in his time who spoke with tongues, but Eusebius hardly referred to the subject, and Chrysostom mentions it only to discourage what he considered as an ecstatic indulgence of doubtful spiritual profit.

141. Were Any of the Disciples Married?

Very little is known regarding the domestic relations of the apostles beyond what is disclosed in the Gospels. Matt. 8:15 clearly implies that Peter was married. Bartholomew is said by tradition to have been the bridegroom at the wedding at Cana, and Philip is mentioned by Clement of Alexandria as having had a wife and children. Nothing definite can be asserted concerning the others, although they are generally assumed to have been unmarried.

142. Who Were the Essenes?

A small community of Jews in the time of Christ, who led a pastoral life and did not marry. They held their goods and took their meals in common, strictly observed the Sabbath, prayed before sunrise with their faces to the East, bathed daily in cold water, never swore, sacrificed no animals, and believed in immortality without a resurrection of the body.

143. Who Were the Gentiles?

Gentiles, which means simply "peoples," was a term applied indiscriminately by the Jews to all other nations than themselves. After a time it acquired a hostile meaning, as the Jews gradually drew themselves apart as a "holy nation." The term is used of "Galilee of the Gentiles," where some five nations other than the Jews were represented; the "Court of the Gentiles" outside the Temple area; the "isles of the Gentiles," etc.

144. Who Were the Pharisees?

The Pharisees were a Jewish sect deriving their name from a word which means "separate" or "distinct." They were disciples of the Jewish sages, who held themselves aloof and claimed to keep rigidly the Mosaic laws of purity. They had many religious observances and believed in a future life of rewards and punishments.

145. Who Were the Sadducees?

The Sadducees were a sect of free-thinkers, differing greatly from the Pharisees on many points. They rejected the oral law and the prophets and only accepted the Pentateuch, and Josephus says they denied the resurrection from the dead.

146. Who Were the Herodians?

The Herodians were a class of Jews in the time of Christ, who were partisans of Herod, either of a political or religious sort, or both. It appears that when the ecclesiastical authorities of Judea held a council against the Saviour, they associated with themselves the Herodians, and sent an embassy to Jesus designing to trap him in his speech. As tetrarch of Galilee, Herod Antipas was the ruler of the province which was Jesus' home, and the Jews doubtless argued that Herod would be pleased if they could convict Jesus of being a rival claimant to the crown. The Pharisees were a Jewish sect who held rigidly aloof from other sects, claimed to be free from every kind of impurity and united to keep the Mosaic laws, to which they gave the closest study. They were frequently denounced by our Saviour for their self-righteousness and their assumption of superior piety. The Sadducees were another sect, originally a religious body, but which had developed into a body of freethinkers. They rejected the oral law and the prophets, but believed in the Pentateuch; they denied the resurrection and they held different views from other Jews on various other important points while claiming to be the most aristocratic and conservative of all the bodies.

147. What Is Known of the Early Life of the Author of the Epistle of James?

Nothing authoritative. He was probably brought up with Jesus and the other children in the Nazareth home. It is believed that he did not become a follower of Christ until after the resurrection. Christ seems to have appeared specially to him, and as Paul mentions the fact (I Cor. 15:7) we may presume it was generally known, though it is not related in any of the Gospels. James was a strict Jew before becoming a Christian, and was highly esteemed among the Jews for his piety. It looks as though he never quite shook off his Jewish ideas (Gal. 2:12), and his epistle shows that he could not cordially endorse Paul's way of stating the Gospel.

148. Was It a Whale That Swallowed Jonah?

Nowhere in the book of Jonah are we told that the fish that swallowed Jonah was a whale. In Matt. 12:40 the word "whale" is used, but the revised version gives "sea monster" in the margin. There is absolute proof that sea monsters large enough to swallow a man have been found in the Mediterranean and other seas.

149. Who Were the Karaites, or Readers?

They were a small remnant of the Sadducees, "the Protestants of Judaism," formed into a sect by Anan-ben-Daniel in the eighth century. They rejected the rabbinical traditions and the Talmud, and accepted the Scriptures alone. The origin of their name is uncertain. Some of the sect exist in the Crimea, Poland and Turkey.

150. How Long Did Lazarus Live After Being Raised from the Dead?

There are no authoritative data on the subject. An old tradition, mentioned by Epiphanius, says that Lazarus was thirty years old when restored from death and that he lived thirty years thereafter. Still another tradition declares that he traveled to Southern Europe, accompanied by Mary and Martha, and preached the Gospel in Marseilles.

151. Who Was Lydia?

She is mentioned in Acts 16:15 and was a resident of Thyatira, a city celebrated for its purple dyes. She seems to have been a business woman, engaged in the sale of dyed goods, and she evidently had an extensive establishment, as she was able to accommodate the missionary party. She was a proselyte to the Jewish faith, but became a believer under Paul's ministry.

152. Was Mary, the Mother of Jesus, of the Tribe of Judah?

It is not proved, except inferentially. The Jews, in constructing their genealogical tables, reckoned wholly by males. Some of the best modern authorities, however, observing all the rules followed by the Hebrews in genealogies, have reached the conclusion that in Zorobabel the lines of Solomon and Nathan unite, and that Joseph and Mary are therefore of the same tribe and family, being both descendants of David in the line of Solomon and that both have in them the blood of Nathan. David's son, Joseph, has descent from Abiud (Matt. 1:13) and Mary from Rhesa (Luke 3:27), sons of Zorobabel. The genealogies of Matthew and Luke are parts of one perfect whole; the former bearing the descent of Mary and Joseph from Solomon—the latter the descent of both from Nathan.

153. Who Were the Parents of Mary?

Many scholars are of opinion that she was the daughter of the Heli mentioned in Luke 3:23. As the Jews reckoned their genealogy by the male side only, it was customary to set a man's son-in-law down as his son. This would account for Joseph being described by one evangelist as the son of Jacob and by the other as the son of Heli. Apart from that theory there are no data for ascertaining the parentage of Mary.

154. How Many Marys Are There in the Bible?

The Marys spoken of in the New Testament are: Mary the mother of Christ, Mary Magdalene, Mary the sister of Lazarus, Mary the wife of Cleophas (John 19:25) and Mary the mother of John (Acts 12:12).

155. Who Are the Nestorians?

They are the descendants of a sect of early Christians, named after Nestorius, a theologian of the fifth century A. D. They claim also to be descended from Abraham, and sometimes call themselves Chaldeans. They are probably the oldest of the Oriental churches. They are found in Persia, in India, East Indies, Syria, Arabia, Asia Minor, and even in Cochin China, the principal settlements, however, being in and near Persia. They believe Christ to be both divine and human—two persons, with only a moral and sympathetic union. They do not believe in any divine humiliation nor any exaltation of humanity in Christ. They acknowledge the supreme authority of the Scriptures and believe they contain all that is essential to salvation. The main body of Nestorians is nominally Christian, but it is a lifeless Christianity. They have no images, but they invoke the Virgin and the saints and are ignorant and superstitious.

156. Who Were the Nicolaitanes?

Though they are mentioned in Rev. 2:15 it is not positively known, but from the context it would appear that they were people who abused Paul's doctrine of Christian liberty, which they turned into license. It is supposed that Jude 4 refers to them. They appear to have attended the heathen rites and shared in the abominations there practised. Some suppose them to have been followers of Nicolas of Antioch, but if so, they falsely claimed that he taught such things. It is more probable that the name, if relating to a person at all, has been confused with some other Nicolas.

WORDS AND TERMS

157. What Significance Has the Word "Abba," as When It Precedes the Word "Father"?

"Abba" is the Hebrew word for "father," in the emphatic or definite state, as "thy father." Its use in referring to God was common among the Jews; but in order that it might not seem too familiar or irreverent, the New Testament writers gave it the two-fold form, which has become a recognized phrase in Christian worship. It is as though they said: "Father, our Father."

158. What Are We to Understand by the Battle of Armageddon, Referred to in Revelation?

Armageddon is the name given to the last great battle to be fought in the world's history, in which the whole human race is arrayed on one side or the other. It is to be the final struggle of Antichrist. When it will be fought no one can tell; but that there will be a great struggle we are assured. Before that day comes "many false prophets shall arise and lead many astray . . . iniquity shall be multiplied and the love of many shall wax cold." There are to be false Christs, false teachers doing signs and wonders, and leading astray "even the elect if such were possible." It is to be preceded by a period of apostasy, in which the authority of the wicked one will be fully demonstrated, with the assumption of divinity and the demand for universal worship as God. In the present stage of the conflict between good and evil, when mighty forces are arrayed on both sides, we can see the foreshadowing of the fierce struggle that is to come; but we may rest assured that righteousness will triumph in the end. (See the parallel passage in Joel 3:2-12.) Armageddon is "the mountain of Megiddo," west of the Jordan, a scene of early historic battles and the place that would naturally suggest itself to the mind of a Galilean writer to whom the place and its associations were familiar.

159. What Is Meant by the "Prince of the Power of the Air"?

It refers to Satan (Eph. 2:2), the "prince of evil," who assails men on earth with trials and temptations. The word "power" is used here for the embodiment of that evil spirit which is the ruling principle of all unbelief, especially among the heathen. (See I Tim. 4:1; II Cor. 4:4; John 12:31.)

159A. What Is to Be Understood by Being "Baptized for the Dead"?

Beuzel translated the familiar passage in I Cor. 15:29 thus: "Over the dead," or "immediately upon the dead," meaning those who will be gathered to the dead immediately after baptism. Many in the ancient church put off baptism till near death. The passage probably referred to some symbolical rite of baptism or dedication of themselves to follow the dead even to death. Another view held by some expositors is that it was a custom to baptize certain persons with the names of the dead, in the hope that they might inherit their spirit and carry on their work.

160. What Is the Baptism of Fire?

It has been variously interpreted to mean: (1) the baptism of the Holy Spirit, (2) the fires of purgatory, and (3) the everlasting fires of hell. Modern theologians take the view that the baptism of fire and that of the Holy Ghost are the same, and that it may be rendered "baptized with the Holy Ghost through the outward symbol of fire," or "as with the cloven tongues of fire," referring to the Pentecostal baptism.

161. Have Automobiles and Airships Been the Subject of Biblical Prophecy?

Nahum 2:4 has been quoted as referring to automobiles, but this appears to strain the meaning of the passage, which was written as a direct prophecy of the destruction of Nineveh. The verse describes the mad rush of those in chariots to escape the enemy. Isa. 60:8 has been thought by some to be a reference to the coming use of airships, but here again the direct meaning is obvious, that in the time of Judea's prosperity ships shall flock to her shores as doves to the windows of their dovecotes. Hab. 1:8 might be thought to presage manflight, but the figure is used to express the terrific haste with which the Chaldeans shall come against Judea.

162. What Is Meant by the "Beast and His Mark"?

The Seer of Revelation appears to have had his visions in the form of a series of scenes, as in a panorama. Almost at the close (Rev. 14:9) he saw the beast you refer to. It is evidently identical with the beast described by Daniel (7:7). It is representative of the power which is said to have throughout the world's history opposed God. It appears in John's narrative in a series of forms, and is sometimes identified with a persecuting church, and sometimes is the civil power. At the culmination of its career, John saw it as the great Antichrist, who is yet to arise, who would attain to such power in the world that he would exclude any many from office and from even engaging in trade, who did not acknowledge him. Only those who bear the mark of the beast can buy or sell in that time. This mark may be a badge to be worn on forehead or hand, or as some scholars think, merely the coins to be used in business, which will bear Antichrist's title symbolized by the number 666.

163. How Was the Brazen Serpent a Type?

"As the serpent was lifted up in the wilderness, so must the son of man be lifted up." These were the Saviour's words. Jesus' death on the cross was an uplifting, and in this sense it is compared to the uplifting of the brazen serpent. In both cases the remedy is divinely provided and there is another striking similarity: As death came to the Israelites in the wilderness by the serpent's sting and life came by the uplifting of a serpent, so, in redemption, by man came death, and by the death of the God-man in the likeness of sinful flesh comes life eternal. In the first instance the cure was effected by directing the eye to the uplifted serpent; in the other, it takes place when the eye of faith is fixed upon the uplifted Christ.

164. Were the Giants Mentioned in Genesis 6:4 the Descendants of Angels, As Some Fanciful Interpreters Claim?

This has been answered by a notable authority as follows: "Gen. 6:1-4 forms the introduction to the story of the Flood. All races have preserved the tradition of a flood; whether it was universal or local is a moot point. The Jewish Scriptures leave the investigation of natural phenomena to human research. The Bible is not a scientific treatise. Its sole concern is religious and moral. Its aim is to justify the ways of God to man, and to show that natural phenomena, being controlled by God, are in harmony with divine justice. Hence, before relating the story of the Flood, Holy Writ sets forth the universal corruption which justified the destruction of the human race, with the exception of one family. Chapter 6:1-4 describes the violence and immorality prevalent in the antediluvian period. Mankind had, in course of time, fallen into two divisions—the classes and the masses. The masses were the common multitude of toilers, the ordinary 'sons of men.' The classes were the 'supermen,' 'the sons of God,' 'the mighty heroes.' The latter formed the aristocracy; they were the ruling class, the children of judges and princes. Small in number, they were physically strong and mentally vigorous, and had, moreover, appropriated a large portion of the wealth of the then known world. They should have used their power and position for the benefit of their kind, and set an example in chastity, temperance, self-restraint, justice and kindliness. Instead, they gave way to unbridled lust, to indulge which they resorted to violence. 'They saw that the daughters of men (*i. e.,* the common folk) were fair, and they took (*i. e.,* by force) whomsoever they chose.' This abuse of power was punished by the destruction of the race. 'The Eternal said: My spirit shall not abide in man forever.' The Hebrew word may mean 'abide as a sword in a sheath'; or it may mean 'contend with man'—the higher with the lower nature—the spirit of heaven with the body formed of dust and its instincts, of the earth, earthy; or it may mean 'My spirit shall not rule in man.' The struggle is too severe. 'Since he is but flesh, his days shall be one hundred and twenty years.' On account of the moral infirmity incident to human nature, time will be given for repentance. If the opportunity is not taken, destruction will follow the respite. *Nephilim* literally means 'the fallen.' On the principle of *lucus a non lucendo,* the term refers to the men of gigantic stature who existed in ancient times. They were the mighty men who yielded to licentious passions. The children of these illegitimate unions were also, for some generations, Nephilim of gigantic stature, famed for their physical and mental development, but morally degenerate. They were the renowned heroes of old—the mighty warriors, like the berserkers of the northern sagas."

Another view is that "the sons of God" were the Sethites, who had mantained in some measure the filial relationship to God, and who now intermarried with the Cainites, who had been spiritually disowned on account of their godlessness and unbelief. All the evidence leads to the conclusion that the whole arraignment of wickedness upon the earth related to beings of flesh and blood (see Gen. 6:3) and not to supernatural beings, who, we are elsewhere told distinctly, have no distinction of sex and never marry (see Luke 20:35, 36). In this view, which seems to be the correct one, the appellation "sons of God" refers to men's moral and in no sense to their physical state. There are many passages elsewhere that bear out this belief. (See Acts 17:28; Ex. 4:22, 23; Deut. 14:1; Hosea 11:1, etc.)

165. What Is Meant by "Casting Out Devils?"

The question has been the subject of dispute for many generations. The plain meaning of the narrative, however, seems to us to be that Satan had gained absolute possession and control of the afflicted persons and that Christ evicted him by his superior power. It seems to us impossible on any other assumption to satisfactorily explain the words of exorcism Christ used, the words uttered by the afflicted persons and the effects which followed. The symptoms described very closely resemble those of some forms of epilepsy and insanity of our time. Science, however, does not now ascribe the affliction to demoniacal possession. Nevertheless some of the patients do occasionally display a degree of malignity and cunning which could scarcely be exceeded if they were really possessed by the devil.

166. What and Where Is the "Kingdom of God?"

There are several senses in which the word "kingdom" is used. It may be taken in general terms as the kingdom which is set up in the heart (as Christ told the Pharisees, Luke 17:21, "The kingdom of God is within you") and the kingdom which is set up in the world (see Daniel 2:44) and the kingdom Christ will establish at his second coming (II Timothy 4:1), and there is the kingdom in heaven where God reigns. In the first of these senses we enter the kingdom at conversion when we give our allegiance to Christ.

167. What Is Being "Baptized Unto Death"?

The passage in Rom. 6:3, 4, 5 implies that those who have gone through this experience have formally surrendered the whole state and life of sin, as being dead in Christ. Verse 4 is more accurately interpreted "by the same baptism which makes us sharers in his death we are made partakers of his burial also," thus severing our last link of connection with the sinful condition and life which Christ brought to an end in his death. Possibly immersion was alluded to in this verse as symbolical of burial and resurrection. Verse 5 is self-explanatory.

168. In What Sense Is the Believer "In Christ"?

The reference is exclusively to the relation of the believer to the risen Lord, and expresses a peculiar spiritual connection. Rev. David Smith, the distinguished theologian, defines it as a spiritual way of four connecting links, viz.: (1) Christ for us (see II Cor. 5:21), which is substitution; (2) We in Christ (II Cor. 5:7; Rom. 6:11), which is justification; (3) Christ in us (Rom. 8:11; II Cor. 13:5; Gal. 2:20), which is sanctification, and (4) We for Christ (II Cor. 5:10), which is consecration. This is the condition of Christ's true disciple. He stands in the world as representative and witness-bearer for Christ. It is not merely a question of his own salvation; he must be a shining light to guide others, and must live the Christ-life, under whatever circumstances he may be placed. One who lives the Christ-life and all of whose thoughts, acts, influences and hopes are centered on carrying on the work of Christ, and who is guided by his will, can be said to be truly "in Christ."

169. What Is It to Be "Risen with Christ"?

Paul had described himself as having been crucified with Christ (Gal. 2:20). He was dead to the world through the death of Christ, dead to sin, to worldly ambition, and to all the worldly principles and motives. But he might have been asked, "Was he really dead?" and, in Col. 3:1, he answers that, like Christ, he had received a new life, having been raised with him, as he had been crucified with him. This was the resurrection life by which he had become transformed, and was a new creature in Christ Jesus. It was this that Augustine meant when he was greeted by a dissolute companion of his youth, whom he had passed on the street without recognition. "August, it is I, do you not know me?" He replied: "I am August no longer." Having become a Christian (risen with Christ) he had abandoned all his old life with its companions and associations.

170. What Is the Bible Definition of a Christian?

A Christian is (1) one who believes in Jesus Christ the divine Son of God, and that through his life and atonement we have everlasting life; (2) the Christian through his fellowship with Christ receives the adoption of a child of God (see I John 3:2 and 5:1); (3) he enters into fellowship and communion with God. See Heb. 2:11, 16; I John 1:3; Prov. 18:24. (4) He is sanctified and separated. See Rom. 1:7; I Pet. 1:14, 15; I Thess. 5:23. (5) He is a soldier. I Tim. 6:12; II Tim. 2:3, 4. (6) He is an heir of glory. Rom. 8:17; Gal. 3:29; Gal. 4:7; Titus 3:7; I Pet. 1:3, 4.

171. Who Were the First Christians?

See Acts 11:26; 26:28 and I Peter 4:16 which make the earliest mention of the term "Christian" being used to distinguish this from other religious sects. Thus, though the three Magi or Eastern princes, who came, led by the star, to worship the infant Christ (see Matt. 2:1-5), and the shepherds who also worshiped (see Luke 2:15, 16, 17) and the aged Simeon and Anna (same chapter) doubtless believed, they were not Christians in name; nor does it appear that either the divine nature of the Master or his mission were clearly comprehended until John the Baptist proclaimed him as Messiah. His disciples were *literally* the first Christians, being both believers and followers. The first Christians known as such by name, were those of the church founded by Paul and Barnabas at Antioch about A. D. 34. The term "Christian" is said to have been first used in the Episcopate of Evodius at Antioch, who was appointed by the Apostle Peter as his own successor.

172. When Was the First "Church" So Called?

The word "church" is first applied by Luke the evangelist to the company of original disciples at Jerusalem at Pentecost (Acts 2:47), and is afterwards applied in Acts, Epistles and Revelation to the whole Christian body or society, as well as the sanctified of God (Eph. 5:27), and to those who profess Christian faith under pastors (I Cor. 12:28). It was also applied to early societies of Christians in cities and provinces (Acts 8:1), to Christian assemblies (Rom. 16:5), and to small gatherings of friends and neighbors in private houses (I Cor. 11:18 and 14:19, 28). In those early days and for a long time afterward, there was no distinctive body and certainly no denomination; the church was simply an appellation describing groups of believers anywhere. Later, these groups were organized into congregations and districts and parishes were defined. Then they were called "Christians," the first use of this appellation being at Antioch. The Romanist claim to priority is an old one, but it does not stand the test of history. The title "Catholic Church" (meaning the "church universal") was originally given to the Christian Church on account of its not being confined to Jews but embracing other nationalities. The earliest use of this title was about 166 A. D., whereas the Roman Catholic Church as such did not come into existence until several centuries afterward, when the original church divided in consequence of the rivalry between the bishops of Rome and Constantinople.

173. Who First Fixed the Date of Christmas Day on December 25th?

There does not seem to have been any special observance of the nativity until the celebration in the Eastern Church (or Greek Christian Church) in A. D. 220. The Western (or Latin) Church began to celebrate it about a century later. Both adopted the uniform date about A. D. 380. There are some writers, however, who affirm that it was solemnly celebrated among the early Christians in the second century. Chronologists disagree as to the exact year of the nativity, but the majority believe it was B. C. 5. The celebration was at first held on January 6, but toward the end of the fourth century it was changed to December 25. The Christmas tree, it is said, was first used in Europe in the eighth or ninth century, and was introduced by a German or Hungarian princess.

174. How Are We to Understand the Act of Creation?

"Creation" means, in the orthodox sense, that God of his own free will and by his absolute power, called the whole universe into being, evoking into existence that which before was nonexistent. See Rom. 4:17; Ps. 33:6, 9; Heb. 3:4; Acts 17:24; Acts 14:15; Ps. 102:5; Jer. 10:12; John 1:3; Rev. 4:11. It is needless to speculate on these matters. If we concede the absolute power of God, we must accept his power both to create and annihilate, as stated in the Scriptures. There are many problems which the finite mind cannot wholly grasp and which must be accepted by faith or left alone.

175. What Is Demoniac Possession?

Whether or not there are evil spirits and the fact of demon possession has often proved baffling to believers. Ephesians 6:12, for instance, is a recognition of the existence and power of evil spirits. It is intimated that there are kingdoms of evil, ruled by wicked beings, which are fighting the powers of good. Against these forces the Christian, protected by the armor of God, is called to fight. The expression "in high places," or as translated in the margin, "heavenly places," may mean in the "upper air," as some interpret it, or as others hold, that even in the highest Christian experiences we are subject to temptation (which is, of course, the case), and that we must contend with the evil spirits for the possession of these high places in the spiritual world.

Although many rationalistic teachers have held that the Biblical cases of demon possession were nothing more than forms of epilepsy, violent hysteria, lunacy and other kinds of permanent or temporary mental derangement known at the present day, nothing has been actually proven which discredits the Scripture accounts and statements. Specialists today recognize the existence of recurrent mania, which sometimes assumes a destructive character. The Bible recognizes a form of lunacy different from demon possession. See Matt. 4:24. We know there are evil persons who, while alive in the flesh, do harm to others. Some have the definite experience of feeling themselves impelled to do wrong by an influence outside their own minds or bodies. Some present-day cases of insanity are really cases in which there are features that furnish a close parallel to demon possession. It is only fair to state, however, that present-day theological opinion is divided on the subject. It is certain that the belief in demon possession was held in early Christian times, and for long ages thereafter, and included at one time almost every form of mental disorder. On the other hand, it is urged that it is just as rational to believe in devils as to believe in angels. Angels are a race of personal holy beings; demons a race of personal vicious beings, both existing in a form other than human and corporeal.

176. In What Sense Was Man Created in the Divine Likeness?

Man's likeness to God, referred to in Gen. 1:26, is the great fact which distinguishes him from the rest of creation. He is a "person" with power to think, feel and will, and with the capacity for moral life and growth. Still further, at the beginning, man had not only the capacity for moral life, but his moral disposition was such that he loved God, loved the right, and hated the wrong. The tragedy of the fall reversed this. Man was still a person and still had the capacity for righteousness, but his spirit was so changed that he feared and distrusted God, and, to a greater or less extent, loved the evil and disliked the good. Jesus came to undo this calamity and to restore us to a moral likeness to God.

177. What Is Meant by the "Elect"?

"Elect" is a term variously applied. It sometimes meant the ancient church, and the whole body of baptized Christians; again, it was those elected to baptism; and still again, it was the newly baptized who had just been admitted to full Christian privileges. Further it is applied to those especially chosen for the Lord's work, like his prophets and evangelists, and to those who had undergone tribulation and even martyrdom. It has been applied to the whole Jewish people as chosen of God. Finally, it is applied to individuals who, not of their own merit, but through God's grace, through Jesus Christ, are chosen not only to salvation, but to sanctification of the spirit and who are holy and blameless before the Lord. They are individuals specially chosen out of the world to be heirs of salvation and witnesses for God before men. This is not of works, but of free grace. In a general way, the "elect" are the sanctified—those chosen to salvation through sanctification of the spirit, as explained in Peter 1:2 and similar passages. They are the special vessels of the Spirit chosen in God's good pleasure to carry out his purposes. This election is of grace and not of works (see Rom. 9:18, 22, 23). In all ages such men have been evidently chosen by the Lord as his witnesses. This choice is at once an expression of his sovereignty and his grace. Paul himself was so chosen. On the other hand, it should not be forgotten that salvation is by grace. The whole subject of election has been one of acute controversy for ages and has given rise to many differences of opinion. The attitude of Christians with regard to the Second Coming should be one of prayer, expectancy and constant preparation.

178. What Is Meant by "Saved, Yet As by Fire"?

The apostle in I Cor. 3:15 speaks of mistaken teachings and concludes that the man whose work was not of genuine character, who had been seeking worldly gain and popularity and not trying to win and build up souls, would lose the reward which would be given to the preacher who built on the foundation of Christ, "gold, silver, and precious stones." The unprofitable worker's work he likens to wood and stubble which would not stand the day of judgment. Even though his soul should be saved, he would miss the reward promised to the faithful worker, while his own work, being false, will not escape the destruction.

179. What Is Meant by "Strange Fire"?

The "strange fire" mentioned in Lev. 10:1, 2 is understood to mean that Nadab and Abihu, instead of taking fire into their censers from the brazen altar, took common fire which had not been consecrated, and thus were guilty of sacrilege. They had witnessed the descent of the miraculous fire from the cloud (see chapter 9:24), and they were under solemn obligation to use that fire which was specially appropriated to the altar service. But instead of doing so, they became careless, showing want of faith and lamentable irreverence, and their example, had it been permitted to pass unpunished, would have established an evil precedent. The fire that slew them issued from the most holy place, which is the accepted interpretation of the words, "from the Lord." Besides, the two young priests had already been commanded (or warned) not to do the thing they did (verse 2). They had undertaken to perform acts which belonged to the high priest alone, and even to intrude into the innermost sanctuary. See the warnings in Ex. 19:22 and Lev. 8:35.

180. What Was the Forbidden Fruit?

There have been many interpretations of the Fall, and the books on the subject would fill a small library. The majority of the early Christian fathers held the Mosaic account to be historical, and interpreted it literally, believing that an actual fruit of some kind, not definitely known, was eaten by our first parents. A few early writers, Philo among them, regarded the story of the Fall as symbolical and mystical, shadowing forth allegorical truths, and that the serpent was the symbol of pleasure, and the offense was forbidden sensuous indulgence. Whatever the "fruit" may have been, its use was plainly the violation of a divine prohibition, the indulgence of an unlawful appetite, the sinful aspiration after forbidden knowledge. Professor Banks, several years ago, while traveling in the region of the Tigris and Euphrates, found in a little known district a place which the natives declared to be the traditional site of Eden and a tree (name and species unknown) which they believed to be the successor of the original tree of knowledge, and it was venerated greatly. It bore no fruit.

181. What Are the Spiritual Gifts?

For an enumeration of the spiritual gifts see Acts 11:17; I Cor. 12 and 13; I Peter 4:10. The gift of healing is held by some denominations as having belonged exclusively to apostolic times, while others claim that it is granted even now to those who have sufficient faith.

182. What Is a "Generation"?

"Generation" is used in a variety of senses in the Scriptures. In some cases, it means a period of limitless duration; in others it means the past (Isa. 51:8), and still others the future (Ps. 100:5); again, it means both the past and future (Ps. 102:24). In Gen. 6:9 it means all men living at any given time. In Prov.

30:11, 14 it refers to a class of men with some special characteristics, and in Ps. 49:19 it may be interpreted to mean the "dwelling-place." A generation, in modern phraseology, means thirty to thirty-five years, but there is no instance of the word being used in this particular sense in the Bible. Thus, "the book of the generation of Jesus Christ" is a genealogical record extending back to Abraham. In I Peter 2:9 it means an elect race.

183. What Was the "Gift of Tongues"?

It is understood to have been not only the power of speaking various languages which the speaker had not previously studied or acquired, but also the power to speak a spiritual language unknown to man, uttered in ecstasy and understood only by those enlightened by the Holy Spirit. Paul, in I Cor. 12:10, is writing not to depreciate this gift, but to warn the Corinthians not to be led away by unprofitable or doubtful manifestations of it. Even in those early days of the Church, the leaders had difficulty in controlling the tendency to fanaticism among its adherents. The gift of tongues at Pentecost was given because of a great and urgent need. It is supposed by some authorities to have been speaking so that under the direction of the Holy Spirit it sounded to the ear of every auditor as though it were his own mother-tongue. There were many nationalities represented in the throng, but no confusion or misunderstandings. The gift of tongues on this particular occasion was the miraculous method employed to bring into the Gospel fold the strangers from other lands. The lesson is that God is not the author of confusion, and he never gives a message to his children that is unintelligible. Any "gift" or message that is incapable of being understood is *not of God.* We should try the spirits by this simple but decisive test.

184. What Does "God's Image" Mean?

In discussing spiritual things, to be right, no one can go beyond the word of Scripture. The Bible tells us that God gave to man a living soul. In this sense he was in the image of his Maker in his dispositions, temperament and desires, and in his obedience to the divine will; but this condition was forfeited through sin. It could only be said thereafter of those who walked uprightly before God and were inspired of him, that they were "his offspring." (Matt. 13:38; Mark 7:10. See John 12:36; Acts 13:10; Col. 3:6.) Jesus himself drew the distinction when he told the wicked scribes and Pharisees that they were the children of the evil one, and this is the actual condition of every one living in sin, unrepentant and unforgiven. Thus while in his perfect condition man was like his Maker, in a condition of sin he is no longer so, nor has he any of the spiritual attributes and qualities that belong to the perfect condition, or even of the pardoned sinner, who has the hope through Christ of reconciliation and restoration. The Bible nowhere declares that man is of himself and inherently immortal. "The soul that sinneth, it shall die." When sin entered, then came physical decay and death; man's first condition was lost and with the continuance of sin, and unrepentant and unforgiven, he also forfeited spiritual immortality. Eternal life is the gift of God. Paul declares that Jesus, through his Gospel, brought life and immortality to light for fallen man and showed the path to restoration through repentance, forgiveness and acceptance.

185. Where Did the Jews Get the Name "Hebrews"?

It is held by the best authorities and by the Jews themselves that the name is derived from Heber, or Eber (which means "from the other side," or a sojourner, or immigrant). Heber was the son of Salah and the father of Peleg (see Gen. 10:24, 11:14, and I Chron. 1:25). Abram was the first to be called a Hebrew (Gen. 14:13), presumably in the immigrant sense. The name is seldom used of the Israelites in the Old Testament, except when the speaker is a foreigner, or when the Israelites speak of themselves to one of another nation. Some writers have held that Hebrew is derived from Abraham (Abrai), but this explanation is not generally adopted.

186. What Was the "Heresies" of Apostolic Times?

The Greek word translated "heresies" in Gal. 5:20 means either an opinion or a party. As used in the New Testament it stands for an opinion "varying from the true exposition of the Christian faith" (as in II Peter 2:11), or a body of men following mistaken or blameworthy ideas, or, as a combination of these two meanings, "dissensions." This latter definition "dissensions" is the rendering given by Thayer in this passage. The American revision translates the word "parties," leaving, however, the expression "heresies" as the marginal reading. The three last words of the verse, "strife," "seditions," "heresies," are, in the American revision, "factions, divisions, parties."

187. What Is an Indulgence?

An "indulgence" is a spiritual bill of health or official act of pardon granted by the Church of Rome. It has no warrant in Scripture. There are indulgences to ease the way of souls out of purgatory, indulgences for the living, permitting them to eat meat on holy days; indulgences for the forgiveness of past sins, and, in Spain at least, and probably in other countries, indulgences for those who have committed crimes, by which they are relieved of the responsibility of their acts. Indulgences are usually purchased with a fee, although in some cases they are granted in consideration of undergoing some form of penance. A recent illustration is the distribution of indulgences during the Eucharistic Congress in Vienna, where they seem to have been granted free to many people as a reward for their loyalty and devotion to the Catholic Church on that occasion.

188. What Is Meant by "Because Thou Hast Left Thy First Love"?

These words (in Rev. 2:4) were addressed to the Christian believers at Ephesus. The "first love" does not refer to any person or influence other than Christ, but simply means that the Ephesians had lost the intensity of their affection and zeal for Christ. The Ephesian Church had had special opportunities and blessing. Under Paul's ministrations its members had received the gift of the Holy Spirit (Acts 19:1-6); the apostle had resided with them for three years (Acts

20:31); he had later written to them what is perhaps his most spiritually exalted epistle. Their experience of love for Christ had been warm and keen. In his message sent them through John the Master is reproving them for having allowed their love for him to grow weak and cold.

189. How Did Satan Receive the Name "Lucifer"?

There have been at different times various interpretations of the famous passage in Isa. 14:12: "How art thou fallen from heaven, O Lucifer, son of the morning! how art thou cut down to the ground, which didst weaken the nations!" "Lucifer" means "light-bringer," and has also been translated "son of the morning," "morning star," "brilliant," "splendid," "illustrious." Tertullian and Gregory the Great interpreted the passage in Isaiah as referring to the fall of Satan, and, since their time, the name "Lucifer" has been almost universally held by the Christian Church to be an appellation of Satan before the fall. Dr. Henderson, a famous commentator, simply interprets it "illustrious son of the morning," and holds that it has no reference to the fall of the apostate angels. Some later authorities claim that the passage has a prophetic reference to the fall from power of the great and illustrious King of Babylon, who surpassed all other monarchs of his time in splendor.

190. What Were the "Marks of the Lord Jesus"?

It was a practice to brand slaves with their owners' initials. A slave by showing the brand proved to whom his service was due and that no one else had a claim upon him. The marks of the Lord Jesus which Paul bore (Gal. 6:17) were the scars received in his service —the marks of the rods with which he was beaten and the wounds he received in fighting with wild beasts. He showed them as evidence that he belonged to the Lord Jesus.

191. Who Were the Magi?

These wise men were from either Arabia, Mesopotamia, Egypt, or somewhere else in the East. "East" is not to be understood in our wide, modern sense, but referred to those countries that lie to the east as well as north of Palestine. Thus, Persia is referred to as the "East" (Isa. 46:11). While it is true that the Gospel account does not state the number of wise men, but simply says they were from the East, many ancient traditions have been preserved from the early days of the Christian Church, among them one which states that there were three Magian princes, and gives their names as Caspar, Melchior and Balthasar, who came with a large retinue of servants and camels. Magism is supposed to have originated in Chaldea and thence spread to the adjacent countries. The Magians are believed to have been originally Semitic. Among the Greeks and Romans they were known as Chaldeans. Daniel sympathized with the order during his exile, and probably became one of their number. They believed in God, hated idolatry and looked for a Messiah. The latter fact alone would almost be regarded as conclusive evidence of their Semitic descent. There are no absolute data, however, for asserting it positively. For many generations the Magi has looked for the fulfillment of the prophecy contained in Numbers 24:17 ". . . there shall come a star out of Jacob . . ." and when the light as guiding star indicated the direction of Judea they knew the prophecy had been fulfilled. "His star" can be interpreted as "his sign." Whatever form it assumed, it was sufficiently marked as an astronomical phenomenon to claim attention. Some writers have contended that it was visible to the Magi alone; others hold that it was a heavenly light, standing as a beacon of glory over the manger; still others, that it was the luminous figure of an angel. Tradition asserts that "the star" guided the Magi both by day and by night. The infant Saviour was probably over two months old when the visit of the Magi took place. They had seen the phenomenon of the star long before their arrival in Jerusalem, two months after Jesus had been presented in the temple, and it was some time after this that the Magi arrived in Jerusalem and went thence to Bethlehem to worship him and offer gifts. It must have taken them many months to accomplish the journey from their own country to Palestine. The Magi brought the first material Christmas gifts when they presented their love offerings.

192. What Did Paul Mean by "The Revelation of the Man of Sin"?

Paul evidently believed that immediately before the second coming of Christ there would be fierce temptation and persecution (II Thess. 2:3). Christ referred to the same event (see Matt. 24:20-25). The man of sin is the Antichrist or Pseudo-Christ, who is to deceive many. He is described in Rev. 13:11-18.

193. When Was the Sabbath Changed from the Seventh to the First Day of the Week?

The New Testament indicates that the Jewish Christians held both days holy. Paul evidently preached in the synagogues on the Sabbath, but it was on the first day of the week that the Gentile Christians met to break bread (Acts 20:7). This second sacred day was called the Lord's Day to distinguish it from the Sabbath, and was probably the only one observed by the Gentile converts. There is a hint of their being called to account for observing that day only, in Col. 2:16, where Paul bids them pay no heed to their critics. *The Teaching of the Twelve Apostles,* written certainly before the year 100 A. D., speaks of the Lord's Day and refers to it as a day of holy meeting and the breaking of bread (chapter 14). The primitive Christians everywhere kept it so solemnly. Pliny, the historian, refers to this fact in his letter to Trajan about A. D. 100. Justin Martyr (A. D. 140) describes the religious worship of the early Christians, their sacramental observances, etc., on the "First Day." Other early writers who make clear and unmistakable reference to the Lord's Day are Dionysius of Corinth, Irenæus of Lyons (who asserted that the Sabbath was abolished), Clement of Alexandria, Tertullian, Origen, Cyprian, Commodian, Victorinus, and lastly Peter of Alexandria (A. D. 300), who says: "We keep the Lord's Day as a day of joy because of him who rose thereon." These evidences cover the first two centuries after our Lord's death and indicate that the Lord's Day is an institution of apostolic sanction and custom. All grounds of doubt are swept away by the fact that Constantine in an edict issued in A. D. 321 honored that day by recognizing it as one sacred to the Christians, and ordered that business should be intermitted thereon. Finally, the Council of Nicæa (A. D. 325) in its official proceedings gave directions concerning the forms of Christian worship on that day, and the Council of Laodicea (A. D. 364) enjoined rest on the Lord's Day. Thus by apostolic usage, by law and custom, by imperial edict and by the highest councils of the early Christian Church the change has been accepted and approved.

194. What Is the Distinction between Sabbath, Sunday, and Lord's Day?

The word "Sabbath" is derived from the Hebrew "Shabua," meaning "seven," or a heptad of seven days. It was employed to designate the seventh day of the Jewish week (from sunset on Friday to sunset on Saturday). Under the Christian dispensation the day of rest is changed from the seventh to the first day of the week, in memory of Christ's resurrection, and its true designation therefore is neither Sabbath (which is the ancient Jewish term) nor Sunday (which is the heathen appellation, *i. e.*, "the day of the sun"), but "the Lord's day." It is not with us, as with the Jews, a day of rest and absolute abstention from all employment, but a day of spiritual recuperation and religious activities in a thousand different directions, and a period of withdrawal from secular pursuits. Under the Mosaic law, one might not walk beyond a certain distance, nor light a fire, nor even carry a handkerchief. With us it is rather a day of celebration and glad Christian work, wholly unhampered by the ancient restrictions and obligations which were designed to apply to a different age and dispensation. The use of any one of the three terms—Sunday, Sabbath or Lord's Day—is, however, with most people, rather a matter of habit than of principle, as the historical facts are thoroughly well established.

195. What Are We to Understand by the "Secret Place"?

The "secret place" (see Ps. 91:1) is interpreted as meaning "the covert" of his tabernacle—"the beatitude of the inner circle, or secret shrine, to which that select company of the faithful have access, and where they may taste the hidden wisdom." One commentator writes that this passage applies "to those who are more at home with God than other Christians, and who are also more alone with God. In this inner circle the childlike spirit is made one with the will and the love of the almighty Father. It is a security and a refuge against whatsoever may await us in this world or elsewhere, and those who belong to it bear on their countenances the seal that they are free from fear of evil and that they have gained the victory over terror and dismay." In brief, it is only those who live closely to God who find those divine attributes which to others are majestic and overpowering, transformed into a sure shelter and a joy that lifts all care forever from the soul.

196. Who Were the "Sleeping Saints"?

The "sleeping saints" (see Thes. 4:14 and Matt. 27:52, 53) are held to be Old Testament believers who, having served the Lord faithfully according to their lights, and who looked forward to the promise of the

Messiah's coming, were quickened at the moment of Jesus' death, although they did not come out of their graves until his resurrection. The opening of the graves was symbolic proclamation that death was "swallowed up in victory"; and the rising of the saints after Jesus' resurrection fittingly showed that the Saviour of the world was to be the "first" that should rise from the dead. (See Acts 26:23; Col. 1:18; Rev. 1:5.)

197. Who Are We to Understand by the "Spirits in Prison"?

The passage in I Peter 3:19, 20 is one which has been much discussed. It is generally interpreted as meaning that the preaching to the spirits "in prison" implies not the preaching of the Gospel, but the announcement of Christ's finished work. Nor does it imply a second day of grace. The spirits were clearly those of the Antediluvians. The passage, however, is mysterious and has puzzled Bible students in all times. Peter is the only Bible writer who mentions the occurrence, whatever it may have been, so that there are no other passages to shed light upon it. The apostle was speaking in the context of the operation of the Holy Spirit and it has been generally thought by Augustine among the Fathers and by Dr. Adam Clarke and other modern commentators that he referred to the Antediluvians as having, like others who lived before Christ, been under the Spirit's influence, though they repelled it. In that case his meaning would be that Christ had from the beginning been preaching through, or by, the Spirit, to men in all ages, as he preaches to men now by his Spirit through his ministers. Other theologians, Dean Alford among them, contend that somewhere in the universe these Spirits were imprisoned and that Christ preached to them in the interval between his death and resurrection, though that view is surrounded by other difficulties which are obvious. The reference is incidental and does not practically concern us so much as does the lesson Peter is enforcing, that through the Holy Spirit we are enabled to live to the spirit and not to the flesh.

198. What Does the Word "Spiritual" Really Mean?

The word is one which Christians ought to guard zealously in religious phraseology. There is a recent tendency to use the word in a loose sense, giving it merely its philosophical or scientific meaning rather than its real Bible and theological significance. In secular phraseology the word means: relating to spirit, rather than to matter. Many varying shades of meaning grow out of this basic idea: one poet may be more spiritual than another; one artist than another; one musician than another. In this sense the word implies a relation to thoughts, emotions, impulses, connected with the soul of a man rather than his body. But the Christian use of the word is distinctive. It is given as the third definition of the word in the Standard Dictionary: "Of or relating to the soul as acted on by the Holy Spirit." An apt quotation from Henry Drummond is given: "The *spiritual* life is the gift of the living Spirit. The *spiritual* man is no mere development of the natural man. He is a new creation, born from above." In Christian phraseology, then, a man is spiritual as he is possessed, filled and dominated by the Holy Spirit.

199. What Was the Purpose of the "Tree of Knowledge"?

The tree of knowledge of good and evil (Gen. 2:8) was designed as a test of obedience by which our first parents were to be tried, whether they would be good or evil; whether they would chose to obey God or break his commandments, and the eating of the fruit of the tree revealed to them their new condition as sinners under divine displeasure.

200. What Is Known Concerning the "Tree of Life"?

Gen. 2:9 and 3:22, 24 tells practically all that we know of the "tree of life," although a vast amount of speculative literature has appeared on the subject. Various references to the "tree of life" elsewhere in Scripture show that it was regarded as the means provided by divine wisdom as an antidote against disease and bodily decay. Access to it was conditioned upon our first parents obeying the injunction against eating the forbidden fruit of the "tree of knowledge," which was the test of obedience. Certain Hebrew writers have called the two trees "the trees of the lives," holding that the wondrous property of one in perpetuating physical life and conferring perennial health was in direct contrast with the other, the "tree of knowledge," which was sure to occasion bodily suffering and death. "The tree of life was, in short, a sacramental tree," writes one commentator, "by the eating of which man, in his state of innocence, kept himself in covenant with God."

201. What Is It to Be "Unequally Yoked"?

The passage in II Cor. 6:14 may have a wide interpretation. "Unequally yoked" may mean bound together with one who is alien in spirit, although it might also mean that the disparity in culture or possessions, the difference in race, or in religious belief, are to be regarded as insurmountable barriers. In early Israelitish times, marriages with heathen were forbidden; so in Christian times, unions of believers and infidels, or unbelievers in any form, were to be avoided. Righteousness and wickedness cannot pull in the same harness, and as our first duty is to God, we should put away from us all avoidable contact that would hinder its performance. Paul in the passage in question clearly had in mind the union of believers with unbelievers.

202. Who Are the "Witnesses" Who Surround the Believers?

They are probably the worthies referred to in Heb. 11 chapter, whose triumph through faith are recalled. The word "witnesses" (Heb. 12:1) has two meanings and it is not certain which of the two the writer of the epistle had in his mind. A witness may be a spectator, or he may be one who testifies as in a court of justice. If the word in this passage is used in the former sense, it implies that departed and glorified saints are observing the trials and victories of the Christian on earth. If the word refers to a testifier, it means that the Christian has good reason for making the effort mentioned in the passage, because of the testimony of the Old Testament saints cited in the previous chapter.

JESUS' LIFE AND DEATH

203. Does the Doctrine of Jesus' Divinity Depend on the Miraculous Conception?

Even if the doctrine of the miraculous conception were abandoned, it would be difficult, if not impossible, to account for the facts of Christ's life, by any other theory than that of his being the incarnation of God. If you regard him as man, you must explain how he, a plain peasant, trained as a carpenter, brought up in an obscure Oriental town, could live such a life as he undoubtedly lived, and give utterance to truths which have thrilled the world for nineteen hundred years. Besides this he spoke with authority, making claims to a higher nature, which if he did not consciously possess that higher nature, would be false claims. His whole life was consistent with his divinity, and, therefore, even persons who reject his miraculous conception, have good ground for believing him to be divine. It is the only theory that explains such a life. There is no need, however, to reject the doctrine of the miraculous conception. The more you study the life of Jesus, the less you will be surprised to learn that the promise of God through the prophets, of the union of divinity and humanity, was literally fulfilled in him.

204. Was Christ Born in the Year 1 or in 5 B. C.?

As we are told in the Gospels that Herod was living and slaughtered the children after Jesus was born (see Matt. 2:16), and as it is claimed by chronologists to be a matter of record that he died in 750 U. C., which corresponds to B. C. 4, it is obvious that Jesus was born before that date. Then, on the other hand, he was born after the decree for the census (Luke 2:1) was issued. From Tertullian we learn that the decree was issued in 748 and the enrollment began in 749 U. C., which corresponds to B. C. 5. Thus the birth is fixed by those two occurrences.

205. Is There a Real Conflict in the Evangelists' Genealogies of Christ?

The purpose of publishing the Saviour's genealogy was to show that he had descended from David. If the genealogy of Mary had been given, it would have carried no weight with the Jews, as they would not admit the divine conception, and regarded Joseph as the head of the family. It was necessary, on their account, to show that Joseph had descended from David. It really, however, includes the others, as the descendants of David were so proud of their distinction, and of the Messianic promise involved, that no man of that family would take a wife of any other family. Mary, undoubtedly, therefore, was descended from David. The theory has been propounded and supported by Weiss and other scholars that the genealogy of Luke is that of Mary. Luke says (3:23) that Joseph was the son of Heli, whereas Matthew says (1:16) that he was the son of Jacob. It is suggested that Luke's statement should read, "who was the son-in-law of Heli," that is, married the daughter of Heli. Luke traces the descent through David's son Nathan, while Matthew traces it through Solomon. Even that explanation, however, has its incongruities, of which there is no clear explanation. The fact that Mary before her marriage went to Bethlehem to be taxed or registered (Luke 2:5), would indicate that she was of David's house. It is noteworthy, too, that Christ's claims to Messiahship were never challenged on that ground. If there had been any flaw in his pedigree, the Jews would have seized upon it without a doubt, because the prophecies clearly stated that Messiah would be descended from David.

206. Who Were the Brothers of Jesus?

The brethren of Jesus are named in the New Testament as James, Joses, Simon and Judas. In Matt. 12:46; Matt. 13:55; John 2:12, and Acts 1:14 they are generally understood to be proper brothers, all being named together conjointly with the mother of Jesus, and the same is inferred from John 7:5. Some of the early church writers, however, held that they were merely relatives or cousins (sons of Mary the sister of Jesus' mother), it being a common custom to call all immediate relatives, nephews, cousins and half-brothers, by the general designation of "brothers" or "brethren." Further, the early fathers of the church held that Mary, the mother of Jesus, had no other children. The question still remains open whether they were not the sons of Joseph by a former marriage, and therefore half-brothers to Jesus. On the other hand Matt. 1:25 and Luke 2:7 favor the view that they were brothers and that Jesus was the "first-born." Sisters of Jesus are also mentioned in Matt. 13:56 and Mark 6:3, but their names are not given. Much has been written on the subject without positive determination, although most modern commentators hold to the opinion that the "brethren" in question were the sons of Joseph and Mary, and that Mary's mother's sister had two sons, named James and Joses.

207. Is There a Rational Explanation of the Star of Bethlehem?

There was a remarkable conjunction of Jupiter and Saturn about that time, which must have been a very brilliant spectacle, and which would be very impressive to astrologers. It might lead them to the belief that some mighty potentate was born, and probably to make inquiry as to such birth. The fact, that would doubtless be known to all Orientals, that the Jews expected a Messiah, may have led the Magi to Palestine. Their inquiry for "the King of the Jews" seems to imply that it was there they expected to find such a being as the conjunction portended. The difficulty, however, is to explain the star going before them (Matt. 2:9). As they traveled westward, it might have had that appearance, but not so definitely as the account implies. Another explanation is that it was possibly a meteor divinely directed.

208. Did the Parents of Our Lord Take Him After His Birth to Jerusalem or to Egypt?

According to some, the accounts in Matthew and in Luke do not agree. But there is really no discrepancy. After the birth of Jesus, the parents remained at Bethlehem until the time arrived for presenting the Babe in the Temple, being the end of the days of purification. After the presentation, Joseph and Mary with the child went to Nazareth, adjusted their affairs and returned to Bethlehem, where they were dwelling —no longer in a stable but in "a house"—when the incident of the Magis' visit occurred. These wise men had first gone to Jerusalem, whence they were directed to Bethlehem. After their visit Joseph was warned by an angelic messenger and the flight into Egypt followed. To get a clear idea of the order of events, the records of the four evangelists must be taken as a whole, as one records incidents which another omits. Thus Mark and John contain nothing relative to the childhood of Jesus, while Matthew and Luke taken together, give a clear outline of these events, though Luke omits all reference to the return to Bethlehem and the journey into Egypt, the latter of which Matthew relates with considerable detail. In no sense did any one of the four evangelists intend to present a complete chronological record of the Saviour's earthly life, but each designed rather to supplement what the others had written.

209. How Could Jesus, Being Already Perfect, Increase in Wisdom?

The statement in Luke 2:52 is explicit and there is no reason for doubting it. Jesus was subject to human conditions and limitations so far as the divine nature could be subjected. We read of His being weary, of his being hungry and thirsty, and we are assured that He was tempted in all points like as we are, which all show that in His physical nature He was human. Doubtless He would be educated like other boys, and probably His consciousness of divinity would be gradual, and possibly not complete until the forty days in the desert. His questioning the doctors in the Temple (Luke 2:46) is supposed by some authorities to have been not catechizing them but to obtain information.

210. How Old Was Jesus When He Began to Understand the Nature of His Mission?

Although one cannot trace with any degree of precision the various stages of development of the consciousness of his mission, it is evident from the Gospel record that it must have begun early and gradually increased to complete appreciation as manhood approached. We are told that even in childhood he "grew and waxed strong in spirit, filled with wisdom," and the "grace of God was upon him." (Luke 2:40.) In youth we find him questioning and expounding to the rabbis in the temple and "increasing in stature and in wisdom and in favor with God and man." His wonderful knowledge, his amazing questions and his discerning answers to the elders must have become more and more accentuated during the passage of these early years, and we may gather that Mary had already premonitions of the future career of her Divine Son, since she pondered over and "hid all these things in her heart." There are indications that seem to warrant the conclusion that long before the opening of his public ministry, Jesus was absorbed by the thought of the mission to which he was destined. He knew his Father's business and did it, and he frequented his Father's house. His life and surroundings in Nazareth brought him in contact with a simple, earnest people and with sorrow and suffering. These were years of character-building and development. They bore fruit when the time was ripe for his public ministry and prepared him for the baptism at John's hands. This was the last act of his private life and the first that marked the beginning of his public mission, when the heavenly voice proclaimed him as the "Beloved Son" and the Baptist bare record that he was the Son of God.

211. Why Is Christ Described As a High Priest After the Order of Melchizedek?

The writer of the Epistle to the Hebrews, whether Paul or some other person, was showing the superiority of Christianity to Judaism. It too had its priest and sacrifice. The Jew might answer that Christ could not be a high priest as he did not come of the tribe of Levi, to which the priesthood was confined. The answer is that there was another order of priesthood—that of Melchizedek, which Abraham recognized (Gen. 14:20) by paying him tithes. Christ belonged to that order as the Psalmist had predicted (Ps. 110:4), and Levi, through his ancestor, had thus indicated his superiority. It is an argument that would have weight with a Jew. It is a curious fact, that among the recently discovered Tel el-Amarna tablets, are letters from one Ebed-tob, King of Uru Salim (Jerusalem), who describes himself as not having received the crown by inheritance from father or mother, but from the mighty God. We know nothing of Melchizedek beyond the scanty references in Genesis, but this tablet appears to intimate that the ancient Kings of Jerusalem claimed this divine right.

212. As God, How Could Jesus be Weary, Hungry and Thirsty?

In his divinity, no; but in his humanity he could be all of these. Scripture tells us that in his human aspect he was "in all things as we are." What we have in the Gospels is the report by his hearers of what he said. As John tells us (21:25), it is a very imperfect and meagre report, but sufficient for the purpose the writers had in view. At the same time, it is doubtful how much of the Godhead Jesus may voluntarily have laid aside when he became man. Paul says (Phil. 2:7, R. V.) that "he emptied himself," from which we infer that in order fully to enter into human feeling he divested himself of such qualities as would have kept him from feeling hunger, etc. It behooved him to be made in all things like unto his brethren, and he could not be that unless he temporarily relinquished some portion of his divinity.

213. Why Was Jesus Baptized?

The Saviour evidently ranked baptism as one of the acts inseparable from his Messianic calling (see John 1:31). By being publicly baptized he entered into John's community, which was introductory to his greater Messianic work. Further, it was the means of revealing himself to the Baptist and through him to the people. John was the forerunner of the Messiah, and it was especially fitting that he should personally serve at Jesus' consecration to his Messianic work, and assist at the beginning of his public career.

214. Did Christ Make Wine at the Cana Feast or Was It Grape Juice?

The fact that the ruler of the feast pronounced the miraculous wine "the best," showed that it was really wine, but we are not justified in concluding that it was alcoholic or intoxicating. There has been endless discussion on this point, but we are satisfied that divine power never gave any gift to man that would degrade or hurt him.

215. What Was Jesus' First Sermon?

Luke tells us (Luke 3:23) that Jesus was about thirty years of age when he began his ministry. During his sojourn in Galilee (chap. 4, v. 14) he had already spoken in the synagogues. Mark 1:14, 15 mentions these instances, though very briefly, and so also does John 2:11. His first recorded sermon is mentioned in Luke 4:16-28. It was on the Sabbath day, and he took his text from the prophet Esais. He had passed through his forty days' preparatory vigil in the wilderness and was filled with the Spirit, and ready for his work.

216. Did Christ Sing Any Hymns?

While there is no record of such a thing in Scripture, or anywhere else, it does not seem improbable. See the passage in Matt. 26:30 and Mark 14:26. The closing hymn here referred to was probably the chant called by the Jews "the great Hallel," and which consists of parts of Psalms 115, 116, 117 and 118, these parts being sung at the close of the Passover. "It is hardly conceivable," writes one commentator, "that the eleven disciples should have been singing to cheer their sorrowing hearts and that their Lord should have stood silent beside them."

217. Was Jesus Really Tempted As We Are?

Unquestionably he submitted to all the liabilities of the human condition; we are told expressly that he "was in all things as we are." The appeal of the tempter was to his ambition, and the purpose, as some commentators conclude, was to excite in his mind the desire for worldly power and dominion. Even his own followers had cherished visions of an earthly kingdom. The question whether he could by any possibility have yielded has often been asked, but it is one that must remain unanswered. To say that it was impossible would imply that he was not wholly subject to human conditions and temptations; while to admit its possibility would make him less than divine. The incident shows to us that while the vision of sudden power may have been alluring, it could not move him from the fixed and beneficent purpose of his great mission, which was to establish his kingdom in the hearts of men by love and sacrifice, and by the example of his perfect humanity. Contrasted with such a kingdom, all the glory of worldly pomp and power are trivial, transient and unsatisfying.

218. Could Jesus Sin?

The Christian Church has always held that Christ was absolutely free from sin. This is in accordance with the explicit teachings of Scripture, which states that he was in all things "as we are, yet without sin." (Heb. 4:15.) He is also described as the Holy One, the Just and Righteous (Acts 3:14, 22:14; I Peter 3:18; I John 2:29, 3:7). See also I Peter 11:21, 22; I Peter 1:19; II Cor. 5:21 and other passages. One of the earliest of Church councils (A. D. 451) formulated the doctrine of his sinlessness thus: "Truly man, with a rational soul and body, with like essence with us as to his manhood, and in all things like us, with sin excepted," and this has remained unchanged as the accepted Christological doctrine of the Christian Church. Whether he *could not* sin has been much discussed. Doubtless he *could* have yielded; but the fact remains that he *did not* yield to temptation and continued to the end an example of perfect purity and sinlessness—the condition of man before his fall.

219. Did Satan Own the Kingdoms Which He Offered in the Temptation?

No; Satan did not own them. But it is still true that they were in his hands to offer to Christ; he had usurped them. At Creation, Man was placed in the Garden of Eden as lord over all. "Thou hast put all things under his feet," was true of the first Adam (see Ps. 8:4-9), while it will only be carried out permanently under the second Adam. (See I Cor. 15:25; Eph. 1:22; Heb. 2:6-9.) But when Adam listened to Satan and fell, he transferred his allegiance, and through that Satan became the "prince of this world." (See John 14:30; 16:11; 18:36; Luke 22:53; II Cor. 4:4). The consequence of this has been that the empires of the world have been truly delineated as wild beasts. (Dan. 7:3.) It was universal empire Satan offered to Jesus, but which he refused to take from his hand. When Satan said, "to whomsoever I will I give it" (Luke 4:6), the Lord did not deny it, but was content to go on in the path of obedience until the time should come for the Father to give it to him. (Matt. 11:27.) Then "the kingdoms of this world shall become the kingdoms of our Lord and of his Christ, and he shall reign for ever and ever" (Rev. 11:15). The fact that "the powers that be are ordained of God" Rom. 13:1, does not conflict with this. God did put authority in the hands of Noah, Gen. 9:6, but this has been usurped by Satan, through the willingness of man to be led by him. The fact that the devil has so much to do with the affairs of men in the world is a proof of this. On the other hand, the kingdoms and glory of the world were not his to give. He has no valid claim or right to anything in God's material universe. "The earth is the Lord's and the fulness thereof." The temptation of Christ in the wilderness, according to the best critical authorities was of a subjective character. That is to say, it was a mental appeal to do wrong. It was a phantasy, a deception, a sham. This is the way Satan tempts us, and Christ was in all points tempted as we are. Satan does not need to take us up on a high mountain to show us the kingdoms of the world. He can put a mental picture before us. When we are tempted to do as he bids us and think that certain things will come to pass, we soon discover that the devil has deceived us. When he speaketh a lie he speaketh of his own, for he is a liar, and the father of lies. His tempting promises of glory, greatness and prosperity are all false. Obedience to him, in the end only pierces the soul with many sorrows. He makes the thief believe that his acts will never be known. But God says, "Be sure your sin will find you out." The sensualist, who gratifies his lust, in the end becomes a moral leper. Lastly, he makes the sinner believe a lie that he may be eternally ruined.

220. What Became of the Nine Lepers Who Did Not Return After Being Cleansed?

The inference to be drawn from the Gospel narrative (Luke 17:11-19) is that the nine, being healed merely in body, were so elated and overjoyed with their new-found health that they ungratefully forgot the source of their restoration, whereas the one leper who returned, had learned the deeper lesson of Christ's divinity, and had experienced that inner cleansing and clearness of spiritual vision which, after the first exuberant outburst was over, brought him back grateful and loving to the Saviour's feet to pour out his thanks. The nine are not again mentioned.

221. In What Kind of a Body Did Moses Appear at the Transfiguration?

Probably the spiritual body, to which Paul refers (I Cor. 15:44). It is difficult for us to conceive of such a body because we are so accustomed to recognize the soul only as it manifests itself through the senses. But it would be rash to conclude that the soul is dependent on the physical senses for its powers. It may have, or may acquire after the death of the body, new and perhaps superior means of communicating thought and feeling.

222. Were There Two Anointments by Two Different Marys, She of Bethany and Mary Magdalene?

There have been many conflicting interpretations of the Scripture narrative concerning Mary of Bethany and the woman spoken of in Luke 7:37. The majority agree that there were two anointings, one during Jesus' Galilean ministry (Luke 7), the other at Bethany before the last entry into Jerusalem (Matt. 26, Mark 14, John 12). There is not the slightest trace in the Scripture story of any blot on the life of Mary of Bethany. The epithet, Magdalene, seems to have been chosen for the especial purpose of distinguishing the one to whom it was applied from other Marys. Mary or Maryam was a common name, which seems to have led to misunderstanding. Some of the earliest Church writers entirely reject the identification of the two Marys, although it is an error into which not a few have fallen. It is to be noted that Luke 7:37 speaks of a woman "which was a sinner," but gives no name, while Luke 10:38, 39 speaks of Mary and Martha as though neither had been named before and without any evidence of previous reference. The whole question is one concerning which no one can speak with final authority although the reasonable inference is, as we have said, that they were different individuals.

223. What Prayer Did Our Saviour Ask at the Last Supper?

The words Jesus employed are not recorded, but the blessing pronounced may have been that which was customarily asked by the head of the household at all Hebrew paschal feasts. It is in these words: "Blessed art thou, O Lord our God, King of the universe, who hast created the fruit of the vine! Blessed art thou, O Lord our God, King of the universe, who hast chosen us above all nations, and exalted us above all peoples, and hast sanctified us with thy commandments. Thou hast given us, O Lord our God, appointed seasons for joy, festivals and holy days for rejoicing, such as the feast of unleavened bread, the time of our liberation, for holy convocation, to commemorate our exodus from Egypt." As Jesus gave to the Last Supper a broader spiritual significance than the Passover possessed, it is probable that he gave to the opening words of blessing a character in keeping with his high purpose. The new Passover was not to be for the Jewish nation alone, but for the whole world.

224. Was Judas at the Institution of the Lord's Supper?

It is doubtful whether Judas was present at the institution of the Lord's Supper. He was present at the foot-washing and at the early part of the feast, but he could not remain after Christ spoke of his imminent betrayal and showed his knowledge of the identity of the guilty man. Then Judas went out, but we do not know whether the breaking of the bread and the blessing of the cup had already taken place: from Luke's narrative it would appear that they had; Matthew and Mark, however, mention the ceremony after the conversation about the betrayal, which would imply that Judas was not present at the ceremony. The Evangelists were concerned more about the spiritual significance of the events of that agitating night than about presenting those events in consecutive order.

225. What Was the Value of the Thirty Pieces of Silver That Judas Received?

The pieces of silver were probably shekels. The value of the whole sum in our modern reckoning was about eighteen dollars. Zechariah had predicted the whole transaction (see Zech. 11:12, 13): "They weighed for my price thirty pieces of silver and the Lord said cast it unto the potter," etc. It is not likely that Judas acted from avarice only, though he was fond of money. He probably meant to force Christ's hand. He may have thought him backward in claiming the kingdom, and supposed that if he was driven to bay, he would deliver himself by a miracle and declare himself king. That theory is confirmed by his committing suicide when he discovered the consequences of his act.

226. How Did the Sleeping Disciples Know What Word Jesus Uttered in the Garden?

One of the functions of the Holy Spirit was to bring all things to the remembrance or knowledge of the Apostles. Though the Evangelists record most fully the events they witnessed, they record other matters of which they could have had no knowledge except by revelation. This may have been one of them. But it is not stated that they slept all the time they were with Christ in the Garden. The account rather implies men struggling to keep awake. Christ said of them that their spirit was willing. They may have heard the few words they record, though missing the remainder of what may have been, and probably was, a long prayer.

227. Who Was the "Certain Young Man" of Mark 14:51?

There has been much speculation as to who this young man was. It has been suggested by some commentators, perhaps rightly, that inasmuch as he is mentioned only by Mark, he was Mark, the evangelist; himself. Mark's family was prominently connected with incidents of the Lord's last days and following the resurrection. Thus the "upper room" where the Last Supper was eaten and which later witnessed the descent of the Holy Spirit was in the ownership of that family and Mark's mother was the sister of Barnabas, a wealthy Levite of Cypress.

228. Was the Pain the Saviour Suffered on Calvary Physical or Mental?

Pain is a difficult thing to measure. The sorrow of Jesus will always be one of the awe-inspiring, baffling events of the world story. It is impossible to read the Bible deeply, particularly after one has become personally acquainted with Jesus and observed the amazing power that the facts of his suffering and death possess over human souls, without realizing that there must have been far deeper anguish than can be accounted for by the mere facts of his humiliation, rejection, torture and death. If we consider the merely physical pain we must acknowledge that others have apparently borne as much, though we must also acknowledge that there are almost infinite degrees of susceptibility to pain. A wound which will cause little pain to a man of a certain temperament and organization may be excruciating to one of finer and more acute sensitiveness. But the real agony of Jesus must have been different from either physical or mental. There is a sane note, a moral note in his suffering that puts it altogether beyond our comprehension. Matthew, Mark and Luke all record the fact that as he died he cried out with a loud voice. That seems strange from what we know of the dauntless courage of Jesus. Some immeasurable, inconceivable suffering must lie back of that cry. So also his appeal in the garden for deliverance at the last hour. There must have been an infinite anguish ahead to compel him to ask for another way. We get the clearest hint in the grievous prayer from the cross: "My God, my God, why hast thou forsaken me?" There must have been some definite, conscious, agonizing break in the eternal love which had bound the Father and the Son together. Perhaps there was deeper truth than the ancient formulators of the creed knew in those strange words: "He descended into hell." No—of all the griefs in the world that of Jesus while he was on the cross and while his body lay in the grave, is unique. Its depth, its duration, none can know. They counted the hours he spent on the cross and the hours in the grave. But what eternities of spirit anguish he underwent we may never know. But, praise God! they were enough to shock every penitent soul that hears of it into a new life, a life in which sin is hated and righteousness loved, a life of which the crucified and risen Saviour is the eternal Light and the never-failing hope and joy.

229. Why Was the Inscription Used on the Cross "The King of the Jews"?

From the fact that the evangelists give us three different forms for the inscription over the cross it has been argued that they were not accurate in their portrayal of things and events. There is, however, nothing here to disturb anyone. Matthew 27:37 has it, "This is Jesus the King of the Jews," using probably the Greek form; St. Mark 15:26, "The King of the Jews," and Luke 23:38, "This is the King of the Jews," availed themselves of the Roman form, and John 19:19, "Jesus the Nazarene, the King of the Jews," probably employed the Hebrew form. Since the four accounts of the inscription do not differ in import the exact language of the insulting designation is of little or no consequence.

230. How Many Hours Was Jesus on the Cross?

It is uncertain how long Jesus lived after he was nailed to the cross. At the longest it could not have been more than six hours. Mark says (15:25), "It was the third hour (or nine o'clock), and they crucified him"; and again (15:34), "And at the ninth hour (3 p. m.), Jesus cried," etc. John, on the other hand, describing the proceedings before Pilate (19:14), says: "It was about the sixth hour." But John was probably reckoning the hours by the Roman method from midnight, which, allowing for the subsequent judicial farce and the journey to Golgotha, would bring him into accord with Mark. Matthew also (27:46), represents Jesus as being alive at the ninth hour (three o'clock). Matthew, Mark and Luke, referring to the darkness, say that it lasted from the sixth hour (noon), till the ninth hour (3 p. m.), but it does not appear to have begun until Jesus had been some time on the cross. The ancients had not the means that we have of accurately reckoning time; so that we cannot be certain of the hour, and it may have been later than nine when Jesus was nailed to the cross. He evidently did not live long after three, probably not many minutes.

231. At What Hour Did the Crucifixion Take Place?

Mark says (15:25) it was about the third hour, or, as we should say, nine o'clock. Again, the sixth hour is referred to by three of the evangelists (Matt. 27:45; Mark 15:33; Luke 23:44), when Jesus had apparently been three hours on the cross. In the next verses, in all three cases, the ninth hour is mentioned as the time of death, which would be three o'clock. The statement of John (19:14) is believed to be due to a copyist's error, or to his using the Roman method of reckoning.

232. Was Jesus Happy on His Way to the Cross?

We cannot suppose so, although some have held that, because he was doing the Father's will, therefore he must have been happy even in the midst of suffering. But in the narratives of the evangelists we find only the impression that he was filled with sorrow. From the time of the agony in the garden (see Matt. 26:37) till the last cry on the cross, this cloud was not lifted. On the way to Calvary, together with his sorrow for the people who "knew not what they did"

—who were now as ready to mock and revile him as they were only a short time before to joyfully acclaim him—there must have been a deeper burden of sadness for his base betrayal and for his utter desertion by all of his panic-stricken disciples, even by Peter, that weighed down at every step. Yet, wounded, bleeding, and subjected to the worst indignities, he bore it all without a murmur even while his heart was breaking. He was sustained by the sense of his high mission and bore his suffering with such fortitude that even his enemies remarked it (Luke 23:47). Thus, to the last moments of his earthly life, he was "a man of sorrows and acquainted with grief."

233. Who Were the More Guilty of Christ's Death, the Jews or the Romans?

Both were guilty, although the onus of the malevolent persecution of Christ rests with the Jews. When they brought him before Pilate and that official, although representing the power of Rome, and even admitting that he could "find no fault" in Jesus weakly yielded to the fanatical clamor for the sacrifice, he became a principal with a full share of responsibility for the tragedy that followed. A stronger man, backed by the Roman authority and convinced of the injustice of the mob's demand, would have resolutely refused to permit the innocent to suffer. History is full of passages recording the nobility and justice of men whose firmness checked the commission of crimes in the name of law. Roman justice, even in that day, was proverbial. It was therefore the duty of Pilate to have executed justice as Governor of Judea. When he had examined Christ and declared that he "found no fault in him" (John 19:6), and again when he declined to acknowledge responsibility for the "blood of this just person," he was pledged by his judicial oaths to execute not injustice in obedience to clamor, but justice, even in the face of the whole Jewish nation. Roman laws governed Judea; the native laws, secular and ecclesiastical, could only be recognized and enforced where they did not conflict with those of Rome. Pilate stifled the voice of conscience, set aside the result of his judicial inquiry, disregarded the warning of his wife, and basely consented to a murder in obedience to Jewish clamor. The priests, it is true never wavered in their demand for the Saviour's death, and even warned Pilate that if he refused to order the execution he would not be Cæsar's friend. This touched the Governor's weak point: his ambition. To stand well with Cæsar he gratified the populace and ordered his troops to carry out their wishes.

234. What Became of Pilate After He Judged Jesus?

There are various legends and traditions concerning Pilate's further history. The *Acta Pilati,* an apocryphal work still extant, contains some of these. One tradition is to the effect that the Emperor Tiberius, alarmed at the universal darkness which had suddenly fallen on his empire upon the day of the crucifixion, summoned Pilate to Rome to answer for having caused it. Pilate was condemned to death, but pleaded ignorance as his excuse. His wife died at the moment of his execution. Another tradition is that Tiberius, having heard of Christ's miracles, wrote to Pilate bidding him send Jesus to Rome. Pilate was compelled to confess that he had crucified him, and was thrown into prison and committed suicide. Earth and sea refused to receive his body, and it was repeatedly cast up, finally being sunk in a pool at Lucerne, under the shadow of Mount Pilatus. Josephus, the Jewish historian (in *Antiquities,* 18 chap. 4:1), states authoritatively that Pilate met with political disaster. The Samaritans complained against him to Vitellius, president of Syria, who sent Pilate to Rome to answer to Caligula, the successor of Tiberius, and he soon afterward killed himself. The scene of this act is uncertain.

235. Could Pilate Have Done Other than Condemn Jesus to Death?

Yes, as Pilate told Jesus (John 19:10), he had power to release him. His difficulty lay in his own bad record. If he refused to oblige the Jews in this matter, they might go to Rome and accuse him before the Emperor of many acts of misgovernment. It would have done him no harm for them to complain of his letting Jesus go. In that matter, his defense that the prisoner was innocent, would have been sufficient. But they would probably say nothing about Jesus; they would bring charges against him for which he had no defense and he would lose his office. He concluded that he could not afford to set them at defiance, although he ought to have done so.

236. Could Christ Have Come Down from the Cross?

Christ had done many miracles, as when he healed the blind, stilled the storm and raised the dead. His remark to Peter (Matt. 26:53) that his Father would give him twelve legions of angels if he asked for deliverance, showed that he believed he could be delivered if he wished. The only reason why he had no desire to come down from the cross was that love of the human race held him there. He knew that his voluntary sacrifice was essential to the great atonement for the sins of the world. He had foreseen his own death on the cross and on several occasions had spoken of it.

237. How Many Appearances Are Recorded of Christ After His Resurrection?

Eleven. 1 Mark 16:9-11; John 20:11-18; 2 Matt. 28:8-10; Mark 16:8; Luke 24:9-11; 3 Luke 24:34; 4 Mark 16:12, 13; Luke 24:13-35; 5 Mark 16:14; Luke 24:36-49; John 20:19-23; 6 John 20:24-29; 7 Matt. 28:16-20; Mark 16:15-18; 8 John 21:1-24; 9 Matt. 28:16; 10 Acts 1:3-8; 11 Acts 9:4; 1 Cor. 15:8.

238. Christ's Garments—Where Did He Get Those Which He Wore when He Appeared to Mary on Resurrection Morn?

The question has often been asked, but never satisfactorily answered. We must conclude, in the absence of any Scriptural statement about the garments, that they belonged to that strange mysterious life on which Christ entered when he rose from the dead. That they were not of the ordinary materials seems clear from the Gospel narratives, which represent Christ as "vanishing out of their sight" (Luke 24:31), appearing among his disciples in a room the doors of which were shut (John 20:19), and being seen now at Jerusalem, now at Emmaus, and in Galilee, at least forty miles distant. Whatever the garments were, and wheresoever they came from, they were clearly not of the substantial kind, which would have prevented these disappearances.

239. In What Body Did Jesus Appear After the Resurrection?

The language of Luke 24:39 is clear and explicit. The resurrection body proved that Jesus was "the Son of God with power" in taking to himself the same identical body which had been crucified and laid in the grave, and yet which had been glorified "by some such inscrutable change as took place at the transfiguration." The very fact attests him as the Master of life and death and as divine. He continued forty days on earth after the resurrection, taking again to himself that life which he had laid down, in order that his followers and the whole world might be convinced of the completeness of his triumph over the grave and that he had not "seen corruption." He ascended to heaven a spiritual body. (Phil. 3:21, Col. 3:4.)

240. How Long Was Jesus in the Grave?

In Matthew 12:40 he said that he would be three days and three nights in the heart of the earth. The passage has long perplexed Biblical students. The most probable explanation is that Christ adopted a mode of expression common among the Jews, and said that he should be in the grave three "evening-mornings," which the translators rendered three days and nights. The Jews also had a rule, of which there are several examples in other parts of the Bible, that any part of the *onah,* or period, counted as the whole. Thus the interval between the crucifixion and the burial on the Friday would be part of Friday, and would count as one "evening-morning"; from sunset on Friday to sunset on Saturday would count as the second; and from Saturday sunset to the resurrection on Sunday morning as the third. The disciples evidently regarded the Sunday as the third day, as is seen by the conversation on the way to Emmaus, when Cleopas said: "This is the third day since these things were done." (Luke 24:21.)

Professor Wescott, a great New Testament scholar and one of the editors of the most widely used text of the Greek New Testament, held the view that crucifixion and burial occurred on Thursday; but practically every other authority disagrees with him. The celebration of Friday as the day of our Lord's death and burial dates back to extremely early times in Church history. It is true that the expression "three days and three nights" in the passage you mention sounds very emphatic to our Western ears, accustomed to the sharp distinction conveyed by the words in our time and speech. But, as Dr. Whedon comments here, "the Jews reckoned the entire twenty-four hours in an unbroken piece as a *night-and-day.* They counted the odd fragment of a day, in computation, as an entire night-and-day. Our Lord, therefore, was dead during three night-and-days."

241. Did Jesus Die of a Broken Heart?

That is the opinion of many who have written on the subject, physicians included. It is certain that the crucifixion did not kill him, as that was a death by exhaustion. Jesus was not exhausted, for we are told (Matt. 27:50) that he "cried with a loud voice" when he yielded up the ghost. The fact that when the soldier pierced his side there came thereout blood and water (John 19:34) indicates, according to eminent surgeons, that the heart was ruptured. The most probable way of accounting for the blood and water flowing from a wound in the side of a dead body is that the spear pierced the pericardium—or sac which contains the heart—which would contain blood and water if the heart were ruptured. The severe strain in the Garden the night before, the intensity of which was indicated by a sweat of blood, probably prepared the physical nature of Jesus for the sudden collapse, which caused Pilate to "marvel that he was dead already." (Mark 15:44.)

242. Why Did They Cast Lot for Christ's Garment?

When the soldiers cast lot for the Saviour's garment (John 19:24) they had no design to fulfill a prediction of the Old Testament. They had probably never heard of the prophecy. They simply perceived that if they tore the garment into four pieces they would spoil it, and it would be of no value. It was the most natural course for such men to cast lots for it. The evangelist, in writing that it was done "that the Scripture might be fulfilled" meant that in God's providence the fulfilment took place. The soldiers were unconsciously doing the thing that it was predicted they would do. John was anxious to show that Christ was the predicted Messiah, and he mentions this incident to show that the details of the prophetic writings were fulfilled in him.

243. Why Did Jesus After His Resurrection Say: "Touch Me Not"?

It was not a time for the old familiar greeting or handclaspings. He had not come to renew the former human associations with his followers. A great change had taken place. The crown of his life-work was not yet complete. He must show himself in his resurrected body to his disciples before he ascends to the Father. Mary evidently comprehended the significance of the change and went and told the disciples.

244. Was the Ascension in Human Form?

The visible resurrection was essential as a demonstration of his victory over death. The facts of the ascension are so well authenticated in numerous passages, that they are accepted by all denominations of the Christian Church. It was a bodily ascension, visible to the multitudes, as far as human eye could penetrate. What change may have occurred in the spiritualizing of his body, in its preparation for his place on God's right hand, we may only conjecture. The best commentators hold that "though Christ rose with the same body in which he died, it acquired, either at his resurrection or at his ascension, and without the loss of identity, the attributes of a spiritual body, as distinguished from a natural body; of an incorruptible, as distinguished from a corruptible, body." See Phil. 3:21; Col. 3:4.

245. What Were the Characteristics of Jesus That Made Him So Worthy of Following?

He was altogether lovely, Song of Solomon 5:16; holy, righteous, good, faithful, true, just, guileless and sinless, spotless, innocent, harmless (Luke 1:35; Acts 4:27; Is. 53:11; Matt. 19:16; Is. 11:5; John 1:14; John 7:18; Zec. 9:9; John 5:30; Is. 53:9; I Pet. 2:22; John 8:46; I Pet. 1:19; Matt. 27:4). He was forgiving, Luke 23:34; merciful, Heb. 2:17, and loving, John 13:1, 15:13; compassionate and benevolent, Is. 40:11; Luke 19:41; Matt. 4:23, 24; Acts 10:38. He was meek, lowly in heart; patient, humble and long suffering, Matt. 11:29, 27:14; I Tim. 1:16; Luke 22:27. Though zealous, he was resigned, resisted temptation and was obedient to God the Father, even as he had been subject to his parents in his youth (Luke 2:49, 22:42; John 4:34, 15:10; Luke 2:57).

246. Why Is Jesus Sometimes Called the Son of Man and Sometimes the Son of God?

It is held that Jesus, in applying to himself the title Son of Man, intended to emphasize his humanity and his representative character. The Jews were looking for a Messiah who would raise Israel to the head of the nations; Jesus wished to impress the disciples with the fact that he was representative of the whole human race and not of the Jews only. Then, too, to have spoken openly of himself as the Son of God would have been at once to exasperate the Jews and bring upon himself a charge of blasphemy, as in the end it did (see John 10:36). The title, Son of Man, was not open to that danger, as it was expressive of lowliness, humility and identification with humanity. In using it, however, Jesus did not withdraw his claim to be the Son of God. When the High Priest put him on his oath (see Matt. 26:63-65) he acknowledged that he was the Son of God.

JESUS—SAYINGS OF JESUS

247. The Meaning of the Name "Jesus."

The name "Jesus" is the name by which the Saviour is preferably known in the Gospels. "Christ" is used as a proper name in the Epistles, but in the Gospels, except in rare instances, such as Matt. 1:1; Mark 1:1; Luke 11:11; John 1:17, there is found not the familiar "Christ" but "The Christ." The later combination of the two names, "Jesus Christ," is found only in John (John 17:3) and after the resurrection (Acts 2:38, 3:6). "Jesus" is the Greek form of the Hebrew name "Jehoshua," or in its abbreviated form "Joshua." Its variants are found in "Jeshua" and "Hoshea." "Jesus" means Deliverer and the divine selection of the name is indicated in Matt. 1:21—"He shall save his people from their sins."

248. In What Language Did Christ Speak?

The common language of Palestine at that time was Aramaic, a Syro-Chaldaic dialect. After the Babylonian captivity it supplanted the original Hebrew, although the latter continued in use for ecclesiastical documents. It is reasonable to believe that Christ used the Aramaic, as the people would not have understood him had he spoken any other language. Matthew is commonly believed to have been written in Aramaic and the other three in Greek. The commercial and literary language of the day was Greek. Neither Luke nor John was an uneducated man. Both would be likely to know Greek. Mark, too, as a young Jew of some standing, would probably know the language.

249. Why Have We Differing Versions of the Lord's Prayer?

There is no absolute evidence that the prayer was taught on one occasion only. Matthew reports it as given during the Sermon on the Mount, and Luke (who was not one of the twelve) places its delivery after the close of the Galilean ministry, but mentioning no time or place. Many of the best scholars regard the position of the prayer in Matthew as unhistorical and give the preference to Luke, although it by no means follows that even he gives the original form. If delivered on more than one occasion, the prayer may have had one form for a small group of disciples, and another form for the whole body of Jesus' followers. And this might account for the presence of a clause in one version which was absent in the other. The word "trespasses" may be regarded simply as a variant. Furthermore, it is conjectured that Luke made certain changes in the expressions of the prayer, to make its meaning clearer to Gentile hearers. Cyril, Bishop of Jerusalem, is the first writer who expressly mentions the use of the Lord's Prayer in religious worship, but it was not generally used in Christian churches during the early days. There is no evidence that it was employed by the apostles. Luke omits the closing doxology, and although it appears in Matthew's Gospel as we now have it, it is not to be found in any of the early manuscripts, and is probably an interpolation due to liturgical use.

250. Does Any Parallel to the Lord's Prayer Exist?

Some commentators have claimed that the Prayer is based upon expressions and sentiments already familiar to the Jews, and that parallel phrases may be found in the Talmud, but this does not detract from its beauty and originality as a whole.

251. What Is Implied in Jesus' Words "See the Son of Man Coming in His Kingdom"?

This passage is frequently misunderstood. Mark has the better version: "Till they see the Kingdom of God come with power" (which is the more explicit), and Luke: "Till they see the Kingdom." Jesus is believed to have had reference to the realization of the firm establishment and victorious progress of the new Kingdom of Christ during the lifetime of some then present. He did not refer here to his second coming, but to the founding and triumphant extension of that work, the acceptance of which by the world was to be the grand pledge of his return.

252. What Is Meant by "Poor in Spirit"?

The simple meaning of this passage (Matt. 5:3) is that it is the humble soul that gets blessed. And the higher a saint gets in the divine life the more humble he will be. Spiritual progress which is not accompanied by humility is progress in the wrong direction. This is one of the distinctive points of Christ's doctrine; at the very threshold of the Christian life the Christian gives up his self-confidence; he surrenders all hope of making himself righteous, and gives himself to Christ to be made righteous. And his highest attainment can be expressed in the words of Paul: "I am crucified with Christ; nevertheless I live, yet not I, but Christ liveth in me."

253. Did Jesus Abrogate the Law?

In Matt. 5:17-20 Jesus was explaining that he did not come to abrogate but to fulfil the law—to unfold its true spiritual meaning. In verse 19, the thing spoken of, as commentators explain, is not "the practical breaking or disobeying of the law, but annulling or enervating its obligation by a vicious system of interpretation and teaching others to do the same; so the thing threatened is not exclusion from heaven and still less the lowest place in it, but a degraded and contemptuous position in the present stage of the kingdom of God—in other words, they shall be reduced, by the retributive providence that overtakes them, to the same condition of dishonor to which their false system of teaching has brought down the eternal principles of God's law." On the other hand, those who so teach that they exalt and honor God's authority, shall be honored in the kingdom in due proportion. It is therefore a rebuke to the outward and formal righteousness of the Scribes and Pharisees, who neglect the inward, vital and spiritual.

254. What Is Meant by "Whosoever Therefore Shall Break One of These Least Commandments"?

The meaning of the passage in Matt. 5:19 is: Whosoever shall break, or make invalid through deliberate misinterpretation, one of the least of these commandments and shall teach men so (as the Pharisees were doing), shall be called the least in the kingdom of heaven. The penalty was not exclusion from heaven, but the loss of the position of honor in God's kingdom, which they might have enjoyed. On the other hand, whosoever shall teach men to obey the law in its right interpretation, looking to the glory and honor of God, should be honored in heaven. It was a warning to the Scribes and Pharisees that righteousness must be *inward,* vital and spiritual, instead of *outward* and formal.

255. What Are We to Understand by "Lead Us Not into Temptation"?

God does not tempt any one. He may permit us to be placed in positions where, if left to our own resources, we would fall; but he does not tempt us to evil. Eve said, "The serpent beguiled me." (See Gen. 3:1, 4, 5, 13.) She yielded in her weakness and suffered accordingly (vs. 14, 15, 16). In Matt. 4:1, and parallel passages, it is distinctly stated that the devil was the tempter of Jesus. In I Cor. 10:13, also, it is made clear that though God may permit us to be tempted, he is not the tempter. See James 1:13, where it is emphatically asserted that God tempts no man. The withdrawal of the Holy Spirit exposes us to temptation, by leaving the heart open to the attack of the tempter; but nothing is more erroneous than to assume that temptation, or the placing of any agent in man's spiritual path which may cause him to fall, comes from God. If this were true, he would be the author of eternal ruin to multitudes who rush into sin by yielding to temptation. See also Job, 1st and 2d chapters, where Satan is shown as the tempter who pleads to be allowed to test the spiritual stability of the patriarch. The only sources of temptation in any case are the evil spirit, the world and the flesh. Unless we are fortified by the presence of the Divine Spirit, when these assail, we are especially exposed and liable to fall. See further on the subject Rev. 12:9; John 8:44; II Cor. 11:3; I John 3:8; Mark 1:13; Luke 4:2; Acts 5:3; Matt. 26:41. Even when God has made a trial of man's faith, he has done so in every instance by the removal of spiritual safeguards and leaving man to his own resources, when the tempter availed himself of the opportunity. In this sense, it is evident that a test is not a temptation.

Some cannot reconcile the statement that God did tempt Abraham, Gen. 22:1, with the assertion of James 1:13 that God tempts no man. James refers to allurements to sin. Abraham was not tempted in that sense. He was tried and tested. Temptation is a trial and a test because when a man is tempted he learns his strength and weakness, hence the confusion in the meanings of the word. It is obvious, however, that the trial may come in different ways. In Abraham's case he was ordered to do something that was against his nature, and the question was whether he would do what he did not wish to do at the command of God. James, on the other hand, is speaking of a case in which a man is prompted to follow his own inclinations and to commit sin. God tempts no man to commit sin, but he does test our faith in him and love for him by trials. Job must have been tempted to take his wife's advice and curse God; but his trials, as we know, were tests of his disinterested allegiance, not such temptations as James refers to.

256. Who Are the "Angels of the Little Ones"?

The reference in Matt. 8:10 has caused discussion among divines in all periods of the Christian Church, and is by no means satisfactorily explained. Jesus seems to have lifted for a moment the veil over the unseen state, and to have spoken of a matter familiar to him, but incomprehensible to us. The apparent meaning is that even the humblest followers of Christ are ministered to by angels, who have access to the presence of God himself.

257. What Is Meant by "The Children of the Kingdom Shall Be Cast Out into Outer Darkness"?

In this passage (Matt. 8:11-12) Christ was evidently referring to the Jews. His remark was called forth by a Roman officer exhibiting more faith in him than had ever been done by a Jew. He therefore warned his Jewish hearers that, although they prided themselves on being children of the kingdom of God, through their descent from Abraham, they might be excluded from the kingdom because of personal unfitness; while others, who could not claim that illustrious pedigree, would be admitted because of their personal fitness. The present application of his words appears to us to be not to converted persons, but to nominal Christians, who have never been converted, but expect to enter heaven because they belong to Christian families, have been baptized and admitted to membership in a Christian church, but have not the spirit of Christ and Christ's words here also apply to people in Christian countries who having a knowledge of the things of God, do not live according to their knowledge. They, too, will see people who had not their advantages admitted, while they themselves are excluded.

258. What Is Meant by "Let the Dead Bury Their Dead"?

The language employed by Christ (Matt. 8:22) on the occasion in question is to be accepted figuratively as in many other instances of his teachings. He was speaking of the characteristics of true discipleship, and particularly referred to those who permitted themselves to become so entangled in worldly affairs, that they persistently procrastinated in spiritual things. To these, Jesus showed that all other claims were inferior to the divine claim upon their energies and the paramount command to "preach the kingdom of God." These should take precedence even of the highest claims of nature. While immortal souls are in peril, the true disciple must not hesitate, but must go even at the sacrifice of all he holds dear. Those who remain, being dead to the spiritual call, may well be relied upon to fulfill all needful natural duties to the dead or the dying among themselves. The disciple's duty is to obey the call, leaving the consequences with God.

259. Why Did Jesus Want the News of His Miracles Kept Quiet?

It was probably out of consideration for his followers, as there might be a popular rising which might lead to slaughter. The people were expecting the Messiah to be a king and, if they had recognized Christ, and still held that notion they would probably have risen in rebellion against Rome. On one occasion (John 6:15), he hid himself to prevent such a rising. It was safe after his death to preach him as the Christ, because then the spiritual nature of his kingdom would be understood; but while he lived, it was necessary to avoid publicity. Even the disciples expected that he would make himself king and did not understand his real purpose until after the resurrection.

260. What Is Meant by "Who Is Able to Destroy Both Soul and Body in Hell"?

Stier and some other writers contend that it is Satan to whom Christ refers in Matt. 10:28, but the context disproves this theory. The whole tenor of the chapter is directed to encouraging men to trust in God and to fear offending him. Christ shows in the following verse how God's control covers all life, and that without his permission no life is lost. Christ does not teach us anywhere to fear Satan, but to rejoice that, through himself, Satan has been overcome. In this passage the contrast is between the fear of man on the one hand, which might lead us to keep away from Christ or desert him lest we should be persecuted; and the fear, on the other hand, of God whose power is infinite in extent, and whom we should dread to displease.

261. What Is Meant by "I Came Not to Send Peace, but a Sword"?

Christ's work on the individual soul may help you to understand his meaning (Matt. 10:34). The converted soul enjoys a peace passing all understanding;

but how is it attained? The first stages of the process are those of fierce conflict. See the agony, the distress, that the majority of men pass through when they are under conviction. It is through conflict that peace is attained. It is so with the evil in the world. Christ's kingdom is one of peace; but not the despicable peace with wickedness and oppression. With those evils there must be war. If a father wisely loves his son, he does not ignore that son's bad ways; he punishes him in order to save him. You may say how do we reconcile the rod in the father's hand with his love for his child. There is no need to reconcile. The rod is a sign and proof of the father's love. So Christ's coming brought a sword to smite the evil that is cursing the world.

262. What Is Meant by "For I Am Come to Set a Man at Variance with His Father"?

This statement (Matt. 10:35) showed the result of his coming, not the purpose of it. Christ was warning the people who came to him of the sufferings they would have to endure, among which was this of the hostility of their near relatives. Many were offering themselves as his disciples who expected that he would become the King of Israel, and that they would share his glory, and he wished none to come with any such idea. He wanted them to count the cost, and he told them of the trials awaiting them if they followed him. They must be quite sure that they loved him so well that if their fathers or their brothers cast them off for being Christians they would be faithful to Christ, even at the cost of losing the love of their relatives.

263. What Is Meant by "This Is Elias Which Was to Come"? Matt. 11:14.

There was a prophecy that God would send Elijah or Elias to turn the hearts of the people (Malachi 4:5). When John appeared the Jews asked him if he was Elias, and he answered that he was not (John 1:21). They evidently expected that the literal Elijah, who is represented as ascending to heaven without dying (II Kings 2:11), would be sent to earth. John knew he was not that. He regarded himself as a humble messenger, a mere voice, with no distinction but that of preparing the way. The character of his preaching, however, shows that, like other messengers from God, he underestimated his dignity. When Christ spoke of him he settled the question definitely in the passage you refer to. John, he said, was the Elias to whom the prophecy referred.

264. What Are the "Idle Words" that Men Shall Give Account of?

The passage in Matt. 12:36 means unseemly or improper conversation, levity, slander, scoffing, boasting, swearing, mocking at sacred things. The Saviour had been speaking of blasphemy and of the scoffing attitude of the Pharisees, who imputed his miracles to Beelzebub. The "idle words" presumably referred more particularly to their sceptical way of accounting for the miracles, of which they had spoken slightingly.

265. What Are We to Understand by Christ's Parable of the Return of the Unclean Spirit?

Its first application, as the closing words show, is to the Jews of that time. (See Matt. 12:43, 45.) They were rid of the evil of idolatry, but were worse than their fathers, who worshiped idols, in that they rejected Jesus and finally crucified him. In modern times, the same evil is seen when a nation abandons its superstitions, but instead of turning to Christ, and becoming Christian, becomes atheistic. Its application to individuals is of the same character. Christianity is positive as well as negative in its effects. It forbids and condemns sin (that is negative); it also enjoins love, kindness, service (that is positive). If, for example, a man who has been a drunkard overcomes his propensity, that is, gets rid of his unclean spirit, but does not go forward to faith in Christ, he is liable to become Pharisaic and intolerant, and perhaps sceptical. In that condition he is liable to fall into worse sin. The throne of the soul is never empty. If Christ does not rule, some evil spirit takes possession.

266. What Are the Tares Mentioned in Matt. 13:25?

The tares in the parable refer to the seed called "darnel," a rank and widely distributed grass, and the only species that has deleterious properties. It is poisonous and its grains, if eaten, produce vomiting, purging, convulsions and sometimes even death. Before it comes into the ear it resembles the wheat so closely that it can hardly be distinguished from the latter, hence the command to leave it to the harvest. Grain-growers in Palestine believe the tares, or *zuwan*, to be a diseased or degenerate wheat. The seed resembles wheat in form, but is smaller and nearly black.

267. What Was the Power Conferred on Peter by Christ's Commission of the Keys?

The keys and the power of binding and loosing referred to a common Jewish custom. When a man had passed his examinations for the high position of a doctor of the law, he received as his diploma, a key which was handed to him with the words, "Receive authority to bind and to loose," that is to permit or forbid. Having mastered the law, he could say whether some act was lawful or unlawful. Peter's declaration that Jesus was the Son of God was the evidence of his having reached a state of spiritual faith and perception which Christ recognized (Matt. 16:18, 19). The keys may also have had reference to Peter's opening the doors of Christ's kingdom to the multitude on the day of Pentecost and to the Gentiles by preaching to Cornelius. It is clear that the Apostles did not recognize Peter as superior to themselves. It was James who passed sentence in the council (Acts 15:13, 19) although Peter was present; and Paul "withstood Peter to the face." (Gal. 2:11.)

268. What Is Meant in Jesus' Advice "Turn to Him the Other Also"?

Christ's teaching in this and other passages was intended to inculcate principles, rather than blind, literal, servile obedience. He would have his followers patient, gentle, non-resistant, forbearing, submitting to be wronged rather than resisting. His own example in yielding himself to death, when by the exercise of his miraculous powers he could have delivered himself, is an illustration of his meaning. Yet he scourged the traders in the Temple, and in denouncing the Scribes and Pharisees he showed that he was not deficient in vigor. There have, however, been many instances of men literally obeying the command to turn the other cheek, and in some, the effect on the striker was to produce shame and humiliation greater than could have resulted from a fight. There have been many, too, who after painful experience have wished they had submitted to a wrong instead of going to the courts. (See Matt. 18:15, 16, 17.)

269. Who Are the People to Whom Christ Referred as Being "Joined Together of God"?

We may understand the remark better by reading the whole passage (Matt. 19:1-12). The Pharisees were trying to draw Christ into a controversy which, at the time, was raging between the schools of different Jewish teachers. One school contended that a man was justified in divorcing his wife for any cause as, for instance, if she burnt the food she was cooking for his dinner. Another school held that physical defects alone justified divorce. There were other schools holding other opinions. Christ refused to identify himself with any and lifted the question into the higher plane by showing the origin of marriage in divine institution.

270. What Was the "Needle's Eye"?

The "needle's eye" (Matt. 19:24) was the small gate or wicket at the side of the big gate at the entrance to the city wall. When the big gate closed for the day, all entrance had to be gained through the small gate, and to a loaded camel, or indeed to any body of considerable size, passage was impossible.

271. What Is Meant by "A Rich Man Shall Hardly Enter the Kingdom of God"?

To rightly understand the full significance of the passage in Matt. 19:23 read Luke 18:24-27. It may be liberally interpreted: "How hard it is for those who trust in riches to enter! Unless this idolatrous trust and confidence in mere wealth is overcome, they cannot enter" except by a miracle of divine grace, which changes the heart. Jesus found no fault with the young man because of his riches, since wealth, and the power and influence it brings, may be made a means of great blessing if used in the right spirit as a trust committed to our stewardship. He found, however, that the young man's wealth was to him of greater moment than his eternal welfare, since he could not grasp the great opportunity offered him by the Master. Paul in I Cor. 6:10 also has a bearing upon the love of wealth and the hard and merciless means that are sometimes adopted to acquire it. Where extortion begins may be defined by statute, but it must really be determined by the conscience, since what is a fair return in one case may be a cruel extortion in another. We must carry the Christ idea into our business relations, and deal not only justly but generously and humanely, never making gain of another's necessity, and if with all we pile up riches, we are apt to rely on them to put us into heaven. This was the case of the young man who came to Christ. The sincerity of the young man was obvious; yet he himself felt that although he had lived a clean, moral life, keeping the letter of the law in absolute strictness, there was yet something wanting. He was not satisfied with his own blameless life. It was to find out what this hidden need was that he came to the Master, and asked, "What lack I yet?" Jesus, reading his heart, knew that his wealth stood as a barrier between him and the spiritual life he craved; that the influence and social position it gave were so dear to him that he could not bear to part with them, even to attain his ideal of a perfect life. His riches were his idol, and this the Master knew. So when Jesus in his wisdom put the test, forcing the young man to choose between riches and heaven—that he must himself cast aside the stumbling-block in his spiritual path—he failed at the crisis, turned his back upon the Master, and went away sorrowful. Jesus demanded an absolute surrender of the heart and the whole life, the placing of all in the scale as a heart offering. Good works could not save, but sacrifice of our works and our wealth brings us into a new and divine relationship as true heirs to the kingdom. See Matt. 19:29, in which the spiritual compensation for such sacrifice is promised. The rich young ruler came very near to the kingdom, but without entering in. His own estimate of his obedience was not justified, for if he had indeed kept the first commandment he would have placed God first, above even his much-prized earthly treasures, and he would never have gone away from Christ.

272. What Is the Parable of the Laborers Intended to Teach? Matt. 20:1-6.

There has, probably, been more difference in explaining this parable than any other. To us it appears that the incidents of it are not intended as laying down a business principle, but as a commentary on the events in the preceding chapter. Peter had asked, "What shall we have, therefore?" showing a bargaining spirit. Christ shows him by this parable that, not they who stipulate for reward, but they who trust in God, leaving their reward for him to fix are treated best. That was a prominent characteristic of Christ. He craved personal trust and personal faith in himself. Where does the injustice of the householder come in? He kept his agreement with the early laborers, who had stipulated for a penny a day. They had the amount they had demanded and had no grievance. The householder chose to deal more liberally with the others, who had left their remuneration to him, but that was in no sense a wrong to the early laborers. If an employer knows something about one of his employees—perhaps that he has been sick, or that he has a large family—and chooses to give him a double wage, is he bound to go all round his factory and double the wages of every man in his employ? It is the hireling spirit, the spirit of the man who bargains, who resents the kindness done to another as a wrong to himself, that Christ reproves here. He condemns it, as he condemned the elder brother in the parable of the Prodigal Son, who resented the feast to the prodigal and reminded the father of his own claims. Many of the first (not all) shall be last because of the spirit in which they have performed their work.

273. In the Parable of the Laborers What Is the Principle Taught?

This parable in Matt. 20:1-16 stands in close connection with the preceding chapter, and its evident purpose was to illustrate the sentiment of the closing verse: "Many that are first shall be last, and the last shall be first." The parable has reference to rewards, and illustrates the method of their bestowment upon the followers of Christ, namely, in such a way that the last shall be equal to the first, and the first last—a way that rewards faithfulness of service, rather than length of service or the amount accomplished in the service. The purpose of the parable, being understood, it cannot properly awaken any question as to discrimination in the matter of the pay of the laborers. As to the transaction of the householder, as represented in the parable, there was no injustice in it. He agreed with the first laborers for "a penny a day," while with the others no specified amount was agreed upon, and he could pay them what he pleased. Further, the Saviour does not necessarily approve the course of the householder, and we are not required to show that it was either right or wise, as an act of man toward men, but only that rewards in the kingdom of God are thus bestowed without reference to the time of service, another and very different consideration actuating our Heavenly Father in this matter—namely, faithfulness.

The parable was an answer to Peter's question (Matt. 19:27), "Behold, we have forsaken all and followed thee: what shall we have therefore?" In a word, it was a rebuke of the bargaining spirit. Those who follow Christ for the sake of the reward, and not from love of him, will not be defrauded. They will have all that God has promised them, but they are not those whom he most loves. A parent who promises a child a reward for a certain service, or for good behavior, and notices that the child performs the task or behaves himself better than at other times, when no reward is promised, does not approve of the child's spirit. He does not like to see the child doing for money the thing that he does not do for love, as he ought to do. Still, he keeps his promise and pays, as he agreed. But the child who does cheerfully and readily, as the parent requests, without any promise of reward, is the one whom the parent approves. That child would surely be rewarded, though no reward had been promised.

The householder in the parable makes his bargain with the first party of laborers. The phrase, "when he had agreed with them," clearly implies negotiation. With the others he made no bargain, merely giving his promise to pay whatsoever was right. They trusted him, and went to work. He liked the confidence they showed, and he gave them more than they expected. The early morning laborers had no just ground of complaint. They received all they had stipulated for. All through Christ's ministry he showed the same spirit. He craved personal love and confidence. He wanted people, above all things, to trust in him. Peter's question must have chilled Christ's spirit. It might have been interpreted as showing that this man who Christ supposed was following him for love, was there for what he could make out of it. Hence, the rebuke of the parable.

274. How Are We to Interpret "The Son of Man Came Not to be Ministered Unto but to Minister"?

This passage in Matt. 20:28, is the elevation of the duty of Christian service. Of course Christ did come to earth to win all men to his service, but it was for their sakes rather than his own. To serve him meant salvation; it was sin that kept them from their allegiance to him. And he came to save them from their sins. All the time he was in the flesh he gave rather than accepted service. He was moved by love. Even when the people would have taken him by force to make him king he would not accept it. That was not the kind of service he wanted. He wanted men to serve him in holiness and spiritual power. He gave his body in humiliation and sacrifice in order that they might be lifted up to this higher plane of service. The whole message of the New Testament is that Christ came to earth for the sake of mankind, not for his own sake. And he taught by example the life of humility, self-sacrifice and service which he wishes all men to lead.

275. What Did Jesus Mean by Faith That Could Remove Mountains?

This is the language of similitude and figure which Jesus frequently employed to illustrate and emphasize his teaching. A leading commentator writes of this passage (Matt. 21:21): "From the nature of the case supposed—that they might wish a mountain removed and cast into the sea (a thing very far from anything which they could be thought to actually desire)—it is plain that not physical but moral obstacles to the progress of his kingdom were in the Saviour's mind." What he designed to teach was the great lesson that no obstacle should be able to stand before a firm faith in God—that it would enable us to overcome all difficulties, if we absolutely trusted in him.

276. Was the Man without the Wedding Garment Harshly Dealt with?

No; he was treated as he deserved. At a wedding feast in an Oriental land such as Christ was describing, the king would provide garments for his guests, suitable to the occasion. A guest who declined to wear the wedding garment and went in wearing his ordinary attire, would be conspicuous and his conduct would be an affront to the king. He would naturally be considered as despising the dress which the king had provided and preferring his own. Christ, in the passage in Matt. 22:11-13, was warning his hearers against trusting in their own righteousness and rejecting God's way of salvation.

277. Why Should We Call Jesus "Master"?

Because he himself has told us to do so. It is a very beautiful and inspiring title which Christians everywhere may apply to their beloved Lord. (See Matt. 23:10.) This passage is a part of Jesus' denunciation of the Scribes and Pharisees, who were given over to formalism and regarded the *letter* rather than the *spirit* of Scripture. They sought personal honors and the applause of the multitudes. They carried strips of parchment of Scripture texts, bound to arm, forehead and side, in time of prayer, and they loved to be addressed by ecclesiastical titles. *Rabbi* (Master) was a title which they particularly affected and which their whole spiritual conduct discredited. Had they been true teachers and guides, instead of false, he would not have reprobated them, nor would they have belied the title they bore. Titles in the modern Christian Church are vain distinctions, except where they are worthily worn. All should be brethren in Christ, the highest dignitary of the church and the humblest follower. Unfortunately, in every age there has been a desire for ecclesiastical distinctions and, while in many cases these have been merited and gladly accorded, in others the honors were not deserved. The ecclesiastical system of the Jews lent itself to this vanity to such an extent as to arouse the divine indignation. The title "Rab" was originally Babylonian and that of "Rabbi," Palestinian. It was given to learned men, authorized teachers of the law and spiritual heads of the community.

278. What Is Meant by "Heaven and Earth Shall Pass Away"?

The expressions "heaven" and "the heavens" mean not only the spiritual, eternal world, but also the stars and the spaces of ether surrounding the earth. Jesus used the word frequently in both these senses. He spoke of "the kingdom of heaven," signifying the eternal kingdom, and then spoke of the stars as "heaven" or "the heavens" in passages like the one you mention. Paul speaks of "the house not made with hands eternal in the heavens." (II Cor. 5:1.) The teaching of the Bible is that the material universe, including the earth itself, will be transformed, but that the spiritual universe will endure forever.

279. What Is the Lesson of the Parable of the Talents?

The parable in Matt. 25 was given to explain the principle of the judgment. From one who had been well endowed much would be expected, and a smaller result would be looked for from one who had received less. Only he would be punished who had made no effort to turn his talents to account. Christ probably intended it to apply to every kind of gift. Men of wealth, of education, of spiritual privilege, with any kind of opportunity for doing good, were affected by it. A man must do the best he could in his circumstances, and if he could not do as well, or as much as, another who was better equipped, he would not be blamed. The distinction between worldly and spiritual is somewhat vague in this instance. The man who gives to a starving family is not exactly doing spiritual work, but it is the kind of work that this parable would apply to.

280. Was the Story of the Rich Man and Lazarus a Parable or an Actual Fact?

It was a parable—an illustration of the kind made familiar in the teachings of Christ. It is the only parable in which a proper name is employed, and Lazarus was probably chosen because it was a common name. By some both men in the parable have been considered as real personages, and one tradition even gives the name of the rich man as Dobruk, while another gives it as Nimeusis. Neither tradition is deserving of credit, and the best commentators agree that the two characters were described by the Saviour simply to illustrate two type of men.

281. Did Jesus in Any of His Parables Make Allusion to Historical Characters?

He is thought by some to have done so in the parable of the talents (Matt. 25). Dean Farrar points this out as follows: "It is the only instance in which we can connect a parable of the Gospel with historical events. The man who goes into another country to seek a kingdom is Archelaus, son of Herod the Great. Left heir of the chief part of Herod's kingdom by the last will of his father, altered within five days of his death, Archelaus had to travel to Rome to obtain from the Emperor Augustus the confirmation of his heritage. During his absence he had to leave the kingdom under commission to his kinsmen and servants, some of whom were wise and faithful, and others much the reverse. The circumstances of the succession of Archelaus would be recalled to Christ's memory as he passed the magnificent palace which the tyrant had built at Jericho. Archelaus was absent at Rome for some months. Jesus calls him a 'hard man.' The grasping character of Archelaus made him unpopular from the first, and the hatred felt for him was increased by his deadly cruelties. The event to which our Lord here distinctly refers had occurred in his own infancy."

282. What Is Meant by "New Wine in Old Bottles"?

Mark 2:21, 22 is designed to illustrate the difference between the old and new economies, and the result of mixing up one with the other. The "new wine" was the evangelical freedom which Christ was introducing into the old spirit of Judaism. It was as though he had said, "These inquiries about the difficulty between my disciples and the Pharisees, and even John's disciples, serve to point out the effect of a natural revulsion against sudden change, which time will cure and which will be seen to be to the better advantage."

283. What Is Meant by "Unto Them That Are without, All These Things Are Done in Parables"?

In the passage in Mark 4:11, 12 Jesus meant apparently that he made the difference between his teaching of disciples and of the ordinary people because of the spiritual insight of the former. It was of no use to give the latter the direct teaching that he gave the disciples. But he taught them by illustrations to which they would listen and which would remain in their minds. They would thus learn more than they knew at the time. The meaning of the stories was not clear to them then, and they probably thought there was no particular moral to them, but the influence of the teaching would be felt afterwards. Sometimes a child may play at a game that may teach him geography or history and his teacher is aware that the child has learned more than he has any idea of. The child may be interested in a fable and see nothing in it applicable to himself, but in future years the moral meaning of the fable may be perceptible to him.

284. What Did Our Lord Mean When He Spoke of "The Mystery of the Kingdom"?

The word "mystery," found in Mark 4:11, 12 as in certain other places in Scripture, is not used in the classical sense of religious secrets or things incomprehensible, but of things of purely divine revelation—matters foreshadowed in the ancient economy and then only partially understood, but now fully published under the Gospel (see I Cor. 2:6, 10; Eph. 3:3, 6, 8, 9). The mysteries of the kingdom meant those great Gospel truths which at that time none but the disciples could appreciate, and even they only in part, while to those without (whose hearts had not yet been opened to the Gospel) they were like tales and fables, subjects of entertainment rather than divine truths. Such persons saw but recognized not, and heard but understood not, for their spiritual sight and understanding were judicially sealed by sin. From obdurate rejection of the Gospel, and their obstinacy in preferring darkness to light, they had become morally incapable of acceptance and totally indifferent. (See prophecy of Is. 6:9, 10, then read contrasting passage in Matt. 13:16.)

285. How Should We Interpret Jesus' Words "The Damsel Is Not Dead, but Sleepeth"?

The Saviour's language in Mark 5:39 was as though he had used the familiar figure "she hath fallen asleep" —the same figure that is frequently employed in the Scriptures in describing death as sleep. (See Acts 7:60; I Cor. 15:6, 18; II Peter 3:4.) Some have interpreted the language of Mark 5 to mean that the maid was in a trance or swoon; but most commentators agree that Mark 5:35 is a clear affirmation that all the signs of death were evident, that the life had already fled and that the reassuring words of the Master (in verse 36) before he had even seen the maid, were intended to strengthen the ruler's faith and prepare him for the manifestation of divine power that followed. The last nine verses, read as a whole, bear out this conclusion.

286. What Kind of Baskets Were Used in the Miracle of the Loaves and Fishes?

The Gospel accounts say: "They took up what remained over of the broken pieces twelve baskets full" (Matt. 14:20). "They took up of the broken meat that was left seven baskets" (Mark 8:8). There have been some differences among scholars as to the translation of the word (in the original) denoting "baskets." In describing the earlier miracle, that of the feeding of five thousand, a word is used which indicates large fishing baskets made of rope, while in the narrative of the later miracle, there is used a term which translated means smaller hand-baskets. It might well be asked how could the apostles have carried around with them seven large fishing baskets? A comparison between the two accounts will clear up a seeming difficulty. Many Jews carried small hand-baskets in which they kept their food supplies free from pollution. Each apostle may have carried such a small hand-basket and in the party of apostles there may have been one who carried a large fishing basket. This large fishing basket was filled seven times and again twelve times, for the phraseology used seems to indicate that, whereas in the one instance each apostle filled his small hand-basket with broken pieces, in the other the one large fishing basket was filled seven times.

287. Who Was the Little Child That Jesus Took Up and Blessed?

The details of these incidents in the life of Jesus, have been preserved to us only by tradition. It is said that the little child of whom the Saviour remarked, "of such is the kingdom of heaven" (Mark 9:36), afterwards became known to the Christian Church as Ignatius, Bishop of Antioch. He was one of the great company of martyrs who gave their lives for the faith in the time of Trajan, being torn to pieces by lions in the amphitheatre at Rome.

288. What Did Jesus Mean by Saying "Why Callest Thou Me Good"?

The true meaning of the much discussed passage (Mark 10:17) quoted is thus explained by very good authority. Professor David Smith, who writes: " 'Master' or 'Teacher' was the regular appellation of a Jewish Rabbi, and it was accounted so honorable that it always stood alone without qualification. It was a deliberate departure from the established usage, an intentional improvement on the common style, when the young ruler addressed our Lord as 'Good Master.' It showed that he had recognized him as more than a teacher; and when our Lord fastened upon the epithet, his purpose was to elicit what his questioner really meant. He said in effect: 'You have gone a long way in calling me "good." That epithet belongs only to God. You have recognized me as more than a teacher: are you prepared to go farther, and recognize me as divine?' Hence it appears that our Lord's question is not a repudiation of the attribute of deity. On the contrary, it is an assertion of his title to it. It is a gracious attempt to bring home to that anxious inquirer, in conscious realization, the truth which he had dimly perceived and was groping for."

289. Why Was the Fig Tree Blighted?

The fig tree incident related in Mark 11:13 has been a subject of much controversy, and the passage in Mark 11:13 has been claimed by some to be a mistake in the transcription of the record as to the words, "He found nothing but leaves, for the time of figs was not yet." It is explained by some writers (including Pliny and Macrobius) that the fig tree in Palestine produces fruit at two or even three seasons of the year, and Hackett (in his *Scripture Illustrations*) tells us that the fruit precedes the leaves. One might infer from this that if a tree had leaves it might be expected to give evidence at least of having had fruit. In the case of this particular tree, having leaves in advance of the regular time (which "was not yet come") yet with no sign of having borne fruit, it was condemned, as some commentators interpret the case, because of its uselessness. Trench and several others hold that the blighting of the precocious and fruitless tree was designed to convey a rebuke to "the barren traditions of the Pharisees, their ostentatious display of the law, and their vain exuberance of words without the good fruit of works." Still others, believe that our Lord, seeing the early leaves, had a right to expect that they would be accompanied by fruit.

290. Was Christ Omniscient in the Flesh?

It is reasonable to suppose that in the days of his flesh Christ experienced some curtailment of divine attributes. We read of his being weary, of his weeping, of his praying, being hungry and thirsty, and being tempted. We read also of his increasing in wisdom (Luke 2:52). We infer from all these that the divine nature did not have full scope for its powers in the human form or could only express them partially owing to the obvious limitations. Christ seems to have been aware of this while on the earth, for he said, "My Father is greater than I." (John 14:28.) We conclude, therefore, that a part of his humiliation was his voluntarily divesting himself of some part of his divine nature and this may account for such a passage as

Mark 13:32. It is impossible for the human mind to fully comprehend the mystery of the Trinity, but we can imagine that Christ in his loving compassion, voluntarily put from him certain attributes of the Godhead while on earth in order that in all things he might be made like unto his brethren. In what way or to what extent, if at all, the incarnation limited the divine attributes cannot be defined, and the fact of his praying to his Father indicated that in the days of his flesh there was a distinction between them that is incomprehensible to us.

291. Does Christ's Admission that He Did Not Know the Time of the End Imply that He Was Not Divine?

No, the inference (to be drawn from Mark 13:32) does not appear logical. We do not understand the union of the two natures in our Lord's person, and therefore cannot explain many of the difficulties which are presented. If, however, we take the conception that is given in the first chapter of John's Gospel, of an incarnation, we can perceive how there may have been restriction in the exercise of divine power operating by a human brain. The instrument would be necessarily inadequate. The assumption of an unrestricted divine nature would imply perfect knowledge in boyhood, yet we know that as a boy Christ did not know all things; for Luke says explicitly (2:52) that he increased in wisdom, which he could not have done had he been omniscient from birth. In taking our nature he voluntarily submitted to the imperfections of our condition, otherwise he would not have been made "like unto his brethren."

292. If Christ Knew All Things, Did He Not Know that Judas Was Not a True Believer?

Christ did not claim to know all things. He mentioned one thing that he did not know (Mark 13:32). At the same time he is said to have known what was in man (John 2:25), so he may have been aware of the possibilities of evil in Judas, which were probably not developed when he was chosen as an apostle. Christ knew of his intended treachery before it was committed. Doubtless Judas himself, at the time of his call, had no idea that he would commit such a crime. Even at the last, he may have expected that Christ would deliver himself by his miraculous power. He was evidently horror-stricken when he learned the result of what he had done, as is proved by his committing suicide.

293. What Are the Signs Which Jesus Said "Shall Follow Them That Believe"?

Jesus did not promise that the signs referred to in Mark 16:17 should always follow. The speaking with tongues, casting out devils, taking up serpents, etc., were signs suitable for that age when the people, being densely ignorant, expected miracles and signs. Christ reproved the tendency, and on more than one occasion refused to gratify them. He wanted them to learn from the sign to seek spiritual blessings at his hands, which were of much greater value to them. We have entered into that higher and better understanding of him. It is much more wonderful to see a drunkard reclaimed, a vicious man reformed, than it was to see a lame man healed. The power to cast out devils and to speak with tongues and take up serpents would not be nearly so valuable to us as is the power he gives to transform evil lives.

294. Why Did Jesus Say of John "He That Is Least in the Kingdom of God Is Greater than He"?

The passage in Luke 7:28 is frequently misunderstood, as being spoken in derogation of John, because of the doubt his messengers had implied in their question (verse 20). The true meaning, as Weiss and other commentators believe, is that Jesus was speaking of the differences in the success of the Baptist with certain classes. The common people and the publicans, who had repented under John's ministry, and had been baptized by him, understood the meaning of Jesus and were glad (verse 29), but the Pharisees and Scribes—the very class who should have been models of righteousness, had rejected and despised John. That Jesus spoke with this contrast in view is made clear in verses 30 to 35 inclusive. He was speaking of the advancement of the kingdom in the hearts of men.

295. What Was the Special Value and Object of Jesus' Parables?

"But unto others in parables that seeing they might not see and hearing they might not understand" Luke 8:10. Dean Farrar says on this passage: "Lord Bacon says, 'A parable has a double use; it tends to veil and it tends to illustrate a truth; in the latter case it seems designed to teach, in the former to conceal.' Our Lord wished the multitude to understand, but the result and profit depended solely on the degree of their faithfulness. The parables resembled the Pillar of Fire, which was to the Egyptians a Pillar of Cloud."

The truth veiled in the form of parable was withheld from the people because their minds had grown too gross to receive it. "Had the parable of the mustard seed, for instance," says Dr. Whedon, "been explained to the Pharisees as indicating that the Gospel would yet fill the earth, it would only have excited their additional hostility and hastened their purpose of accusing him as intending to subvert the existing government." They themselves, as we learn from Matt. 13:15, had wilfully closed their eyes to the Gospel, and so its real principles must be withheld from them. To some this may have been a mercy, preventing them from using the truth to evil purposes. To others it may have been simply the penalty due them for having insulted the truth and become unworthy of it. While, however, the parable veiled the truth from cavillers, it unveiled it to the disciples (Matt. 13:11). The unreceptive people, "seeing" the narrative, saw "not" the doctrine embodied; "hearing" the literal parable, they understood "not" the secret meaning. "The whole Gospel is a parable to him whose heart has not the key." This solemn teaching is found also in the law and the prophets. Deu. 29:3, 4; Is. 6:9; Jer. 5:21; Ezek. 12:2.

296. How Are We to Understand "Whosoever Hath, to Him Shall Be Given"?

This expression (Luke 8:18) occurs in a number of New Testament passages, Matt. 13:12, Mark 4:25, etc. Its meaning is most evident in Matt. 25:29, and

Luke 19:26, in connection with the parable of the talents, or pounds. Christ is stating in these words two laws which are universal. First, a man must have something to start with before he can do any work. Second, if he does not make good use of what is given he loses it. In other words: something never comes from nothing; neglect means loss. Every man is given something to start with for working out his life plan. If he neglects to use what he has he loses it. It cannot be said that God takes it away from him; the man simply lets it slip through his fingers. Helen Keller had very little to begin with, but she made such amazingly faithful use of that, that she gained much more. She used and developed the sense of touch till it has become almost equal to sight and hearing. But a sense or a muscle unused becomes useless. A man has only to stop walking and he will soon lose the power to walk. It is ridiculous to say that there is anything cruel about this. It is simply the law of life. And the law works no hardship to any one who has a desire to make good use of life. In the passage (Luke 8:18) the law is applied to hearing. When a man hears a truth he must follow it and apply it quickly. If he does not he will forget it, or cease to believe it, or lose it in some other way.

297. Why Did Jesus Allow Evil Spirits to Enter the Herd of Swine?

According to the law of Moses, swine were unclean, and any Jew owning them or using them as food violated this law. The destruction of the herd (Luke 8:26, 36) and the question of the destination of the evil spirits has been well explained by Trench in his famous book on *Miracles*. He wrote: "A man is of more value than many swine," and added that it is not necessary to suppose that our Lord *sent* the devils into the swine, but merely *permitted* them to go, adding further that if those Gadarene villagers who owned the swine were Jews, as may be supposed, they were properly punished by the loss of that which they ought not to have had at all. As for the evil spirits, it is reasonable to conclude that they found a congenial refuge somewhere else. With regard to their recognition of Jesus as divine, we have Scripture assurance that "the devils believe and tremble."

298. What Did Jesus Mean by "Take No Thought for Your Life, What Ye Shall Eat, neither for Your Body What Ye Shall Put on"?

This was a part of the "Sermon on the Mount," and Luke 12:19-34 is intended to illustrate heavenly-mindedness and confidence in God's providence. The particular passage quoted admonishes the believer not to be too anxiously concerned or worried about things that are purely temporal. It is right to make due provision for our own needs and the needs of those dependent upon us; but when we have done so, we should not fret and doubt and make ourselves and others miserable because of our fears of coming trouble. This applies to our food, our clothing and our worldly affairs generally. All such doubts and worries spring from unbelief, and are after the manner of the world. If we really believe and trust our heavenly Father, he will provide all we need. This promise, however, does not relieve us from the natural duty of making reasonable provision, though there are some people who mistakenly think so. The whole passage, broadly interpreted, means that we are to do our work here properly and cheerfully and to trust the Father for the rest and never worry, always keeping in view the greater duty of "seeking first the kingdom," beside which all other things are insignificant. Worry in the sense involved in the passage is a sin against God since it shows absolute lack of faith in his promised providential care.

299. What Is Meant by Hating Father and Mother and Wife for Jesus' Sake?

In Luke 14:26 our Lord asserts his claim to our most loyal service and our supreme affection. In taking up one's cross to follow him, we must be prepared for trials for his sake, and to break even the nearest and dearest ties, if need be. He must have the first place in our hearts. It may come to choosing between Christ and our nearest relations. Compare Matt. 10:37 with the passage in Luke 14. "Hate" is not the preferable word, as the passage in Matthew shows. The passage in Luke obscures the true form of the expression and invests it with harshness while Matthew makes the true meaning clear, that we are to love him better than all else, even those who are nearest and dearest to us, and that this love must assert itself loyally at the crisis, no matter what it may cost us. A loyal soldier will give up all to serve his country; so we too must be prepared to give up all, if need be, to serve Christ.

300. What Was Meant by the "Ninety and Nine Just Persons Which Need No Repentance"?

There was a tendency among the Pharisees (see Luke 15:2) to despise the sinner and make no effort for his reclamation. They prided themselves on their scrupulous observance of the law and on their lives being free from open sin. Christ met them on their own ground, and showed them that the recovery and reformation of the sinner was pleasing to God. He desires that none should perish, but that all should forsake sin and return. They thought that as there were no flagrant sins in their lives to be repented of, that they were God's favorite children. Christ showed them that if, as they contended, they were free from such sins, their self-righteous attitude was not so pleasing to God as was the attitude of the man who knew he had done wrong, and abjured it and asked pardon. There was need for repentance on the part of those who claimed to be just persons, as Christ showed them over and over again; but he was teaching another lesson at that time, and was proving to them, that, even assuming that they were sinless, as they claimed, they were wrong in the position they took toward the sinner.

301. What Were the "Husks That the Swine Did Eat"?

The husks (see Luke 15:16), were the fruit of the carob tree, which is common in Palestine and is used by the poor as food and for the fattening of swine or cattle. When ripe, it is like a cooked beanpod, brown, glossy, and filled with seeds. Children eat it readily and seem to thrive on it. The carob is of the same family as the American locust tree. Its fruit is sometimes called "St. John's bread," as John the Baptist is thought to have lived upon it in the wilderness.

302. Who Is Represented by the "Elder Brother" in the Prodigal Parable?

Primarily, the Pharisees and chief priests, who were scandalized by seeing Christ associate with the lower classes and notorious sinners. It was a rebuke to selfishness and formalism—to those who believe they have the spiritual right of way and that less worthy persons, who had been basking in the divine goodness should be envious or critical of the cordial welcome that is extended to a redeemed sinner. The lesson applies to people in our own day who have no sympathy with the work going on at rescue missions, and are sceptical about the conversion of evildoers. The parable was a reproof to such persons, but it also conveyed a weighty lesson as to the evil of sin. Although the father forgave his younger son and gave him joyful welcome, he said to the elder, "All that I have is thine," thereby intimating that the younger son's lost patrimony could not be restored. The sinner is urged to repent, and is promised pardon, but the time he has wasted, and the health he has injured, and the mischief his example has done, are irreparable evils.

303. What Did Our Lord Mean by Saying to Peter "When Thou Art Converted Strengthen Thy Brethren"?

The revised version renders the passage (Luke 22:32): "When thou hast turned again, stablish thy brethren." We cannot suppose that after Peter's fall, he needed conversion in the sense in which we use the word. He needed repentance and restoration. His words, his actions, and the intense devotion he had previously shown to Christ, all indicated a man already converted. He fell under temptation as Christ had foreseen, but it was a backsliding which Christ forgave. At Pentecost their experience was not conversion, but an enduement of power for service, notably the power of speaking foreign tongues.

304. What Is Meant by the "Impassable Gulf"?

The "impassable gulf," in Luke 16:26, is a figure employed by the Saviour in describing the eternal separation of the good and the evil in the future life. In his parables and discourses, in order to impress upon the minds of his hearers the central objects of the lessons, he invested them with such natural and harmonious surroundings as the subject and the occasion demanded; and to interpret such surroundings literally would be as futile as to translate literally any of the multitudinous passages, full of similar imagery, that abound in Oriental oratory.

305. What Classes of Mankind Did Dives and Lazarus Represent?

In the parable of the rich man and Lazarus (Luke 16:19), the object was to illustrate the result of neglect of duty in commiserating and relieving the sufferings of others; to show how wealth hardens the heart, shuts up the springs of human sympathy and makes the possessor selfish and indifferent to the wants of his fellowmen. The rich man was a type of those who, while possibly generous at times, were yet so centered upon worldly pleasures and self-indulgence that all else was a mere incident. Riches that are used only for our own aggrandizement and gratification become a curse, while the man who employs his wealth in dispensing aid and comfort to those around him and relieving the distressed is a blessing to the land in which he lives. This was the distinction which the Saviour drew in his parable of the division of the sheep and the goats, when the King repudiated those that stood on his left hand with the words: "Inasmuch as ye did it not to one of the least of these ye did it not to me" (Matt. 25:45). Lazarus was a type of the hopeless, helpless, friendless poor who are to be found all over the world, and whose lot could be greatly benefited if people of means held their wealth as a beneficent stewardship. Nothing can be clearer than that it was the Saviour's intention to emphasize by these parables the divine law of love and sympathy which he came to teach the children of men by his own example.

306. What Is Meant by "Easier for Heaven and Earth to Pass, than One Tittle of the Law to Fail"?

The law, in its literalness, endured until the time of John the Baptist. After him the kingdom of heaven was preached, the new kingdom whose law is love, whose king is Christ, and whose members are empowered by the Spirit of Christ to keep the greater and more comprehensive law of love, the law which includes and intensifies all the details of the ancient moral law. The law, while in Jesus it loses some of its ceremonial details, loses nothing of its real power; it is no less powerful, even by the tiniest measurement, than it was before, Luke 16:17. Matt. 5:17-19: Christ fulfilled the ceremonial law; he kept its authenticated details, and in his death all the requirements for sacrifice were satisfied and ended. While he kept the law and was to fulfill it, the Scribes and Pharisees were evading the law. By their interpretations and additions they really deprived it of authority. Jesus told them they must not dodge the law but keep it. He even indicated that those who kept the old law most carefully, as Paul did, would be given high places in the work of his new kingdom. Matt. 19:17: This again was counsel given *before* the Atonement. The way of life then was to seek to keep the law. Rom. 3:31: Here the declaration is made that the Gospel establishes the law. Men without the Gospel had little power to keep the law; the Gospel gives them power to keep it, and thus gives the law its rights, establishes it, makes it possible for its authority to assert itself. Rom. 8:7: The carnal mind is Paul's expression for the natural, evil, willful state of humanity. In that sinful, natural state a man cannot keep God's spiritual law. Paul uses also the term "old man" in the same sense. His teaching is that this "old man" is to be "destroyed" (Rom. 6:6), "put off" (Col. 3:8, 9; Eph. 4:22). James 2:10: This verse is undoubtedly true whether it is applied to law either before or after the Gospel. The judgment of the whole law as an institution came upon the man who violated any part of it; and under the Gospel a man is under the same obligation to keep the whole spirit of the moral law and to obey the words of Christ. We dare not disobey or displease Christ.

I John 2:3, 4: These verses make a good climax. John tells about the "perfect love," which enables humble Christians really to keep Christ's law of kindness. That is the great secret. Paul declares: "Love is the fulfilling of the law." If we love Jesus perfectly we shall not displease him by disobedience; if we really love our neighbor we will do him no harm but all the good we can.

307. What Is Meant by "Making Friends of the Mammon of Unrighteousness"?

Probably no passage has been so often the subject of dispute as this in Luke 16:8, 9. The Revised Version renders it, "Make to yourselves friends by means of the mammon of unrighteousness." Luther thought it was a caution against avarice. Farrar regarded it as an injunction to care and faithfulness. Taking account of the parable that precedes the passage, it would appear that Christ was showing how a wicked man succeeded in getting friends at his employer's expense. Good men were not nearly so much in earnest in their godly affairs as the worldly men in their business affairs. If they used their money in relieving the needs of the poor they would make friends in heaven. It would not open the door of heaven, but it would cause those who had been benefited to give a warm welcome, thus enhancing the joy of that state. Dr. William Taylor used to illustrate it thus: A man whose house has been broken into naturally condemns the burglar; but he would be justified in pointing out to a lazy or incompetent workman, that if he had half the ingenuity the burglar had displayed he would soon make a fortune. We cannot imagine sorrow in heaven, but if there is any man who feels regret, it is he who on earth saw his poor brother suffer for the lack of money that he might have given out of his abundance. In heaven he cannot ease the burden of earth, but he must regret that when it was in his power he did not do it.

In the passage in Luke our Lord was showing how worldly people, "in their generation" and for their own selfish purposes, were prudent and sagacious in the worldly sense, and showed energy and determination in carrying out their mercenary plans, none of which, however, were for God and eternity. They were types of the money-makers of that day. Even from them, selfish and worldly though they were, the children of light might learn the lesson of concentration—not in relation to worldly, but to spiritual, things. It should be noted also that (verse 8) it was not Jesus, but the "lord" of the steward who commended the latter. The Revised Version corrects verse 9, which, accurately translated, reads: "Make to yourself friends by means of the mammon of unrighteousness," etc., implying that they, "the children of light," should use money not as the steward did, for selfish purposes, but in doing good to others. (See Luke 6:38 and Matt. 25:34-40.)

308. When Jesus Asked: "Woman, What Have I to Do with Thee?" Was He Ungracious to His Mother?

These seemingly harsh words (in John 2:4) addressed by the Saviour to his mother at the feast of Cana, have been a subject of much speculation. In English they have a harsher sound than they have in the original. Thus "woman" is in Greek a mode of address used with respect and used even to those high in authority, such as queens. What the Saviour intended by this address was to call his mother's attention to the fact that it was his work he was doing and not one in which she had any concern. He no doubt used a gentle inflection of the voice, and her remark to the servants showed that not only was she not hurt or offended, but that she fully understood.

309. How Are We to Understand the Phrase: "The Zeal of Thine House Hath Eaten Me Up"?

The passage in John 2:17 is an expression which graphically describes the tremendous and inspiring enthusiasm of one who is aflame with a righteous purpose. The disciples were doubtless surprised at the courage of One whom they had regarded as so meek and gentle, setting himself to a task from which the bravest might have shrunk. It was a new side to their Master's character, but thinking it over, they realized that it was one that the prophets had predicted of him. His indignation at seeing the house that had been dedicated to God so prostituted made him regardless of his own safety. It absorbed him, or as John says, "ate him up"—made him forget everything else.

310. What Is Meant by "Except a Man Be Born of Water and of the Spirit"?

This passage in John 3:5 has given rise to much controversy and theologians are by no means agreed as to its meaning. Our opinion is that Christ had reference to the topic then agitating such men as the one he was speaking to. They had a ceremony by which the Gentile was admitted to the privileges of Judaism, part of which was baptism, which signified purification from the sins of his old life. To the astonishment of the Pharisees, John the Baptist had insisted that even they were in need of baptism, just as the proselyte was. But as John intimated that was not enough. There was One coming who would baptize with the Holy Spirit. Therefore Nicodemus would understand Christ's meaning, when he spoke of being born of water and of the spirit. To the new birth it was necessary that a man be purified in heart, his past sins blotted out, which was symbolized by the water, and he must be quickened to a new life, which was done by the Spirit. Both are still necessary to conversion. They are called in theological parlance, justification and sanctification. This element of water and the operation of the spirit are the subject of prediction in Ezekiel 36:25-27.

311. What Is the "New Birth"?

It is an expression frequently used instead of "regeneration," to express the change from the natural state of sin to the new spiritualized life of the Christian. It is dying unto sin and being born again unto righteousness, a complete transformation of our moral nature, a new heart. Following after conversion and justification, the new birth or regeneration brings about a complete change of heart (see Heb. 10:22; Gal. 6:15; II Cor. 5:17; Col. 3:9; Eph. 4:22-24 and other passages).

312. What Is the "Witness of the Spirit"?

The "witness of the Spirit" is the inward assurance which the believer enjoys of his filial relation to God, namely, that the Holy Spirit witnesses to and with his spirit that he is a child of God, and that his sins are forgiven. The immediate results of this witness of the Spirit are set forth in Gal. 5:22, 23.

313. In What Sense Is Meekness a Virtue?

It is a comprehensive virtue. It includes gentleness, readiness to do good to all men, to walk humbly before God and man, and not to overrate ourselves; to be loving as well as lowly-minded, not given to worldly ambition, but zealous to yield willing obedience to God's will; quiet, self-possessed, never quarrelsome nor disputatious. See Matt. 5:5; Matt. 11:29; II Cor. 10:1; I Peter 3:4; I Cor. 6:7; Rom. 12:19; I Peter 2:19-22; Rev. 21:7. Thus the meek, though the "only rightful occupants of a foot of ground or a crust of bread here," are the heirs of all things hereafter.

314. Why Did Jesus Give an Evasive Answer to the Question "Who Art Thou"?

When the question was prompted by mere curiosity, or when it was asked with the object of getting evidence from his own lips for the purpose of prosecuting him, it would have been unwise to satisfy the questioner. When, however, he was speaking to the woman of Samaria (John 4:26), there was no ambiguity: "I that speak unto thee am he." Under the adjuration of the High Priest, too, he answered plainly (Mark 14:62): "Art thou the Christ the Son of the Blessed? And Jesus said, I am."

315. What Were the "Greater Works" to Which Jesus Referred that His Disciples Would Do?

Christ always objected to being regarded as a mere wonder-worker. He wanted the people to look upon his miracles merely as his credentials, and to argue from them that he who could do such things was sent from God. The miracles were intended to lead them to trust in him for eternal life. Consequently when, as he said, he went to the Father and the Holy Spirit was given to his disciples, they were enabled to do those greater works, such as the conversions at Pentecost, which Christ held to be of a far higher order than miracles (John 14:12).

316. Do Public Prayers Violate Christ's Injunction to Enter into the Closet When We Pray?

No. Christ referred to the ostentatious devotion of the Pharisees who chose a public place for their devotions, with the motive that men might see them and honor them as pious people (John 16:23). There are many intimations in the New Testament that God approves of his people meeting together for prayer.

317. What Did Christ Refer to When He Asked Peter Whether He Loved Him More than These?

Peter had made himself conspicuous by his protestations of affection, as when he had said (Mark 14:29), "Although all should be offended, yet will not I." The form in which Christ put the question would appear to imply a delicate reminder of Peter's boast. Did he indeed love Christ more than did the other disciples? When Peter again avowed his love, Christ gave him a new commission to feed or shepherd the sheep and lambs (John 21:15). A commission not of authority, but of service.

318. What Did Jesus Mean by "If I Will that He Tarry till I Come"?

This passage in John 21:20, 22 is frequently misunderstood. John alone of all the disciples survived the destruction of Jerusalem and so witnessed the beginning of that series of events which belong to what are known as the "last days" of that particular age. He may thus be said to have witnessed the foundation of the kingdom in men's hearts, in a greater measure than any of his associates. The language of Jesus (in verse 22) was not a prediction, but a question in which there was, however, an assertion of his divine power to dispose of human life as he willed. It has been made the basis of a tradition which treats it mistakenly as a prophecy.

319. What Is the Lesson Conveyed in the Passage on Footwashing in John 13:10?

The saying like the act was symbolical. A different word is used in the original to express the washing, in the phrase "he that is washed," from that in the other phrase about the washing of the feet. The former refers to the bath, or the washing of the entire body, while the latter refers to the rinsing of the feet, as of one who had soiled them in walking from the bath. The body having been washed, he was clean every whit, when the dirt subsequently collected on the feet was removed. The teaching is obvious. The

Christian who falls into sin does not need another regeneration, but the cleansing of these later sins.

320. Are the Verses "For God So Loved the World," Etc., the Words of Christ or John?

Some scholars have thought that John wrote those verses as a commentary and that they were not spoken by Christ; but the number of such scholars was small and has become smaller as the discussion proceeded. Their theory was based on the fact that there is a change of tense in the verses in question; that the phrase "onlybegotten" was a favorite one with John; and that no further interruption from Nicodemus is reported. These reasons do not appear to us of serious weight. The change of tense occurs only when the topic requires it, and if the words are Christ's the change would occur as certainly as if they were John's. The phrase, "onlybegotten" was, it is true, a favorite one with John, but probably because he had heard it so frequently from his Master. And as to the third reason, it is not likely that Nicodemus broke in on that wonderful revelation, or that if he did, John would interrupt it to report his questions. We cannot believe that Christ ended his talk with the fifteenth verse, because if he had done so, Nicodemus would not have heard the essential facts. Neither would statements so authoritative have been made by John, unless he had distinctly indicated that it was he and not Christ who was speaking. The subject was fully discussed some years ago and scholars so eminent as Alford, Lange and Stier then expressed their conviction that the whole passage, from the beginning of the tenth to the end of the twenty-first verse, was spoken by Christ.

321. How Should We Interpret "Take No Thought for the Morrow"?

Jesus did not have a word to say against industry or prudence. His words in this instance were directed against the anxiety, worry, and foreboding which afflict so many people. Trust in God, he said in effect, do not spoil your lives by this distressing fear. At the worst, you will have clothing and food. Do not be grasping or selfish, but give to those in need. Solomon said a similar thing (Prov. 11:24). The one man whom Christ advised to sell all he had and give to the poor, was a boastful man who wanted to be perfect. Jesus saw the fault in his character and told him that his way to perfection was to eliminate that fault. To other men he probably gave no such advice. He laid his finger on the weak place. The apostles, it is true, were bidden leave all and follow him; but that was necessary to the work to which they were called; yet even with them Peter seems to have kept his house as did John.

322. Who Are the "False Prophets in Sheep's Clothing"?

The warning is against teachers who come, claiming to be authorized interpreters of the mind of God and expounders of his Word, yet who are false leaders, having no spiritual light in themselves and being unfitted to guide others into the light of truth. Coming in sheep's clothing implies that they present a plausible exterior, their lips filled with smooth, persuasive words; but they do not teach nor do they themselves know the Gospel of Jesus. They teach instead a man-made Gospel, and make a great show of liberal ideas.

The "old paths" they discard for new ways of reaching heaven. They cast doubt upon the essentials of the faith and teach the doctrines of error. Any teacher who does not hold fast to the cardinal points of the Gospel, or who does not emphasize the divine nature and the mediatorial office of Christ and his sacrifice and atonement; who would exalt works above faith; who belittles the importance of the revealed Word, and casts doubt upon its genuineness and authority; who compromises with sin and the weakness of our nature; who leads his flock to regard with doubt all that pertains to the invisible realm of faith and the supernatural; who attaches more importance to the operations of the human mind than to all else—such a person is not calculated to lead others in the way of life everlasting. It is therefore of the very first importance that the pastor who is chosen for a church should himself be a Christian, living the Christian life, else, however sincere he may be in his efforts, he will not be able to lead others aright.

323. What Is the Parable of the Ten Virgins Intended to Teach?

The duty of watchfulness and unworldliness. In the East, to this day, at a wedding ceremony, the approach of the bridegroom's procession is heralded by the cry, "The bridegroom cometh," and those who have been invited come out of their houses to join it, and go with him to attend the ceremony. In Christ's time, apparently, they were expected to carry lamps. All the virgins in the parable slept while the bridegroom tarried; but five of them were prepared with oil to trim their lamps, and the others were not. Thus, when the bridegroom came they were ready to meet him, while the others were not. Professing Christians would be similarly divided if Christ were to come to the world now. Some would rejoice and be ready to welcome him, while others, who are leading worldly lives and are not cultivating Christian character, would be unprepared and would be stricken with consternation.

324. What Is Meant to Be Taught by the Case of the Evil Spirit Which Brought into the Unguarded Heart "Seven Other Spirits More Wicked than Himself"?

The corresponding passage, Matt. 12:43-45, appears to indicate that primarily the meaning applied to the Jewish nation. It had repented or reformed under the preaching of the Baptist, "cleaned up," as the modern phrase has it, but had not gone on as it should, to acceptance of Christ and righteousness toward God. The negative goodness was to be followed by a worse national condition, in which the Lord would be crucified. It is as if a nation was led to forsake idols, but instead of becoming Christian became atheistic. In the individual the reference is to a man weaned from some besetting sin, but not taking the grace of God into his heart, and replacing the love of sin with love of God and holiness, leaves the heart unoccupied ready for a return of the sin he had quitted, or the fall into something still worse.

325. What Are We to Understand by "Many Are Called, but Few Are Chosen"?

This is one of Christ's terse and memorable sayings, several times uttered. It is interpreted to mean that many receive the invitation of the Gospel who never reach the stage of spiritual progress where they can be said to be "chosen" to salvation through sanctification of the Spirit and belief on the truth." (See II Thes. 2:13.) The "chosen" were those who were set apart for special duty to become living examples of devoted service. Paul was such an illustration of God's sovereignty in choosing his instrument. It should not be held to imply, however, that salvation is forfeited, except through the fault and wickedness of those who are rejected. Christ's death was all-sufficient, and it is not the divine will that any should perish. Many controversies have arisen over this passage, but we can safely rest upon the language of the Saviour himself, who said: "Whosoever will may come" . . . . and "Him that cometh I will in no wise cast out." This promise is absolute and assures us that saving grace is within the reach of all who will forsake sin and accept salvation through Christ. The broad interpretation of the passage would seem to be that while many are called, or set in the way of salvation, the invitation alone does not save them; they must themselves comply with all the conditions. Thus a means is provided for the salvation of all, except those who willfully reject it. This is the true grace of the Gospel and it is so clear and unmistakable that no human doctrine or interpretation can change it.

326. Why Did Jesus Tell His Disciples to Buy Swords?

He wished them to be forewarned of the world's hostility to the Gospel. He spoke in figurative language, as he frequently did, and they, misunderstanding him, interpreted his words literally, supposing he alluded to present defense. Seeing that they misinterpreted his language about the swords, he closed the conversation with the words: "It is enough." His healing of the high priest's servant's ear simply emphasized the fact that he had not intended to counsel physical violence.

327. Was There Heartlessness in Jesus' Words: "Let the Dead Bury Their Dead"?

No. He meant to convey that the proclaiming of the Kingdom of God was more important even than to bury the dead—an office which could be performed by those spiritually dead as well as by one who had been called to the Master's service. He did not belittle the office of burial, but simply put it in contrast with the more imperative duty of preaching the Gospel.

328. In What Sense Is "The Kingdom of God Is within You"?

The words "the kingdom of God is within you" are to be interpreted in the sense that those who follow Christ and believe in him as Saviour, and whose lives are guided by his example, have already in this life a part and share in his kingdom, which is eternal.

329. What Is the "Sin Unto Death"?

It is believed to be the sin against the Holy Spirit which tends toward or is destined to result in spiritual death. Several commentators make it quite distinct from what is known as the "unpardonable sin"—which is believed to have been attributing the Spirit's marvelous work to Satanic agencies. Alford makes it the act of "openly denying Jesus to be the Christ, the Son of God." Such willful deniers are not to be received into one's house (see II John verses 10 and 11). The apostle's meaning is evidently that this chief sin is one by which faith and love are destroyed and the new life killed by a palpable rejection of grace. When such a person knowingly thrusts spiritual life from him, no human intercession can avail. See James 5:14, 18; Matt. 12:31, 32, as to the obstinate rejection of the Holy Ghost's plain testimony to the Divine Messiah. Jesus on the cross pleaded for those who knew not what they did in crucifying him, not for those willfully resisting grace.

330. What Is to Be Understood by Putting "New Cloth on Old Garment"?

The new is really the unshrunken cloth which, when it became wet and dried, would draw and strain the old garment, making a greater rent. The meaning was that at that time the most intelligent Jews, such as Nicodemus, were hailing Christ as a reformer. They were mistaken. His religion was not a new patch on the old. The old could not be mended, but must give place to his new religion. A specimen of this futile attempt was seen in the struggle to force the old Jewish laws on the Gentiles, which was repudiated (see Acts 15:1-21).

331. Did an Angel Actually Come Down and Disturb the Pool at Bethesda?

It should be noted that the evangelist, in giving an account of the pool, does nothing more than to state the popular belief (probably a legend) as he found it, without vouching for it except so far as it explained the invalid's presence there. Jesus simply put aside as of no moment the alleged healing virtues of the pool, and aroused the man's faith in that power which alone could minister to his need.

A CHRISTIAN'S PROBLEMS

332. Is Being Killed in an Accident a Punishment?

No, it is not right even to think such a thing, and it is a gross slander on God to say it. Jesus was very explicit on that subject. (See Luke 13:1-5.) The tower of Siloam had fallen and had killed eighteen persons and Jesus was told of it. He took occasion to disabuse his hearers' minds of the idea that accidents were to be regarded as punishments. There was another case in which the question was put to him directly. He was asked who had sinned, a blind man or his parents, that he was born blind, and he answered, neither (John 9:2, 3). The whole book of Job is devoted to the subject. Job's friends thought that his affliction was punishment for hidden sin. God himself interferes to reprove them. It is a wicked and a cruel thing to add to the affliction of a bereaved family by suggesting that their loss is a punishment of the dead or the living.

333. Should We Endure Uncongenial Association?

In I Cor. 7:15 the bondage of uncongenial association is meant. In Corinth, unbelievers were of a particularly vicious type. The newly converted Christian would be pained day by day by the conduct of an unbelieving husband or wife. The members of the church inquired of Paul whether it was their duty to separate in such cases. He advised their remaining together, and for the believer to try to lead the unbeliever to Christ. But if the unbeliever went away, the believer was not bound to seek a renewal of relations. Let the unbeliever go. There was no compulsion in cases requiring the believer and the unbeliever to live together.

334. How Can One Have Absolute Assurance of Forgiveness of Sin?

The absolute inward assurance of forgiveness is to be obtained by a perfect surrender of our lives to God. If this is done in prayer, and without one reservation, the Holy Ghost performs its part as surely as God's promises stand. There is an expansion, an uplifting, an inward illumination that ever after establishes an assurance of forgiveness of sin to the individual soul. It is "the Spirit witnessing with our spirit that we are the sons of God." This is the new birth. This assurance of God's forgiveness of sins is given in answer to prayer through Jesus, and is communicated to our souls by the Holy Spirit. The degree or clearness of this assurance is according to our faith. Doubts cloud this consciousness of God's favor. The Holy Spirit imparts to the believer an assurance of pardon and adoption into God's family. "Ye have received the Spirit of adoption, whereby we cry, Abba, Father. The Spirit itself beareth witness with our spirit, that we are the children of God." "He that believeth on the Son of God hath the witness in himself." God "that cannot lie" says through the inspired apostle, "If we confess our sins, he is faithful and just to forgive us our sins and to cleanse us from all unrighteousness."

When the conditions are fully met, faith springs up in the human heart, and to believe "that my sins are forgiven" is without effort, the same as to breathe. Some obtain "absolute inward assurance" of sins forgiven more readily than others. Some souls are most trustful. The doubting and despondent may never in this life have assurance "absolute," yet even these may possess "assurance." The first step to "absolute assurance" is to believe that it is not assurance that saves, but faith. We may not see the bridge over which the train is safely carrying us. So faith saves, though we may not feel safe. The second step is to trust oneself to Christ, as a child lets his father take him in his arms. The third step is to willingly do and bear whatever Christ imposes. Absolute conviction will be found in your own heart after you have questioned it and can truthfully say these words: "I believe in and love the Lord Jesus Christ, enough to lay down my life, if need be, for his sake. I love him well enough, to live as long as he wants me to, a life of idleness or of labor, a life in prison or a life of freedom, a life of suffering or a life free from all care, a life wholly devoid of companionship, wealth, worldly pleasures and friends. I love him well enough to go down to my grave, if need be, branded by the world." When you can freely give such a pledge, then you will feel the blessed peace enter your heart, and God will come and talk with you.

335. Was the Atonement an Old Testament Belief?

The expectation of the coming Messiah, who should redeem his people and should suffer for their sakes, is as old as the beginnings of Hebrew nationality. See Isa. 53; Zech. 11:13. The idea of propitiation, reconciliation and expiation was associated with his coming, and although substitution is not mentioned it is implied. In connection with the sacrificial offerings similar terms are sometimes used, but the broader view of vicarious sacrifice, with special reference to the Messianic atonement, is most fully set forth in Isa. 53. The Messianic mission was the salvation of the race (Isa. 11). This expectation was not wholly confined to the Jewish people. The Samaritans held it; the Magi knew of it; even in the days of Melchizedek and Job it was understood by inquiring souls (Job 19:25). The very first recorded Scriptural allusion to it is in Gen. 49:10. See also Isa. 9:1-7; Isa. 40; Micah 5:2. There were periods in Jewish history during which the Messianic predictions and expectations temporarily ceased, but they were never wholly extinguished. It should be admitted, however, that while some of the Jewish Targumistic writings refer to a suffering Messiah, the greater number deal with a powerful and conquering Messiah. Faith in God, belief in his word and a willing obedience were accounted for righteousness in the old dispensation. See Gen. 15:8 and Rom. 4:3-6, 20, 25 and other passages. Incidentally it may be mentioned that Job is supposed to have lived about the time of Isaac, some 1800 B. C., Daniel 600 B. C., Micah 950 B. C., Isaiah 750 B. C., Zechariah, 520 B. C.

336. Is the Efficacy of the Atonement Limited to Those Who Accept It?

The subject has been discussed for generations, and with no practical benefit. It brings up the old and profitless question of foreordination, which is better left alone. It is sufficient for us to know that whosoever avails himself of the offer of salvation through Christ will be saved. If the ruler of a rebellious people proclaimed amnesty to all who laid down their arms, it would apply to all who complied with the conditions, but those who did not comply would have no part in the amnesty. The limit would not be in the offer but in the disposition of the people.

337. Is Celibacy Commanded in the Bible?

Certainly not, and no enforced celibacy was known in the Church until long after the apostolic age. Chrysostom opposed it, Polycarp, Eusebius, Cyprian, and other early writers mention priestly marriage as a common thing, and in fact, during the first three centuries there is no evidence of celibacy as a rule of clerical life. The Council of Trent (1545-1563) established the rule of celibacy. It originated officially with the edict of Siricius, bishop of Rome (A. D. 385), who argued that the reason why priests in Old Testament times were allowed to marry was that they might be taken exclusively from the tribe of Levi; but as no such exclusive limitation prevailed in the Roman Catholic priesthood, marriage was unnecessary and inconsistent with the priestly office. The Roman bishops who succeeded Siricius sustained this contention and a long line of Popes confirmed it in their decretals. For centuries, however, there was a continuous struggle over it among the Romanist clergy and many lived openly in wedlock in spite of the decrees. Finally, about the sixteenth century it became a fixed rule of the Roman Church. It is a system which ever since its introduction has given rise to many abuses.

338. How Far May People Be Compelled to Accept Christianity?

It is the mission of Christianity to preach the Gospel to all nations, but this does not imply the employment of force to compel a people to adopt the Christian religion against their will. In our own land, freedom of worship is guaranteed under the constitution. Any attempt to force the adoption of a religion would be a violation of the constitution. Lawful persuasion may be used, and there is, of course, no bar to discussion, but the individual and the community must be left wholly free. The attempt to force religion upon any people, and especially to force it upon any nation as such with the ultimate end in view of establishing a religious power in the State or nation, is in conflict with Christ's own declaration that his kingdom is "not of this world."

339. What Is a Spiritual Church?

In order to have a spiritual church, it is essential that there should be spiritually-minded leaders, men of ripe Christian experience and earnest faith, who can communicate their own enthusiasm for service and soul-winning to their fellow members. The true spiritual church is an active, working church, where the congregation vie with each other not merely in living up to their privileges in the matter of church attendance, but in active personal effort in their neighborhood, drawing others under the influence of the Gospel and organizing themselves for works of charity and kindness. An inactive church cannot have spiritual growth. The church should be directly connected with the work of home and foreign missions, hospital and sick visitation, shepherding of the children, keeping up the Sunday School, and doing good at every opportunity. Neglect of prayer meetings marks a decline of spirituality in a church which no amount of social attractions will repair. The ideal church is one in which every member has a share in the general activities of the organization. This means all, large and small, young and old, learned and ignorant for too often the educated try to obtain an ascendency. Intellectuality is not always an aid to spiritual life; on the contrary, there are very many cases in which it has proved a barrier. One does not perceive God through the intellect alone, and this is shown in the fact that many of the most spiritual natures have been found among the simple and unlearned. Intellectual vanity and self-sufficiency—an overweening confidence in the powers of the finite mind—are among the strongest impediments to faith. "Ye must become as a little child."

340. Will the Whole World Be Converted Before the Second Coming?

There is nothing in Scripture to make one believe that the whole world will be converted before the Second Coming. On the contrary, we are told that up to and immediately preceding that event, there will be widespread apostasy and spiritual decline, with false Christs and misleaders of men. We should not overlook the fact, however, that the duty is imposed on all Christians to spread the Gospel throughout the world, and to do everything that lies in our power for the conversion of the nations, but the complete harvest can come only in God's own time.

341. Does the Rule Laid Down by James 2:10 Imply that All Crimes Are Equal in Guilt?

No; it means that the violation of any of God's laws places the offender in the category of sinners. The writer is arguing with proud, self-righteous people who take credit to themselves for not committing certain sins. He shows them that in committing other sins that are not accounted by men so disgraceful, they are nevertheless sinners against God as surely as if they had committed the sins they condemn. A man who tells a lie has broken God's law and in that respect is under condemnation as the man is who commits a murder. Not that both are equally heinous, but that both stand on an equality in not being able to plead innocence before God. Both are sinners in need of mercy.

342. Why Did Paul Advise Timothy to Drink Wine?

We suppose he thought it would do him good. He evidently believed that Timothy's ailment, whatever it was, would be relieved by a stimulant. Perhaps if Paul had known as much as modern physicians do of the human constitution, he would not have given the advice. Drinking habits, in our day, do so much harm, that if he were alive now, we do not think he would counsel a young minister to drink wine. He was too much concerned about the general good to suggest an example which would be mischievous.

343. Can Evil Emanate from God?

This is a topic that has caused much controversy. Evil is the negation of good. God is the source of all goodness, and no evil dwells in him; but with the withdrawal of his guiding and protecting spirit from man, evil comes. In I Sam. 16:14, we are distinctly told that this was the case with Saul. The Spirit of God had forsaken him, and then his soul was an easy prey to the Spirit of Evil. He was hypochondriac and his distemper was aggravated by his wicked temper and his consciousness that as the result of his own sin and folly he was in danger of losing his throne. The passage in Is. 45:7 "I form the light and create darkness; I make peace and create evil" does not refer to moral evil, but to discord or disturbance in the order of the universe as a whole. Thus, as light and darkness are opposites, so in the next clause of the verse, peace and disorder are opposites. Evil is the negation of good and distinction must be made between natural and moral evil. Among natural evils are wars, earthquakes, storms, plagues or whatever disturbs or disarranges the perfection of natural things; whereas moral evil is thought, word or act that is contrary to the revealed law of God and is therefore sin. It is the peculiarity of Hebrew writing to delight in contrasts. You find a long series of them in Proverbs. They are always of the same nature of parallelisms. Thus, in the passage in Isaiah 45, the prophet used the converse of the peace he has been talking of. We should say war or physical disturbance.

He uses the word evil in the sense of punishment or misery. It is the state of the nation that he is considering. It serves God and is faithful to him and is prosperous. The prosperity comes from God. It deserts him and disobeys him and is punished by captivity and oppression. They also come from God. In that sense he creates the condition which they regard as an evil. There is a similar argument in Romans 11:22. Moral evil he never creates.

344. Does God Choose People for Destruction?

Peter was right in saying (II Peter 3:16) that in Paul's epistles there were some things hard to be understood. The verses in Rom. 9:15-20 are confessedly difficult. They appear to be contradictory to the conclusion which Paul reaches at the close of his argument (Romans 11:32) "God hath concluded them all in unbelief, that he might have mercy upon all." Perhaps we would understand his argument better if we knew more of the people to whom he was writing. It may have been, that among them were some who had the audacity to criticize God's method of government, and Paul wanted them to realize that God was not under obligation to save any who rebelled against him. That fact we must admit. No man can claim as a right that God shall forgive him. We know, from Christ's own words and from Paul's own letters, that God does forgive all who come to him in penitence. But when a man defies him, as Pharaoh did, Paul contends that God makes an example of him, that men of all times may see what is the end of defiance of his rule. We do not imagine that Paul meant that God directly hardened Pharaoh, but that the hardening was the effect of the removal of the plagues and was "permitted." The very mercy had the opposite effect on the man that it should have had. Pharaoh misunderstood it, as men now misunderstand God's long-suffering, and think they will escape altogether. Our side of the question is not God's sovereignty, which we can never understand, but the sublime fact that "whosoever will" may come to Christ and be saved.

345. Does Satan Interfere with God's Children?

Paul, in common with the people of his time, had a firm belief in the interference of Satanic influence in human life. Not only in I Thess. 2:18, but in II Cor. 12:7, he refers to it. The "thorn in the flesh," whatever that affliction was, he regarded as a messenger from Satan. The writer of Samuel took another view. He said the evil spirit that troubled Saul was from the Lord. (See I Sam. 16:14, 18:10 and other passages.) The writer of the book of Job thought that the evil fortune might be the work of Satan under express permission of God. The origin of evil has always been a mystery and it is not solved yet. Though we cannot understand it, we may be sure that vexations and hindrances and temptations do not come to us without the divine permission, and they are intended to strengthen the character. Paul himself said that all things work together for good to them that love God. (Rom. 8:28.)

346. What Was the "Sentence of the Serpent"?

The "sentence of the serpent" as the passage in Gen. 3:15 is called, was a far-reaching one. The prophecy concerning the posterity of the woman, who were to be at enmity with the seed of the serpent, "points to the continual struggle between the woman's offspring and the grand enemy of God and man—the mighty conflict, of which this world has ever since been the theater," between sin and righteousness. In the clause in question perhaps the more accurate reading would be: "I will *permit* enmity between thee and the woman," etc. God is not the author of evil; but when his holy Spirit is withdrawn from a man or a community or a nation, evil comes and takes the place of good.

347. Who Created the Devil?

This question has puzzled theologians for ages, and has occasioned discussions which have had no profitable issue. There is no source of reliable information but that contained in Scripture and that is of a very meagre character. See Rev. 12:7, 9, and II Peter 2:4. The inference from those and other passages is that Satan was created by God as man was, that he was pure and innocent, but, like man, liable to fall. That he did fall and was cast out of heaven. It cannot be conceived that God created an evil being, though, as we know to our sorrow, he did create a being who became evil. The whole subject is wrapped in mystery and the Bible writers are more intent on the practical question of teaching us how to be delivered from the power of Satan than in giving us his biography. The less we know of him and have to do with him the better for us. That Satan was an angel of high estate, who fell through ambition, leading to rebellion, is the concrete form of a history which is a combination of Scripture and tradition. See John 8:44; Matt. 4:1-11; Matt. 25:41; Luke 8:12; Luke

10:18; Acts 13:10; Eph. 6:11; I Pet. 5:8; I John 3:8 and other passages. In Job he is the adversary and the tempter. See also I Chron. 21:1. Milton the poet described him as "the prince or ruler of the demons." See Dan. 7:10 and Jude 6. These passages leave much unexplained and conjecture here is useless. His final overthrow and punishment are predicted in Rev. 20.

348. Are We As Christians Bound to Keep the Ten Commandments?

The Christian is not under the law but under grace. That however does not free him from obligation. More is expected of him in the way of righteousness than if he were under the law. You lay down rules for your child and make him obey, but when he grows to manhood he is free from your rules. Do you not expect that he will behave without rules? That was your object in training him, to produce in him a disposition which would keep him right when he became his own master. Now, which of the Commandments do you as a Christian, free from law, feel that you are at liberty to break? You would keep them out of love for God, whether you were bound or not. As to commands and injunctions of the Old Testament, when the question was considered in the first apostolic council (Acts 15:5-29) it was decided that Gentile converts were not to be bound by the Levitical law. Christ, also, in his sermon on the mount, said: "It hath been said by them of old time," and went on to say, "but I say unto you," etc., clearly regarding the law as it stood to be subject to his abrogation. It must not, however, be supposed that the Christian dispensation is less stringent. The man who obeys Christ is under obligations higher than those of the law. As an example, the law forbade murder and Christ forbade the anger that leads to murder. As love is higher than law, so Christ, by setting his people free of law and placing them under the obligation of love, inculcated a higher morality.

349. Is the Backslider's Case Hopeless?

The passage in Heb. 6:6, like that about the unpardonable sin, has caused much discussion and apprehension. The description in the previous verses of the persons to whom it refers, appears to indicate a condition of enlightenment and of personal experience such as some attain who do not become true Christians, but return to the world. The writer appears to be speaking of a fact rather than enunciating a doctrine. Every Christian minister and worker knows how difficult it is to win a backslider, especially one who has become a scoffer. The truth seems to have no effect upon them. Any person who fears having fallen into that condition can disprove the theory by going to Christ and asking forgiveness. Christ will receive him. The very fact of his being distressed about it indicates that he has not fallen beyond hope. The man who has need to fear, is he who does not trouble about his state.

350. Is There Any Hope for the Backslider?

See Heb. 10:26-29; John 6:37; Heb. 6:4-6, and I John 1:9. The passage in Heb. 10 refers to those who sin after receiving "full knowledge" of the truth (see I Tim. 2:4), and who after having been "enlightened" and tasting a certain measure of grace and the spirit of truth (see John 14:17-29), apostatize to

Judaism or infidelity. Such is not a sin of ignorance or error, but the result of moral wickedness or a deliberate sin against the Spirit—a presumptuous sin against Christ's redemption for us and the spirit of grace in us. Having fully known the one sacrifice for sin, and having a certain experience of the efficacy of that sacrifice, they have now rejected it. In Heb. 6:4, 6, the same idea is emphasized. Such sinners crucify Christ anew, instead of crucifying the world (see Gal. 6:14). The passage in John 6:37 expresses the glorious certainty of eternal life to those who believe and stand firm—those who are given him of the Father and come to him with full surrender. Not the simply willing, but the actually faithful; not the waverers, but the true and abiding, are to realize the promise. In the backslider there has been no complete dedication, otherwise there would be no apostasy. I John 1:9 emphasizes the assurance of forgiveness and acceptance of the faithful ones. Concerning the possibilities of a return to Christ on the part of a backslider, we can only assert that what to man may and often does seem impossible, is possible with God, and that his grace is boundless. Peter backslid in a most grievous way, and yet was forgiven. By a miracle of divine grace, the backslider, although beyond human hope of recall, may in God's abundant mercy find refuge and forgiveness.

351. Does Every Good Thing Come from God?

It is impossible to say just what impulses proceed from self and what are the direct influence of God in the unconverted soul. Some impulses to kindness seem purely natural, such as the instinctive care of a mother for her child, which is found in beasts as well as in human kind. The affection of animals for people, like the affection of a dog for his master, is sometimes tremendously strong. While all these noble and beautiful things come from God, they do not necessarily indicate the presence of God in the soul. He has planted certain admirable traits both in the instincts of animals and the minds of men; he also has, of course, the power of communicating with men, speaking to their minds and consciences by his Spirit and by his Word. Reason is higher than instinct and conscience is higher than both, but even conscience may not mean that God is dwelling in the soul. Only when it is enlightened or quickened by the divine power does it become a safe guide. Conscience, therefore, is not so much the voice of God as the human faculty of hearing that voice. But at conversion God's Spirit comes into a man's soul. He is no longer outside, but within; mystically though actually linked to the man himself. The great change then is that a man finds himself loving God, eager to get his messages, anxious to please him. The impulses to do good, instead of being vague and weak, become definite and intense. The converted man feels that God is within him, making suggestions, awakening holy, unselfish, beautiful desires, and giving him power to carry out these good desires in vigorous and successful action.

352. Why Do Some Passages of the New Testament Use the Neuter Pronoun in Referring to the Holy Spirit?

In the New Testament references to the Holy Spirit the masculine form is used almost without exception.

In John 14:26 and 15:26 the relative pronoun "which" is employed, a word that in present-day English is always neuter. At the time the Bible was translated, however, the form "which" was used of persons as well as things, for example: "Our Father which art in heaven" (Matt. 6:9) and "these . . . which have received the Holy Ghost." (Acts 10:47.) As a matter of fact it would not have been surprising if the neuter form had crept into the translation of some other passages, as the Greek word for spirit (pneuma) is neuter. This makes it all the more remarkable that throughout the Greek New Testament the pronouns referring to this neuter word are masculine. The fact of the Greek noun itself being neuter has no bearing whatever on the question of personality or sex, as is well understood by any one familiar, for instance, with German, in which the same thing is often true.

353. Will the Jews Ever Return to Palestine?

Will the Jews return to the Holy Land, and will they ever, as a nation, acknowledge Christ as the Messiah? is often asked, and again it is sought to be known how they can be God's chosen people when they reject Christ. There is no doubt that the Jews were God's chosen people and Paul says (Romans 11:1) that He has not cast them off. In that and the two preceding chapters the apostle fully discusses the question. The prophets assure us that they will return to the Holy Land. There are predictions, dating before and during the captivity in Babylon, which were fulfilled when they returned under the edict of Cyrus, but there are others indicating a later and permanent restoration. The passages in Isaiah 2:2-4,

Jeremiah 3:18, 16:14, 15; Ezekiel 36:24, 37:21, 25, 39:28, and many others have not yet been fulfilled. They will probably return in unbelief but will be converted later (see Rom. 11:26).

354. Is Justification the Same Under the Old and New Dispensations?

Justification is the act of God and has ever been so, under both the Old and New Dispensations. Under the Old, those were accepted who rendered a faithful and willing obedience; thus we read, in Gal. 3:6, that Abraham believed God, and this belief (*i e.,* faith) was accounted to him for righteousness. Under the New Dispensation, Jesus "came to bring life and immortality to light," that is, to give us a spiritual illumination which would disclose to man the great scheme of redemption ordained from the beginning. The contention, therefore, that none save those who are in the New Dispensation can attain immortality is untenable. Besides, the evidence of Scripture itself is against such a conclusion. Moses and Elijah were seen at the transfiguration. Paul held that while the race, as a whole, died in Adam's sin, as a whole it received life through Christ's redemptive work.

355. How Can the Kingdom of God Be Established before the Judgment Day?

The Kingdom of the Messiah, which was foretold by many of the prophets and is further explained in the New Testament, is a divine, spiritual kingdom, to be built up in the hearts of men and ultimately to become universal. It is described in the early prophecies as a coming golden age, when the true religion should be re-established and universal peace and happiness should prevail. Unquestionably, it was regarded by the Jews in a temporal sense only, but the Saviour himself declared it to be a spiritual kingdom, and his followers look forward to its highest realization only after his return. Meanwhile, it is being established now; from the beginning of the Christian dispensation, it has progressed in the hearts of men. That Jesus himself intended to convey this is made clear in Matt. 8:12, 11:12, 11:28; Mark 12:34; Luke 11:9, 11, and many other passages which deal with the various phases of the same subject. Matt. 24 describes the condition of the believers at the judgment and their welcome to the *fulness* of the completely established kingdom, with all its blessings and rewards.

356. Can a Christian Keep the Moral Law?

To unfallen man, obedience to the moral law would undoubtedly have been within human reach, but to fallen man it stands as an unattainable ideal, to which he may strive, but in vain. There is none without sin (I John 1:8), and as a perfect obedience to God's law implies entire sinlessness, it is obviously impossible that such obedience can be rendered by mortal man. But to those who are in Christ this difficulty is overcome. (Rom. 4:7.) They are not under the law and consequently are not to be judged by the law. (Rom. 6:15; I John 3:9.) Christ, by his perfect obedience, and his sufferings for their sins, has satisfied the law in their behalf. (II Cor. 5:21.) Thus, when grace enters the heart, its sinfulness is removed. The righteousness and perfect obedience of Christ being imputed to his people, they are accepted of God. (Rom.

3:24; II Cor. 12:9.) Christians, therefore, should not serve in the bondage of fear, as under the law (I Tim. 1:9), but in love, as under grace in Christ Jesus. (Rom. 8:1-15.)

357. Does the Bible Say Anything About Life Insurance?

There is nothing in Scripture bearing on the subject of life insurance, but there are various passages on thrift and on making provision for old age. If you turn to I Tim. 5:8 you will find a very definite statement on the subject. Evidently Paul did not believe that any man claiming to be a Christian was justified in leaving his dependent ones to be a burden on the community, either during his life or afterward. There are birds and other animals that give improvident man a lesson by the way they lay up a store of food against the winter season. Jesus in Matt. 6:31-34 was not rebuking thrift, but worldly-mindedness and vanity. He was referring to those who pursued the things of this life as the supreme object. He wanted his followers to "take no thought (anxious care or worry) for the morrow." He had no word of condemnation for attention to business, but business gains, wealth, possessions, etc., are all of secondary importance, and worry about them springs from the heart's distrust of God, and does no good, but rather evil.

358. Is the Love of God towards Man to Be Interpreted Individually?

This question has often disquieted Christians under affliction. It has often appeared to the godly man, as it did to Job, that the children of God fare no better in the world than the wicked. But we are taught in a multitude of passages in the Bible, that God does know and care for the individual. Christ was very explicit on the subject. (See Matt. 10:29-31.) The promise in the New Testament to Christ's followers is not of prosperity, but that they shall receive strength to bear their afflictions and that those afflictions shall work for good to them. Our prayers would be simple mockeries if we did not believe in God's care for the individual. The Christian, like the worldling, is subject to natural law and other things being equal, a blow that would kill a worldling would kill him. It is often difficult to understand why so many afflictions fall to the righteous which the wicked escape, but God does not explain these particular trials. He expects us to trust him and to be assured that "he does not willingly afflict nor grieve" us, and to patiently wait the revelation which will make all things clear.

359. Does God Work Miracles at the Present Time?

This is a question often asked. The arm of Omnipotence is not shortened that it cannot save. Thousands have been restored in mind and body in answer to the prayer of faith. Yet he never works *unnecessary* miracles. God has given us means and endowed us with intelligence to use these means, and he will not withhold his blessing upon their use when we ask it in faith. We ask him to feed us, but we must labor with our hands and not expect him to bless our idleness nor our lack of effort. So, if we ask him to heal us, we must use in faith the means he has supplied, with all the intelligence he has given us. It is simply "tempting God" to neglect his means. Jesus himself applied the clay and the spittle to the eyes of the blind. Naaman had to bathe in the Jordan. Even in the healing of the soul, which is an operation of the Holy Spirit, we must co-operate, and while he works in us, we ourselves must work with "fear and trembling." And if Divine wisdom should see fit to withhold the boon we crave in the form we ask, we must submit in faith to his will, as he knows what is best for us. Strength is often made perfect in weakness and many things we mistakenly call evils are blessings in disguise.

360. Did Paul Discourage Marriage?

In the 7th chapter of I Cor., Paul had apparently been asked questions by the Church in Corinth which tended to disparage marriage and to regard it as an undesirable state when one of the parties is an unbeliever. His long reply may be summed up in a few words: "Abide in your present station, for the time is short." He believed that, by remaining single, he could devote himself more acceptably to his Gospel work. The passage in I Tim. 5:14 is not inconsistent with the other, for the circumstances of the two cases were different, and in the latter he commends marriage under certain conditions, as an antidote to certain temptations.

361. What Has the Bible to Say About Marriage and Divorce?

The Bible law on marriage and divorce may be learned from the following passages: Gen. 3:24; Matt. 19:5; by Peter in Mark 10:7, 8; Eph. 5:31; Matt.

19:6; Mark 10:8; Mark 10:9; Mal. 2:16; Matt. 5:32, 19:9; I Cor. 7:11; Matt. 19:9; Luke 16:18; Mark 10:11; Luke 16:18; Matt. 5:32; I Cor. 7:11; Rom. 7:2; I Cor. 7:39; Rom. 7:3; I Cor. 7:39.

362. Does God Approve of the Marriage of an Unbeliever to a Believer?

The whole question at issue is fully and fearlessly discussed in II Cor. 6:14-18. This is Paul's interpretation and it stands good today as a general rule of Christian conduct. Nevertheless, we are not to judge those who may ignore the injunction, for in I Cor. 7:14, the apostle shows how such a union may after all accomplish beneficent results. From this verse to chapter 7:1, inclusive, the apostle seems to forbid too much social intercourse generally with idolatrous and heathenish people, rather than to have in view the marriage relation especially. In I Cor. 7:12-16, separation from the unbelieving husband or wife is discountenanced, because the believing spouse may be able to sanctify—that is, make holy—the unregenerate mate, and may effect conversion to salvation. In the same chapter and other passages of the apostolic writings marriage is encouraged without any restrictions. In Gal. 5:1, and Acts 15:10, the word "yoke" is used in a somewhat similar connection to that supposed to contain the implied prohibition. In Phil. 4:3, Paul addresses some unknown individual as "yoke-fellow," and it is quite certain he does not mean his wife. But if it is admitted that the text cited prohibits intermarriage between Christians and unbelievers, it must be construed with reference to the conditions of sensual idolatry universally prevailing at that period in the city of Corinth. Paul was addressing a small community of Christians in a very large heathen city, and it is as if we should advise Christians in China and India not to intermarry with Buddhists and Mohammedans, only more aggravated.

363. Is It Possible that the Miracle of the Incarnation May Be Repeated?

The word "possible" is inappropriate in such connection, because nothing is impossible with God; but when we hear of his doing something utterly inconsistent with his ways, we know that it cannot be true, because he would never contradict himself. All the teaching of the Bible, the Epistle to the Hebrews especially, leads to the conclusion that Christ is the one and final incarnation of God. There is no need of another, because he fully satisfied the Divine purpose and has been found to fully satisfy the need of man. Many have arisen since his time, as he warned us there would, who have claimed to be God in human form, like some who even in recent years have made such a claim; but they were and are impostors. They are deceiving many, as Christ said impostors would (see Matt. 24:24), but not those who look to Christ for light and guidance.

364. What Is the "Call" to the Ministry?

One of the best evidences of a genuine call is the possession of those special qualifications which add in marked degree to the usefulness of the Christian. If, under his addresses in Sunday School, or at prayer-meetings, or at mission churches God has acknowledged his work and souls are led to Christ, there is strong reason to believe that it may be his duty to devote all his time to preaching and pastoral work. A man's own intense desire to preach and the concurrent opinion of experienced Christians that his work would be useful in the pulpit, are also indications. The basis of all qualifications for the ministry, however, is that there must be in the heart an intense love of souls, consecration to Gospel service, and a sense of personal acceptance, pardon and regeneration through Christ. None but one who has himself traveled the road that leads to the Cross can guide others along the same path. See Col. 1:28; Matt. 15:14; Luke 6:39.

365. What Are the Qualifications of a Minister?

A true minister of the Gospel must possess, above everything else, an intense love for Christ and a great love for his fellowmen. These two qualifications will necessarily give him an intense passion to save souls, and this is the true secret of success. He must love Christ so much and love people so much that he will long to proclaim Christ's message to men and win them to him. He must understand the Gospel—must feel its operation in his own heart and must know that "it is the power of God unto salvation, to every one that believeth." He must understand that the Gospel is the message of God's free grace to men by which he forgives and sanctifies them, and he must know how to lead men, not to try to save themselves by efforts and vows, but to accept humbly God's infinite gift of a present salvation. A minister should have common sense and a well-balanced mind. He should have a clear voice and the ability to express himself clearly and forcibly in speech; if eloquently, so much the better. He should have modesty and tact, and these even without much social experience, will lead him to conduct himself correctly and winsomely. His studies should lead him to know more of Christ, to know more of the Gospel, to know more of men, and to acquire more skill in delivering the message. He must study voice culture, rhetoric and some elocution—though this last is dangerous, as it is apt to make a speaker affected, which is fatal to real success. He must study the Bible and should study theology, and psychology. Special emphasis must be laid upon understanding people. A technical theological education sometimes lifts a man away from the people he must help instead of putting him into closer touch with them. He must understand how people live and work and suffer and think and must be sympathetic with and well informed about the movements they are making toward greater liberties and better social conditions. This understanding of people, individually and in groups, will help him to convince them of their need of Christ for their souls and for society. He should, if possible, also have some knowledge of business affairs so that in the conduct of his church he will not fall into financial and legal snares.

366. How Long Have We Had a Trained Ministry?

The Bible informs us that even in the days of Samuel there were "schools of the prophets," in which men were trained for the high function of moral and spiritual teaching. The priests and Levites were trained in the knowledge of the ecclesiastical law and the ceremonies. In later Jewish history, twelve great institutions for educating priests, teachers and elders existed

Jesus himself passed a considerable portion of his ministry in instructing and training his disciples. We read in Acts that the apostles imitated his example in personally instructing the younger disciples. John spent his later years teaching at Ephesus, qualifying youths for the ministry, and Mark did likewise at Alexandria. Early Christian training schools were established in Cesarea, Antioch, Laodicea, Nicomedia, Athens, Edessa, Seleucia, Carthage and in Mesopotamia and there were many minor institutions of the same class. Thus all the evidence goes to show that even from the earliest days, those who were designed to convey God's message to the hearts of men were set apart, consecrated, and fitly prepared. It is so today. A trained and educated ministry is essential to the advancement of religion just as training and preparation are needed in other vocations. The apostles, even if they had nothing more, had a course of several years' personal training with the great Master as their teacher before they were sent out on their full mission. It is true that many converted laymen, and women, too, have done and are doing noble work in soul saving, but they are exceptional and the fact that their labors are owned and blessed of God is not a valid argument against a trained ministry, but rather the reverse. With due training they might have accomplished even more.

367. Is Misfortune a "Judgment of God"?

We have no right to sit in judgment on others, and when some people censoriously announce that a misfortune which befalls a person or a community is "a judgment" of God, they assume undue authority.

We are distinctly warned against judging others. See Christ's teaching on this subject. Luke 13:4.

368. Has a Man Two Natures?

In Rom. 7:25 Paul says: "So then with the mind I myself serve the law of God, but with the flesh the law of sin." The argument of the preceding verses has been the hopelessness of the struggle which that man must fight who strives to obtain salvation through the law. He is defeated by his own body, or the flesh, as Paul calls it. It drags him down and forces him to obey and to yield to its cravings; so that in his despair he cries, "What I would I do not; but what I hate that do I." The picture is one that appeals to every unconverted man's experience. His reason, his pride, his manliness direct him to renounce some sin, such as drunkenness or lust. He resolves, but suddenly the craving arises, and in spite of the resolves of his mind—his real ego—he is swept off his feet, and yields to his passion. The revelation of Christ as a helper crosses Paul's mind, and he thanks God. In the eighth chapter he is going to explain this at length, but he halts here at verse 25, to mark the stage reached by the man he is describing. "With the mind, I myself," the real ego am serving God; while with the flesh, the animal nature, I am serving sin. In Romans 8:10 this problem is solved. Through Christ the spirit is strengthened, and the flesh is controlled and subdued. He is freed by the spirit of life (Romans 8:3).

369. Will the Negroes Be Saved?

The ablest scientists hold to the unity of the race, and in this they are in accord with Scripture, which declares that the Creator "hath made of one blood all nations of men, for to dwell on all the face of the earth" (Acts 17:26), and that the "free gift comes upon all men to justification to life." Climatic variations extending over long periods account for physical differences. The negro is the descendant of Ham, the head of one of the three great divisions of the human race. He was the progenitor of the Egyptians, the Cushites and the African nations, and his descendants were the founders of great empires in Ethiopia, Babylonia, Arabia, Abyssinia and, according to some authorities, in a considerable part of Asia, as far as the Euphrates and the Persian Gulf. No one has the slightest warrant for asserting that the negro has not a soul. Christian converts from Cyrene in Upper Libya were among those who were identified with the formation of the first Gentile church in Antioch. Mark the evangelist labored during a large part of his missionary career in Africa. Simon, who bore our Saviour's cross (Matt. 27:32), was a Cyrenian and a native of Libya. The Copts, who were active in the early days of Christianity, were a mixed race, chiefly negro. The Coptic Christian Church is one of the oldest in existence and possesses some of the most valuable early Christian manuscripts.

370. Do the Pauline Epistles Contain All that Is Essential to Salvation?

It is quite proper to lay special emphasis upon the writings of Paul, because he was especially chosen of God to interpret the life and death of the Saviour to the hearts and minds of men, particularly of those who were not Jews. Furthermore, Paul was authorized to show that the requirements of the ceremonial law, as recorded by Moses, were done away with by the sacrifice of Christ. In this way it is easy to see that the explanation of the salvation wrought by the atonement is of more spiritual value than the precepts of the old law of sacrifices and ceremonies, which are no longer in force. The tremendous value of Paul's writings lies in the fact that he shows men the practical, immediate way of receiving salvation, not by the keeping of commandments, but by faith in the crucified Saviour. Granting all this, however, it is great folly to say that the other parts of the Bible are unimportant. The Pentateuch is full of flashes of God's presence and God's will, containing holy principles which are eternal, and recording the experiences of men who knew God; the historical books show God working in the life of a nation; the poetical and wisdom books give us inspiration and instruction for daily living; the prophetic books give us glimpses of the coming Saviour and are pulsating with direct, personal messages from God to the human soul; the Gospels help us to get acquainted with the Redeemer and to understand the kind of life he wants us to live and his hope for the world; the Acts give us clear pictures of men who were impelled by the power of the Holy Ghost and challenge us to let the risen Christ work through us as he worked through them; the other epistles are full of spiritual help, and the book of Revelation gives us visions of the life to come. All are important; all help us to know Christ better; all lead us to God. We must not slight these other books, even while agreeing that Paul is the direct messenger to us Gentiles to show us the way of salvation by faith.

371. Why Was Polygamy Allowed to the Patriarchs and Why Is It Wrong Now?

Jesus, in speaking of certain provisions of the Mosaic law on the marriage question, said: "From the beginning it was not so." Matt. 19:8. He referred to the original creation of one man and one woman as fixing the moral law that a man should have but one wife. The fact that Abraham and the other patriarchs had more than one wife does not make polygamy right any more than the fact that they owned slaves makes slavery right. The Bible is a truthful record of the lives of the people of whom it tells. They did many things that were wrong; God dealt gently and patiently with his people, leading them by a long process of teaching and development toward the full understanding of his perfect will. There was no particular time at which polygamy became wrong, but it was the teaching of Jesus, more than any other influence, that showed mankind that it is wrong. In the New Testament the love of husband and wife is presented as the highest form of love; it is inconceivable that any outsider, or third person, can enter into this sacred fellowship. Polygamy means injustice to women; the plural wives are outsiders, deprived, from the Christian point of view, of real wifehood

372. Does God Answer Prayers?

Most assuredly he does, but his ways are not as our ways. We are at best but children in spiritual things. Yet there is nothing in this world so clear and so well attested by Christian evidence, as that if we pray with believing hearts and in the right spirit, he will hear us and do what is best for us. No such prayer goes unanswered. The answer may not be as we expected, nevertheless it will be for the best and to the purpose. Says Professor Denney: "When we pray in Jesus' name there is nothing which we may not ask. Whatever limitations there may be, they are covered by the name of Jesus itself. We must not ask what is outside of that name, not included in its promise. We must not ask a life exempt from labor, from self-denial, from misunderstanding, from the Cross; how could we ask such things in His Name? But ignoring this self-evident restriction, Jesus expressly, emphatically and repeatedly removes every other limit. There is nothing which the name of Jesus puts into our hearts which we may not, with all assurance, put into our prayers." In his name, we can ask with assurance for pardon from God; we can ask to be strengthened in temptation and to be kept from falling, and restored when through human weakness we do fall, for we have the assurance that he will not let us be utterly cast down; we can ask for the sanctifying work of the Holy Spirit in our lives. We can ask that our material wants as well as our spiritual needs may be fully supplied. But, in asking, we must have the faith to lay hold, and when we pray with this faith, we shall never pray amiss.

373. Do Prayers for the Unconverted Help?

The most definite Bible passage on this subject is I John 5:16: "If any man see his brother sin a sin which is not unto death, he shall ask, and he shall give him life." The words of Paul in Acts 16:31, "Thou shalt be saved, and thy house," probably mean simply that if all the members of the household believed they would be saved. But we have positive Scripture warrant for praying for our unconverted friends, and countless incidents from present day life and earlier times prove that many hearts have been won to Christ through prayer. The assurance may not always come that those for whom we pray will yield to God, but sometimes the assurance does come very definitely. Prayer for others should be personal, definite, earnest. S. D. Gordon in his *Quiet Talks on Prayer* takes the position that prayer for others, offered in the name of Jesus, has the effect of driving off evil influences from the persons for whom the prayer is being made. It projects the personal influence of the one who is praying to the one prayed for, and clears the spiritual atmosphere so that the voice of God can be heard and the power of God felt. Just as by talking to a person one may be able to persuade him to listen and yield to God, so by prayer one may influence another to submit himself to God. Most important of all is love. We must love ardently, steadily, those for whom we pray. Love will prevent us from doing things that would mar our influence over them or spoil their conception of the religious life. If our friends know that we love them deeply and constantly our words and prayers will have an almost irresistible power.

374. Should We Pray for One from Whom the Holy Ghost Has Departed?

Who are you, to assume to judge that such a one has been forsaken by the Holy Spirit? It would be a fearful responsibility to act on such a conclusion. Of one thing you may rest assured: if the person is at all concerned about his spiritual condition, no matter how deeply he has offended, that very fact is conclusive evidence that the Holy Spirit has not abandoned him, but is still striving with him. When the Holy Spirit leaves a man, that man becomes careless and indifferent and has no desire to pray. It is difficult—almost impossible—for us to understand the operations of the Spirit, but you may be assured that the love and compassion and long-suffering of God are infinite. Christ said that he would cast out none who came to him. With such an assurance, no man need wait to try to solve the mysteries of the Holy Spirit's work. The practical duty of closing with Christ's offer of salvation is the first thing for him to do.

375. Should We Persistently Ask for Blessings?

By all means. The three passages, Matt. 11:12; Luke 11:5-10 (the parable of the friend at night seeking loaves from his neighbor), and Luke 18:1-8 (the parable of the unjust judge), all relate to the subject of earnestness and perseverance in prayer. The argument is that if the unfriendly neighbor and the unjust judge will grant the requests made to them because of the petitioner's insistance, God will surely grant our requests when he sees that we are in desperate earnestness. Matt. 11:12, "the kingdom of heaven suffereth violence, and the violent take it by force," agrees with these two parables in teaching that intensity, of desire and faith and effort, is required for spiritual victory. Faith seems to have two phases: the quiet, restful trust in God; and the aggressive, enthusiastic, energetic, insistent belief that pushes forward through all sorts of obstacles and delays to the victory desired. It is not because God is unjust or unfriendly that he does not answer at once. But our souls are strengthened by the test of waiting, and often human relationships and circumstances are changed as time passes so that the answer is better for the delay than if granted at the first request. God wants to train giants to help him in his work, giants who will believe in him and fight for the right, no matter what obstacles are in the way. And the saints who are strong and rich in faith accomplish most for his kingdom.

376. Is It Right to Ask for Definite Blessings?

There are many passages, such as John 16:23, which warrant definiteness in prayer. Indeed, if a man needs something very badly, and is sure that it would be a blessing to him, he would show a lack of faith if he did not pray for it. There are many, however, who shrink from praying for definite blessings, after a painful experience. They have prayed for some blessing, and God has heard them, and granted their request, and it has proved to be a curse. Emerson said, in a passage which we cannot find, but the gist of which we quote from memory, that all prayers are answered, therefore we ought to be very careful for what we pray. A celebrated divine wrote: "There are millions of Christians day by day imploring God for the salvation of the whole world, and the supplication has never been answered. Does God, then, keep his promise? Is prayer a dead failure? Does God mock the Christian Church? Are we told to bring all our gifts into the storehouse and prove him, only to find out that he breaks his promise? The answer to prayer is only a question of time. So far from there ever having been a million prayers lost, *there has never been one prayer lost.* God not only keeps one promise, but he keeps all the promises, and never since the moment we first breathed the Christian life, have we ever offered an unavailing prayer."

377. Why Should We Agree with Our Adversary Quickly?

The passage is a part of the Sermon on the Mount in Matt., 5th chapter. Jesus had been speaking about quarrels between brothers, and urging reconciliation of such differences in the spirit of love, before coming to the throne of grace. Then (verse 25) he diverges to the question of lawsuits, which were common then as now, and advises his hearers to keep out of the hands of the law and to escape its penalties by settling their disputes between themselves. But he went further than this, for his language pointed to a higher tribunal, to which all must come for judgment and where condemnation awaits them which can only be escaped by their repentance and acceptance of divine mercy.

378. Will God Give Us Anything We Ask?

In John 14:14 (which should be read in connection with its surroundings), Jesus was speaking (in the discourse at table after the Supper) of the way, the truth, and the life, and of how his disciples might render acceptable service for the advancement of God's kingdom on earth. He was about to leave them and he gave them the assurance that they would be endowed with power, after his departure, to do the works that he had done. Verse 14 gave them the assurance of his continuous intercession and that their prayers would be heard and answered. He had already told them that they should seek first the kingdom and all things would be added unto them. This verse also shows his divine equality, in the words "I will do it." Our own prayers should be, as far as we are able to make them so, in line with God's will. There are many of us who may ask for things that would be for our own harm; but if we "seek first the kingdom," we have then the assurance that he will care for all our other needs, supply our wants, comfort our sorrows, relieve our hardships and take us safely through the difficult places of life. We have a right to ask for these, if we have acquired this right by belief on the Son of God and by acting in accordance with the divine will. See John 14:12.

379. Does God Regard Our "Little Things" in Prayer?

Christ assumes toward all his followers the attitude of a friend. He said to his disciples: "Henceforth I call you not servants, but I have called you friends." We "work together" with him as friend with friend; our interests are identical with his and his with ours. On this basis it is perfectly rational to believe that he will give us all the help we need in the work we are trying to do for him. Christ certainly knows all about all the "little things" that come into our lives; also he will allow nothing to happen which will spoil or seriously hinder our work. Paul believed that Satan was trying to hamper him; in one place he says definitely that Satan hindered him, really prevented him from getting where he wanted to go (I Thess. 2:18). The right attitude is to ask God to further our tasks and then heroically and patiently keep at them. We must remember, too, that a certain amount of hardship and suffering is really necessary to develop the most stalwart Christian character. (See Heb. 12:1-11; II Tim. 2:3; Heb. 11, etc.) The Christian must beware of praying selfishly. A brave soldier would hardly pray for fair weather, except as it would aid the battle. We may certainly pray for strength; and the joy will come as we forget self in loving and serving the Master. But we should not forget that when God in his wisdom gave us eyes to see, a tongue to speak, a brain to think and reason to discriminate and guide us in our judgment, he meant these faculties to be of service. He gives us the fertile soil, but we must do the plowing and the planting. Faith in God does not imply that we should look to him to do for us what he has made us capable of doing for ourselves. When we do our part, then we can reach out the hand of faith and grasp his leading hand, which will carry us through in all we cannot do for ourselves.

380. Does God Hear the Prayer of the Wicked?

We have precedent for such a belief. A striking example is that of Manasseh (II Chron. 33:18). A greater sinner than he it would be difficult to imagine. We can understand prayers of sinners for temporal blessings being unheard; "their sacrifice" and perhaps their prayers, too, "are an abomination" (Prov. 15:8); but when the sinner cries to God for pardon and for help to quit his sins, he is surely heard. God does not mock the wicked man when he bids him "seek the Lord." Let the wicked forsake his way and return, for he will abundantly pardon (Isa. 55:6, 7). God heard the prayers of the people of Nineveh (Jonah 3:7-10). The way of approach to God is by repentance and that God gives (Acts 5:31). When the wicked man prays for that, he gets it; then God forgives him and he is in a position to ask for and receive all other blessings.

381. Was the Prohibition against Eating Pork Ever Revoked?

At what is known as the "first church council," described in Acts 15, the decision was definitely made that Gentile Christians were not to be compelled to keep the Jewish ceremonial law. The council sent a letter to the new converts setting them free from all these ceremonial requirements. This was the great burden of Paul's preaching, namely, that we are saved not by keeping the law of Moses but by faith in Christ. Circumcision was the sign of submission to the Mosaic law, and Paul, greatly to the displeasure of the Jews, taught that this was not necessary. The vision of Peter (Acts 10:9-16) while given for the purpose of making him willing to associate intimately with Gentiles, seems also to teach definitely that the Old Testament distinction between clean and unclean meats is no longer in force.

382. When and Why Was the Sabbath Changed to the First Day of the Week?

There is no command recorded, and probably none was given to change, but the change was made in celebration of Christ's rising from the dead. At the first great council of the Church, when the question was discussed whether the Gentile converts should be required to obey the Jewish law, it was decided that only four observances should be required of them. (See Acts 15.) The observance of the Jewish Sabbath was not one of the four, and the Gentile Christians do not appear to have ever kept it. The Rabbis had made it ridiculous by a host of absurd regulations about what a man might, or might not, do on that day. Christ was frequently accused of breaking the Sabbath. The Jewish observance was most vexatious and onerous, and the Apostles very wisely did not attempt to bring the Gentiles under the bondage. The writings of the early Fathers show that very early in the Christian era, if not in Apostolic times, the first day of the week was uniformly the day of religious meeting and abstinence from secular labor, thus celebrating the new Creation as the Jewish Sabbath celebrated the old. Several incidental allusions in the Acts show that even in Apostolic times, the custom was prevalent. But we do not observe Sunday as the Sabbath. It is seldom a day of rest to the earnest Christian, but of holy activity in his Master's service.

383. Is Suicide Wrong?

Life is a precious gift from God and should be so valued. Pain and suffering are to be regarded as discipline. There is no Scriptural authority to justify the view that we have a right to shorten or terminate our existence. Suicide is a crime under human law, and in the early Church it was condemned by repudiation and the denial of Christian burial. See Paul's advice to the Philippian jailer. (Acts 16:28; also Job 14:14.)

384. Is Being Tempted a Sin?

The sin does not consist in the temptation itself, but in inviting it, or yielding to it. Jesus himself was tempted "in all things as we are; yet without sin." Doubtless Satan, in the passage to which you refer, knew that Jesus had been fasting and so tried to tempt him to turn stones into bread. Again, believing that the desire for worldly power might influence him, he tried to tempt him by offering him the dominion of the whole earth, but again failed. It is not strictly correct to say that one cannot be tempted unless he has wrong desires. The tempter is always ready with his lures; but, if we rebuke our own desires and repel the temptation, asking divine strength to do this, the danger will pass. After conversion comes regeneration, and we are enabled to overcome sin. We may still be conscious of a struggle within, but we get strength to stand firm against it. The truly converted man is no longer the slave or bondman of sin, but is kept day by day from its power ever again having dominion over him.

385. What Is the Trinity; How Is It Possible; and What Proof Is There of It?

Are questions that have bothered thousands of earnest believers. No one should feel discouraged if the doctrine of the Trinity seems difficult, because as must be remembered, the facts about God are so much bigger than the brain of man that we cannot be expected in our present human state to comprehend them. The orthodox faith is that God is Triune in person. Christians feel by experience that God is their Father, that Christ is their divine Saviour, that the Holy Spirit is their Comforter, Sanctifier and Strengthener. The Father is a person; the Son is a person; the Holy Spirit is a person; three distinct persons in one eternal undivided and indivisible essence. How this is possible is not beyond comprehension to him that has learned to believe and know that to God all is possible and all doubts may be banished by the beautiful thought that to all others there is here one more glorious mystery into the depths and wherefores of which we are to be introduced in the happy beyond. And the proof! What more convincing proof can be asked than the words of him whom no one doubts, the Son of God and of Man. He tells us "I and my Father are one," "He that seeth me seeth him that sent me." In his farewell address to his disciples he speaks of the Comforter which is the Holy Ghost whom the Father will send in my name. At his baptism, the Father's voice is heard from heaven and the Holy Spirit descends in the form of a dove and lights upon him. Yes, at the very beginning of things God speaks of himself in the plural, "Let us make man after our image," while all the while "the Spirit of God moved upon the face of the waters." Truly proof sufficient for all who would believe.

386. Is Trouble Sent As a Punishment?

The Bible does not teach that all trouble comes from God as a punishment. It recognizes the fact that trouble is in the world, and, while it has some very definite things to say about it, it does not attempt to give a complete solution of the whole problem. Hebrews 12:5-11 declares that God does in some instances, discipline or "chasten," those whom he loves, but this could hardly be called punishment. (See also Deu. 8:5; Ps. 94:12; John 15:2.) Sometimes, however, calamity is a definite punishment, as in many cases during the history of Israel, and particularly in their exile. The book of Job is a beautiful explanation of a form of suffering which has the double purpose of disciplining the soul and glorifying God. Nothing can bring such credit to God as the demonstration made by a soul that trusts and praises him in the midst of misfortune. Paul and the other apostles glorified in their opportunities to suffer for Jesus' sake. They rejoiced "that they were counted worthy to suffer shame in his name" (Acts 5:41). They felt that he had borne so much for them that they wanted to bear something for him. The Bible nowhere encourages people to dodge suffering; it exhorts them to bear it, while at the same time it exhorts them to lessen the sufferings of others, and help them bear their woes. See James 1:2-5; I Pet. 4:12-19; Gal. 6:2.

387. Why Does Not God Save All the Human Race?

It is contrary to the Divine method of dealing with the human race, as we understand it, for him to use compulsion with men. Apparently, his desire is to have a people who, being left free to choose, voluntarily choose righteousness. He draws them, he yearns over them, applies discipline, offers them his help, but beyond this he will not go in this life. A man who is good only because he is compelled to be good, is of a much lower type than he who, being free to become evil, seeks of his own accord to become good. It is this higher type that, as we believe, God is trying to produce.

388. Can an Honest, Moral, Upright Life Save Any One?

People are constantly being misled in this matter because they fail to understand what salvation really is. Salvation is personal friendship and companionship with God. It is hard to see how a man who is not a friend of God at death will become one immediately after death. Being honest and upright does not really get us acquainted with God. Paul was intensely moral before his conversion, but he found out later that he had been an enemy of God all the time. Then, too, salvation means humility and meekness. The man who believes he can save himself puts himself out of the kingdom of heaven by that very attitude of mind. For the kingdom of heaven is made up of people with child-like hearts, who have given up their pride and self-will. Nor will the mere naming of the name of Christ and making a public confession make the necessary change. Jesus said very distinctly: "Ye must be born again." It is extremely unwise and unsafe to quarrel or argue with Jesus. He knows all about the human heart and all about the kingdom of heaven. The only thing to do is to accept his plan of salvation and let him give us the new heart, the heart that is humble and obedient, that is not self-confident but trustful, the heart that loves God and so will feel at home in God's heaven.

Scripture and experience alike teach that it is possible for one to have all the outward marks of religion, yet fail of possessing the real and vital thing. Saul of Tarsus was a most zealous man, trying to do the will of God, but after his conversion he felt that his former life had been very sinful, because he had not submitted himself to the will of God and accepted Christ's righteousness as his own. John Wesley's experience was similar, and countless others of this and earlier days. It must be remembered that it is not outward conduct that makes the real Christian; it is the inner life, the humility, the glad surrender to God's will, the warm love felt for God and for the souls for whom Christ died. It is not our good works that save us, but a simple, self-forgetful trust in Jesus. This faith brings the life and love which constitute religion.

A simple trust in the death of Jesus as the remedy for our sin. A simple acceptance of Christ to be our righteousness and our salvation will bring the joy and power of a new life of real sonship of God and fellowship with Christ. See Rom. 10:1-4; Phil. 3:3-9.

389. Is It Possible for One to Be Saved without Knowing It?

Among the children of Christian homes or among conscientious heathen (see Rom. 2:14, 15; Acts 10:34, 35), there may be cases in which a soul has salvation and is not definitely conscious of it. In the vast majority of cases, however, since the turning toward sin has been definite and voluntary, so the turning from sin and the receiving of forgiveness and a new nature are so definite as to be matters of plain knowledge. The New Testament clearly teaches that those who become converted may receive the witness of the Spirit, assuring them that they have been born again (see Rom. 8:16; I John 5:10). Any one who wants to be a Christian or hopes he is a Christian may receive this assurance if he persists in trusting Christ. Our salvation depends, not upon our feeling, but upon the unchangeable fact of the atonement and upon the plain promises of God's Word. When we definitely trust we become conscious of certain definite changes in our experience. Fear of God changes to love of God; we love God's people and his work. If we continue faithful the witness of the Spirit will be added to these signs and we shall know that we are children of God.

390. What Is Meant by Transfiguration?

"Transfiguration" signifies a change of form or appearance. The forms of Moses and Elijah, when they appeared on the Mount, were spiritualized. Luke 9:31 speaks of the subject of their converse. Some commentators hold that both Moses and Elijah were honored with an anticipatory resurrection, which would seem to be borne out by the fact of their presence at the transfiguration.

391. What Is Transubstantiation?

Transubstantiation (the term applied to the change of the substance of the bread and wine into the body and blood of Jesus Christ at the Sacrament) is a doctrine held by some, but not all, of the Christian churches. The Church of England and a large number of Protestant bodies hold that the bread and wine are sanctified symbols. Chrysostom wrote that after divine grace had sanctified the bread, "it is no longer called bread, but dignified with the name of the body of the

Lord, although the nature of bread remains in it." Theodoret declared that the bread and wine remain still in their own nature, after consecration. Augustine taught that what they saw upon the altar was bread and the cup, as their own eyes could testify; but that their faith required to be instructed that the bread is the body of Christ; and he added, "These things are therefore called sacraments, because in them one thing is seen and another is understood. That which is seen has a bodily appearance; that which is understood has a spiritual fruit." Isidore of Seville said: "These two things are visible, but being sanctified by the Holy Ghost, they become the sacrament of the Lord's body." Luther held the doctrine of the true presence of the body and blood of Christ, saying, "The bread is the body, the wine is the blood of the Lord," according to a sacramental union, but not in the manner of transubstantiation, adhering literally to the language of the Scriptures. The Catholic Church has always held the doctrine of the real, corporeal presence. With a few exceptions, the Protestants interpret the Saviour's language figuratively, and hold that Jesus intended to convey to men the lesson that unless they voluntarily appropriated to themselves his death and sacrifice, so that they become their very life and nourishment, they can have no spiritual and eternal life at all.

392. Can a Wealthy Business Man Be a Practical Christian?

Jesus said it was a hard thing for a rich man to enter into the kingdom; but he also showed, in the parable of the talents and other parables, that riches, properly regarded, and not held as a personal possession to be used for selfish and worldly purposes, but as a trust to be applied conscientiously, may be made a source of blessing. There are many men of large wealth who are useful members of society and who administer their means wisely and conscientiously. Besides, we are not to be the judges of the hearts of men. It has become a habit with many to condemn wealth and its possessors indiscriminately; and it is true that there is much in the present conditions of society that is open to legitimate criticism, but honest men of strict integrity can be found in every honorable line of business, and an active life is as much respected today as when Prov. 22:29 was written. A man who directs his efforts mainly to the acquisition of wealth, without regard to its responsibilities, incurs great spiritual danger. For the use we make of our talents and opportunities we shall be held strictly accountable.

393. Is Wealth an Evil or a Blessing?

There are many passages in the Bible relative to riches and its opposite, poverty. Nowhere is poverty spoken of as a blessing, but rather as a trial and discipline; yet wealth is to be regarded either as a blessing or the reverse, according to circumstances. Riches that are gotten and not by right can never bring happiness or satisfaction, and therefore result in sorrow or disappointment (Jer. 17:11). Christ taught his followers not to lay up for themselves "treasures on earth." He repeatedly warned them against the allurements of wealth. He declared wealth to be a great barrier to many—a hindrance to their eternal welfare. He taught his followers to set their minds on things above, and to take no thought of amassing riches or goods. Usurers, brokers, exchangers, and mere money-getters—those who set their hearts on wealth and made gold their god—he specially denounced. Yet he never spoke, even by implication, a word against the reward of honest industry, but on the contrary commended it. Voluntary poverty was assumed by the earliest disciples and fathers in the Christian Church. There is no duty of this character specifically enjoined, and we are told to "seek first the kingdom" and all needful things will be added. "Neither riches nor poverty" is the ideal meant for a contented Christian life. This is finely set forth in the beautiful prayer in Proverbs 30:8, Agur, the supplicant, being, as is supposed, a symbolical name for Solomon.

394. How Do I Know That I Am Saved?

There are two kinds of "assurance," as taught by the creeds, and both of them are matters of ordinary, everyday experience by many Christians. There are certain clear statements in the Bible as to the kind of person a Christian is. He must bear certain signs and marks and do certain things. He must love God and his neighbor; he must love the Church; he must be earnest and patient and bear the various "fruits of the Spirit." Now, a person can tell whether he is doing those things, whether his soul has these marks or not. Added to this test, however, is the direct "witness of the Spirit," the Spirit himself "bearing witness with our spirit that we are the children of God" (Rom. 8:16; II Cor. 1:22; Eph. 1:13). This is the voice of God, assuring us that we are his. It is important to remember that we should not wait for assurance, but must persistently and with determination believe God's word. Any one who is in doubt whether he is a child of God or not should insist immediately upon beginning to trust him. We become Christians by believing that Christ really does forgive our sins and receive us, remembering that he said: "Him that cometh unto me I will in no wise cast out" (John 6:37). As we continue to trust him we shall find ourselves manifesting the fruits of the Spirit, and God will whisper to us that we are his.

395. Why Is It Wrong to Harbor Angry Feelings?

God forbids it (Ecc. 7:9; Matt. 5:22; Rom. 12:19); it is a characteristic of fools and a work of the flesh (Gal. 5:20; Prov. 12:16; Prov. 14:29; Prov. 27:3; Ecc. 7:9). Anger is connected with pride, cruelty, clamorous and evil speaking, malice and blasphemy, strife and contention (Prov. 21:24; Gen. 49:7; Eph. 4:31; Col. 3:8; Prov. 21:19; Prov. 29:22), and brings its own punishment (Job 5:2; Prov. 19:19). Scripture teaches us that grievous words stir up anger, that it may be averted by wisdom and that meekness pacifies (Judg. 12:4; Prov. 29:8, 15:1). We are enjoined to be slow to anger, to avoid those given to it, to be free from it in prayer and not to provoke children to it (Prov. 15:18, 16:32; Tit. 1:7; Jas. 1:19; I Tim. 2:8; Eph. 6:4).

CHRISTIAN LIVING

396. Can One Be Converted and Saved without Baptism?

Christ commanded baptism, and we cannot understand any person who really desires to serve him neglecting to obey him in so simple a matter. Still, it lowers the reverence we have for God to believe that he would exclude any really repentant, believing person from heaven simply because he had not been baptized. The person might have been converted on his death-bed, or if he was among Baptists he might die between the time of his conversion and the time set for administering the rite. God is not unjust, and would not hold a man responsible in such circumstances. Do you suppose the thief who repented on the Cross was baptized? Yet Jesus promised him an entrance into Paradise. Baptism generally followed conversion in the time of the Apostles, as it does now generally in heathen lands.

397. Can a Person Become a Christian without the Baptism of the Holy Spirit?

As the word is usually understood, the baptism of the Holy Spirit was to confer special gifts for Christ's service. We have no reason to suppose that any man becomes a Christian without the influence of the Holy Spirit. The question is profitless, inasmuch as God gives the Holy Spirit freely. It would be impossible to state positively in what way the first impression comes in any individual case, but we may be sure that in some way the Holy Spirit's power has operated. This does not relieve any one from responsibility, because God is more willing to impart than men are to receive; but he does not force his gifts upon men.

398. What Is the Examination Necessary to Eating and Drinking Worthily at Communion?

A personal self-examination of the heart. If a man is conscious of hatred toward any one, of malice, of sinful purposes, of sinful connections which he ought to sever, but has not severed, or of cherishing any feeling inconsistent with his relation to Christ, he should not partake of the communion. This does not imply that only perfect persons should do so. If a man is honestly and earnestly striving after holiness and doing all that lies in him to live consistently; and sincerely deplores every failure and means to strive to avoid them in the future; if he loves Christ and is trusting in him for salvation, he is right in partaking of the communion although he may be conscious of having fallen into sin. (I Cor. 11:26, 28.)

399. Should All Believers Confess Christ?

Yes. There are very many good Christian people who never realize the true joy that belongs to the followers of Jesus, because they do not live in the sunlight. Some are so exceedingly sensitive about personal religion that they shrink to talk of it, even to their intimate friends. Even though they believe, they yet stand "afar off"; they have not been sufficiently drawn by love for the Master, or by zeal for his service, to come near enough to the Cross to feel the glow that stimulates the ardent believer. When once these timid souls can shake off their reticence and come boldly forward and confess Christ before the world, a transformation takes place. There is a very real blessing which follows the confession of our faith before men. Jesus himself said "Every one who shall confess me before men, him will I also confess before my Father, which is in heaven." (Matt. 10:32.) The knowledge of such recognition, following our open acknowledgment of Jesus as a Saviour, gives courage to the Christian and, like a loyal soldier who sees the flag of his country waving above him and who salutes it, his whole being thrills with zeal for service for the Great Captain of Salvation. Thus, at every fitting opportunity the believer should run up the flag, and let the world see whom he is serving.

400. Believing in Christ. What Does It Imply?

Believing in Christ does not mean merely believing that he is the Son of God. "The devils believe and tremble" (James 2:19). It means true repentance, contrition and an earnest desire for forgiveness, which leads us to look to Christ as the only way by which such forgiveness may be attained. To believe in him means that we are not only to believe in his divine mission and in the efficacy of his atonement for our sins, but to follow in his footsteps and emulate his example in all things wherever possible and to pray for the guidance of the Holy Spirit in our daily lives. Forgiveness is granted to all those who repent and believe and ask in faith. True repentance leads not merely to conviction of sin and to sorrow for our past offenses, but to a complete change in our life, *i. e.,* a turning away from sin to holiness and gradual growth in grace through living near to Christ.

401. Should Believers Associate with Unbelievers?

See II Cor. 6:14; Heb. 3:12; Acts 14:2; II Peter 2:1, 2; also Ch. 3:3, 17. It is not intended, however, that the believer should hold no communication with those who are still in the darkness of unbelief, otherwise he would not be fulfilling the divine command to spread the Gospel, and, "show forth Christ," at all seasons. He should, however, avoid all such associations and relationships—business, social and otherwise—as would bring a discordant element into his own home or business life, and thus antagonize spiritual growth. To put such people on the level of home acquaintances and intimate friends, would be very likely to prove spiritually disastrous to some member of your household.

402. Who Are the "Blessed" We So Often Read About in the Bible?

They are whom God chooses and calls (Ps. 65:4; Is. 51:2; Rev. 19:9); they know Christ and his Gospel, believe and are not offended at Christ (Matt. 16:16, 17; Ps. 89:15; Matt. 11:6; Luke 1:45). Their sins are forgiven and God imputes to them righteousness without works (Ps. 32:1, 2; Rom. 4:6-9). But at times they are chastened, and suffer for Christ, but they are not hurt thereby as they trust in God, fear him, yes have their strength in him (Job 5:17; Luke 6:22; Ps. 2:12; Jer. 17:7; Ps. 112:1; Ps. 84:5). Therefore they delight in his commandments and keep them, they hunger and thirst after righteousness, frequent the house of the Lord waiting for him (Ps. 112:1; Rev. 22:14; Matt. 5:6; Ps. 65:4; Is. 30:18). When in contact with the world they avoid the wicked, endure temptation, watch against sin: are undefiled, pure in heart, just, righteous, faithful, poor in spirit, meek, merciful, bountiful and are peacemakers (Ps. 1:1; Jas. 1:12; Rev. 16:15; Ps. 119:1; Matt. 5:8; Ps. 106:3; Ps. 5:12; Prov. 28:20; Matt. 5:3; Matt. 5:31; Matt. 5:5; Matt. 5:7; Luke 14:13, 14; Matt. 5:9). Watching for the Lord, they die in him, have part in the first resurrection and shall eat bread in the kingdom of God (Luke 12:37; Rev. 14:13; Rev. 20:6; Luke 14:15; Rev. 19:9).

403. What Is Christian Conduct?

Believing, fearing, loving, following, obeying and rejoicing in God (Mar. 11:22; Ecc. 12:13; I Pet. 2:17; Deu. 6:5; Eph. 5:1; Luke 1:6; Ps. 33:1). Believing in, loving, obeying, rejoicing in, and following the example of Christ (Jno. 6:29; Jno. 21:15; Jno. 14:21; Phil. 3:1; Phil. 4:4). Walking and living soberly, righteously and godly, honestly, worthy of the Lord God, in the Spirit, in newness of life, worthy of our vocation as children of light (Tit. 2:12; I Thess. 4:12; I Thess. 2:12; Col. 1:10; Gal. 5:25; Rom. 6:4; Eph. 4:1; Eph. 5:8). Then, when we are striving for the faith, putting away all sin, abstaining from all appearance of evil, perfecting holiness, hating defilement, following after that which is good, overcoming the world, adorning the Gospel (Phil. 1:27; I Cor. 5:7; I Thess. 5:22; Matt. 5:48; Jude 23; Phil. 4:8; I Jno. 5:4, 5; Matt. 5:16; Tit. 2:10), we will show a good example, by abounding in the work of the Lord, shunning the wicked, controlling the body, subduing the temper and living peaceably with all men (I Cor. 15:58; Ps. 1:1; I Cor. 9:27; Eph. 4:26; Rom. 12:18; Heb. 12:14). Then, too, we will attain the Christ-like ability to submit to injuries and forgive them (Matt. 5:39-41; I Cor. 6:7; Matt. 6:14; Rom. 12:20) and by visiting the afflicted, sympathizing with others, submitting to authorities, being liberal to and honoring others, being contented and by doing as we would be done by (Matt. 25:36; Gal. 6:2; Rom. 12:10; Acts 20:35; Rom. 13:1-7; Phil. 4:11; Heb. 13:5); attain blessedness (Ps. 1:1-3; Matt. 5:3-12; Jno. 15:10).

404. Is Joining the Church a Means of Salvation?

Christ demands that his followers confess him before men (see Luke 12:8, 9), and joining the church is the recognized method of doing so. We are ordered not to forsake "the assembling" of ourselves together in the Lord's House. It places us on record. Beside this, it is a means of grace. One who turns his back on God's Church and his people would be a very singular Christian, indeed. In associating with God's people there is mutual help and reinforced service. Then, too, the Christian would naturally wish to obey Christ's request, that his friends would remember him by partaking together of the bread and wine. There may be obstacles in the way of a Christian joining a church, and we would not judge any man for holding aloof, but he should have very weighty reasons to justify him in doing so. Leading a good moral life and believing in God are not, however, sufficient of themselves for salvation. God is not pleased when men ignore the way of salvation he has provided. Jesus saith, "No man cometh unto the Father but by me" (John 14:6).

405. Does the Bible Urge Church Attendance?

Yes. In both the Old and New Testaments there are numerous passages enjoining attendance in God's house as a duty, a delightful pleasure and a great spiritual privilege. See Lev. 8:3; Deu. 4:10; Psalms 23:6; 26:8; 27:4; 84:1, 4, 10; 122:1; Neh. 13:11; Micah 4:2; Matt. 18:19, 20; Acts 4:31; 15:25; Heb. 10:25. Take your reference Bible and look up, through the marginal notes, still other references. Church-going is both a duty and a privilege, and he who neglects it misses a great blessing and much of the enjoyment of spiritual life and growth. The Psalmist tells us that a day in God's courts is "better than a thousand." We are frequently reminded in the Scriptures that it is a duty. See Heb. 10:25; Psalms 111:1; Matt. 18:20, and other passages. True there are other forms of public confession besides that of joining a church, but that is the ordinary and recognized mode. It is the duty of every Christian to identify himself with a Christian church, that he may make it known where he stands, that he may help in advancing Christ's kingdom and that his own soul may be nourished by the association with other Christians.

406. Is the Increase of Church Wealth and Worldly Resources to Be Regarded As a Healthy Spiritual Sign?

History indicates that it is not a healthy sign. The periods of the church's worldly prosperity have usually been periods of moral decadence. There has been a tendency in such times to say, as did the church of Laodicea (Rev. 3:17), "I am rich and increased with goods, and have need of nothing." At the same time, the possession of riches is not incompatible with spirituality. There are, as we in this country have good reason to acknowledge, wealthy men who consecrate their wealth to God. A sincere Christian in business may prosper through the principles of Christianity, which conduce to industry, integrity and clean living. We can imagine a church composed of wealthy men being a church of great power, contributing liberally to the advance of Christ's Kingdom, and doing an immense amount of good in alleviating the burdens of the poor. There is nothing in wealth itself to render a man unfit for the Kingdom of God. It is hard for him to enter, as Christ said, because human nature is apt to love its wealth and to trust in it; but when a wealthy man really gives himself to the Lord, he has opportunities for service which do not lie within reach of the poor man; and if he uses them faithfully, he is more useful, and accomplishes more good. There have been such men, and there still are such men. The church, like the individual, may trust in its riches; and if it does, it is in an unhealthy condition; but it may consecrate its riches, and then it is capable of better service. We must look to other signs to learn if the possession of wealth has eaten into its soul, making it proud, arrogant and sordid, or helpful, beneficent and compassionate, before we can say whether it is the better or the worse for its wealth.

407. Is Confession a Christian Duty?

"Confess your faults one to another" James 5:16. It makes the whole problem of confession simple to remember that the duty is to confess to those whom we have wronged. If we have done any wrong to any person, we must confess it to him, and ask him to forgive us. A wrong that affects no one but God and ourselves needs to be confessed only to God. Often, however, a public confession is helpful. Under the awakening of conscience a Christian may be led to feel that he has been living under false pretenses, and will find a relief in saying so, and in making a new start. After all, we ought not to dread confession so much as we do. The Christian has no righteousness of his own to uphold; his righteousness consists in trusting Christ. Paul liked to declare that he was, to all intents and purposes, so far as the law was concerned, a dead man; he had been crucified with Christ, and Christ lived in him. He had no reputation to sustain. He liked to speak of himself as having been the chief of sinners. Then, too, people are apt to be kinder than we think; our friends will not want to condemn us, but help us. But, on the other hand, this is often a fruitful source of cruel temptation to sensitive souls. They imagine they ought to speak of things which no one but God needs to know about. Remember that God is never unreasonable, nor harsh. Tell him all about it, and then he will tell you plainly and kindly whether any other confessions are necessary.

408. Is There Any Scriptural Authority for the Rite of Confirmation?

The Apostle Paul is represented as confirming the souls of the disciples (Acts 14:22), and again as confirming the churches (Acts 15:41); Judas and Silas did the same thing (Acts 15:32). It does not in these cases appear to have been a rite or ceremony. But there appears to have been some rite of the kind in the early church. The writer of Hebrews speaks (6:2) of "the doctrine of baptisms and of laying on of hands." He may have had reference to the laying on of hands, implying the gift of the Holy Spirit, as in Acts 8:17, and as Paul did (Acts 19:6). It seems to have been a Jewish idea of ancient date, as Jacob thus blessed Joseph's children (Gen. 48:14). The custom continued in Christ's time (see Matt. 19:13), when "there were brought unto him little children that he should put his hands on them, and pray."

409. Is It Not Obligatory to Use Unleavened Bread at Communion?

Nothing could be more foreign to Christ's spirit and teaching than the character which certain churches give to this simple meal. There is nothing occult or mysterious about it. Christ was founding a kingdom or society, and wished his followers to have some way of showing their membership in it. He would not have them forget that they were Christians. He bade them join together in a simple meal, which was a common way of acknowledging equality and brotherhood. They were to come as Christians and eat and drink together in token of their being united in a common bond of love for him. It was not to be an elaborate feast, but to consist of the common constituents of the ordinary meal of that time. As they ate the broken bread they were to think of his body which was broken for them, and as they drank the wine they were to remember how his blood was shed for them. To make a mass of it and invest the details with a significance never intended is to miss the majestic simplicity of Christ's conception and his purpose in instituting the ordinance.

410. What Is Conscience?

It is the moral sense in man, by which he judges between right and wrong, and which approves or condemns his conduct. A man is bound to obey it in all his actions. He must, therefore, be careful to see that it is guided by right principles, that it is educated, and is not biased or warped by sophistry, or prejudice, or by impure motives. It has a standard in the Bible which should keep it true and firm. It is, however, quite possible for a man to do wrong conscientiously; in other words, his unenlightened conscience may mislead him. Paul gives an illustration (Acts 26:9) "I thought with myself that I ought to do many things contrary to the name of Jesus." The revelation on the way to Damascus changed that judgment of conscience and gave him a new principle on which he acted. Peter was conscientious in his idea of food and of associating with Gentiles. It took a miracle to open his eyes (Acts 10:28). The inquisitors were probably conscientious in persecuting protestants; Calvin was conscientious in burning Servetus, and the Puritans were conscientious in executing witches. But we see now, in our more enlightened age, that they erred. When a man is uncertain as to the right course to take, he should pray for guidance and direction, should see what principles the Bible lays down in similar matters, and then let his conscience decide. He will be held responsible for obeying his conscience.

411. Does Conscience Ever Approve Anything That Is Wrong, if so, How Can It Be the Voice of God in the Soul?

Certainly, conscience may, and often does, approve things that are wrong. A conspicuous instance (as already noted), is that of the Apostle Paul, who verily thought that in persecuting the Christians he was doing God service. Many since his time have erred in the same way, while sincerely believing at the time that they were doing right. Conscience is the faculty of the mind which discerns the moral quality of a course of conduct, and passes judgment upon it, according to the standard of right and wrong which it has. If the standard be wrong, the decisions of conscience will be wrong. "There is a way," says Solomon, "that seemeth right unto a man; but the end thereof are the ways of death." Conscience needs to be educated; it must rely on knowledge and reason for its data; it has to avoid being warped by self-interest and being blunted by its environment. Paul speaks (I Cor. 8:7) of a weak conscience, that is one that sees wrong where there is no wrong. As a judge, it represents God in the soul, but it never exercises infallible judgment. It needs divine enlightenment and the development which comes from Bible-reading and prayer. It is, however, the "voice of God" within us in this respect, that it bids us do the right, so far as we can discern it, at any cost; and as we obey or disobey, it rewards or punishes with sweet approval or stern condemnation.

412. Is the Voice of Conscience That of the Holy Spirit?

The facts of experience do not bear out the conclusion that conscience and the Holy Spirit are the same. Conscience is a faculty of the soul which approves or condemns according as one has or has not done what he believes to be right. By study of the Bible, prayer and the counsel of Christian friends one often finds that what seemed formerly to be right was in reality wrong. Paul believed he was doing right while persecuting the Christians. The Hindu mother throwing her babe in the Ganges believes she is doing right, and her conscience approves; but when she becomes a Christian she knows that such a sacrifice is wicked. In all nations and times certain souls have been alert and humble enough to hear the direct messages of the Holy Spirit, but it is through the written Word, the message of the Gospel and the knowledge of Jesus that the Holy Spirit comes to be a positive and constant fact of experience. The Christian tests the messages that seem to come from him by the Bible, by the personality of Christ, by the advice of Christian friends (see I John 4). The messages of the Holy Spirit are clear and positive, not hesitating and confusing. In the enlightened Christian, the voice of conscience and the voice of the Spirit will always agree.

413. How Can Consecration Be Accomplished?

This question of consecration is one that frequently arises, yet when we stop to analyze it, it seems strange that there should be any difficulty about it. If you possess anything which you wish to give to another, you simply give it to him; it is just as simple as that to give your whole heart and life to God. We already belong to him absolutely; in consecration we are only returning what is his. This is the "one thing" lacking in countless lives to give them full spiritual meaning and direction. (See Rom. 12:1). The question how we can take ourselves out of God's hands should really be more difficult than the question how we may submit ourselves to him. Remember that God is always reasonable, always kind. Many of the things sometimes suggested to our minds when the subject of consecration is brought up are not the suggestion of the Holy Spirit, but of our own minds, or of disturbing spirits. There is no uncertainty about the voice of God. He only asks us to obey him when he makes duty clear, and has promised to give us grace and power always for the duties he lays upon us. There surely should be no unwillingness to submit our lives to him; he can care for them and direct them much better than we. Consecration becomes simple when we approach the cross of Christ. We realize there that he gave himself for us because we were sinners—because of this very unwillingness in our hearts to surrender ourselves to him. Knowing this it is not hard to commit ourselves absolutely to his love, trusting him to forgive our sins, to cleanse our hearts, to guide and to keep us.

414. Is Conversion the Same as Regeneration?

Conversion, when the term is used theologically, is the turning away from sin to God. It is the reversal of a man's course of life. After his conversion his desires and aims and principles of life cease to be toward enjoyment or self-gratification or worldly ambition and tend toward God and holiness. Regeneration is the new birth wrought by the Spirit of God upon the man. Thus conversion supposes some activity on the man's part, while in regeneration he is passive. As the Spirit operates on the spirit of man "making it willing in the day of his power," the difference between the two terms is not of moment.

415. How Is Conversion Accomplished?

By prayer, by repentance of our sins, by sincerely accepting Christ as Saviour, by surrendering ourselves to him in all things as our guide, and by proclaiming our new allegiance and striving, with his help and in his strength, to regulate our lives according to his teachings. Conversion is a turning from sin to righteousness, producing thus a change in our thoughts, desires, dispositions and daily lives, which is the work of the Holy Spirit upon the heart as the result of saving faith. Conversion, however, in the sense of turning from sin and accepting Christ as Saviour, is distinct from regeneration, which is the work of the Spirit only.

416. Are Impure Thoughts a Sign of Non-Conversion?

Every man has some avenue by which temptation most easily besets him. His duty is to exercise special vigilance at that avenue. He should study himself and find out how best to deal with the temptation. It is well to ascertain by recalling our periods of trial, what were the exciting causes, and avoid them in future. Plenty of hard work, physical and mental, the pursuit of some absorbing subject of study, constant occupation, the avoidance of reverie, and of suggestive books, a careful attention to diet, and, above all, earnest prayer, especially whenever the evil thoughts arise, are the means we should use. But we must be continually on our guard against sudden temptation. We have to fight our battle, and it will be a hard one, but we may count on divine help, and if we are really in earnest, we will win the victory. We must act intelligently, as we would if we were afflicted with some physical disease and were seeking a cure. Thousands have fought the same battle and have won it. We should not doubt the reality of our conversion. That would undermine our strength.

417. Does the Bible Anywhere Prohibit Dancing?

Not specifically, but it condemns frivolity, folly and wickedness in every form. There are various points of Christian behavior applicable to modern life for which no specific rule or authority can be found in the Bible, as social conditions have greatly changed. Modern vices and indulgences have sprung up and these must be dealt with by the Christian as his conscience and judgment dictate. Dancing, though not in itself necessarily sinful, is exceedingly apt to degenerate into sin. Had promiscuous dancing, as it exists in society today, been prevalent in Bible times (instead of the comparatively innocent amusement then known, and the ceremonial or religious dances), it would unquestionably have been a subject of denunciation as sweeping as that applied to any of the vices of the time. The purpose of the Scriptures is to give general principles for the new life and so leave us the great benefit of deciding for ourselves how to apply them. In modern dancing, the evil so far overbalances the good that it is indefensible and should not be sustained by Christians.

418. Does God Send Disease?

God governs the world by the natural laws which he has established, and it would be impossible to define the extent to which he uses those laws to work out his providential purposes. It is probable that, in some cases, where he sees that a child of his needs discipline, or to be laid aside from worldly work and association so as to be drawn nearer to him, he may permit sickness to come upon him. In some passages sickness is threatened as a punishment. (See Deu. 28:27, 59, 60 and 61.) An instance is mentioned in Acts 12:23. On the other hand, it is certain that many diseases which afflict humanity are the result of disregard of sanitary laws, and although they may be used for the spiritual benefit of the sufferer, should not be attributed to God.

419. How Can I Get Rid of Doubt?

The only way out of any form of spiritual darkness is a firm faith in Christ. Spiritual darkness always means that in some way or other we are doubting him. We are often tempted to think that something else is necessary to be done before we begin to trust him, some sacrifice to make, some duty to perform, some problem to be solved. But these things come after faith, not before it. Of course if some positive wrong has been committed this wrong must be righted before we can believe that Christ fully saves us. But where no such positive wrong has been done and no clear duty neglected, the first, and indeed the only requirement is to trust in Christ. Any other advice would be false. "Christ died for the ungodly." There is our only place of peace and light. When you believe that he died for you, that he died to make possible the forgiveness of your sins and the cleansing of your heart; when you believe that because he died your sins are forgiven and your heart is cleansed, you will have peace, and you will find the Saviour near you, with his light and comfort and power. After all, it is no wonder that we feel sad while we are doubting him. You would feel sad if you were doubting your friend, your brother, your parent. And remember that he, too, is saddened by our doubt. Read some of the rich promises of God's Word, and refuse any longer to doubt that they were written to you as well as to any other of his children: Isa. 55; Ezek. 36:25-27; Matt. 5:8, 10; Matt. 7:7-11; John 7:38, 39; John 8:36; Acts 2:14, 16-21, 39; Rom. 6; Rom. 8:11; II Cor. 7:1; Gal. 3; Eph. 3:14-21; Col. 3; I Thess. 5:23; Heb. 4:9-11, 7:25, 99:11-14; Heb. 10:1-22, 35; Heb. 11; I John 3:1-9, 22; I John 5:4; Jude 24, 25.

420. Does a Truly Converted Person Have Evil Thoughts?

Thoughts of evil may enter the minds of even the most saintly. So long as we are in the body we are subject to temptation, and there can be no temptation without a thought of the evil that is suggested. Every time we hear or see or read of an evil word or act we have the thought of evil. These thoughts are stored in the brain, become items in the great storehouse of memory, and are apt to recur to us at any time. There can be no sin in a thought itself; it is only our feeling about the thought and our decision what to do with it that has any moral quality. When our hearts have been filled with love for God and love for people we find this love making us repel the evil thought and turn toward the good. It is helpful to remember that what makes a thing evil is that it will harm somebody. When we love people, we shall not want to harm them in body, mind or soul, and the thought of love will conquer and expel the thought of evil. It is in this sense that "love is the fulfilling of the law," and that "perfect love casteth out fear," as well as other sinful emotions. We may thus *bring into captivity* every thought to the obedience of Christ.

421. Is It Possible to Rid Oneself of Inherited Evil Tendencies?

We are not quite sure that we are justified in holding our ancestors altogether responsible for our evil tendencies. Some people like to hold Satan responsible for a share. It is, however, always advisable to inquire how far a man himself is deserving of blame. Probably, if it can be proved that he had nothing to do with the origin of them, still he may have assisted in their development. There is no doubt that he can, at least, be delivered from indulging his evil tendencies, even if they are not entirely extirpated. That is what Christ came to do. He offers us the power we need to bring our natures under subjection. The Holy Spirit in the heart so reinforces the better part of our nature that it gains power enough to hold the evil tendencies in subjection. They then so lose their power that they cease to be a danger, and, like any other part of our being that is not used, become weak. We must help in working out our own salvation. We must avoid temptation, and must be vigilant in preventing outbreaks. God will help us if we are sincere, and with Almighty help, what is there that is not possible?

422. What Does Faith Do for Us?

"Faith is the substance of things hoped for, the evidence of things not seen" (Heb. 11:1). We are commanded to have faith in God and in Christ (Jno. 14:1; Jno. 6:29) and yet it, of itself, is the gift and work of God in us, through the Holy Ghost by the Scriptures and preaching and other means (Rom. 12:3; Eph. 2:8; Acts 11:21; I Cor. 2:5; Heb. 12:2; I Cor. 12:9; Jno. 20:31; Jno. 17:20), causing by these means of grace, repentance and thereafter conversion (Mark 1:15; Acts 11:21). Through faith we obtain remission of sins, justification, salvation, sanctification, adoption of and access to God, the gift of the Holy Ghost, spiritual light and life, edification, preservation, eternal life and rest in heaven (Acts 10:43; Rom. 3:25; Acts 13:39; Mark 16:16; Acts 15:9; Jno. 1:12; Gal. 3:26; Rom. 5:2; Eph. 3:12; Acts 11:15-17; Jno. 12:36, 46; Jno. 20:31; Gal. 2:20; Jno. 3:15-16; Heb. 4:3). Faith is essential to the profitable reception of the Gospel; it makes the Gospel effectual in those who have faith; it is necessary in the Christian warfare, and without it it is impossible to please God (Heb. 4:2; I Thess. 2:13; I Tim. 1:18, 19; Heb. 11:6). The effect of faith in us is to produce hope, peace, confidence, boldness in preaching and testifying and, as Christ is precious to those having faith and dwells in their heart, they live, stand, walk, obtain a "good report," work in love, overcome the world, resist the devil (Rom. 5:2; Acts 16:34; Rom. 15:13; Is. 28:16; I Pet. 2:6; I Pet. 2:7; Eph. 3:17; Gal. 2:20; Rom. 4:12; Heb. 11:2; I Jno. 5:4, 5; I Pet. 5:9; Ps. 27:13; I Tim. 4:10). Therefore we should be sincere, strong and steadfast; holding our faith with a good conscience and not only praying for the increase, but having full assurance of it (I Tim. 1:5; II Cor. 8:7; Acts 14:22; Rom. 4:20-24; I Cor. 16:13; Col. 1:23; I Tim. 1:19; Luke 17:5; II Tim. 1:12). Then will we be known by our fruits, as without fruits our faith is dead (Jas. 2:21-25; Jas. 2:17, 20, 26), and as all difficulties are overcome by faith, so all things should be done by it, never fearing as we are fully protected by our shield and breastplate (Matt. 17:20, 21:21; Rom. 14:22; Eph. 6:16; I Thess 5:8).

423. What Is Faith?

Faith is trust. It is the gift of God, wrought in the heart by the Holy Spirit, which quickens and directs all our faculties toward the one object. We must pray to have faith, and to have our faith increased. It will be strengthened, too, by the frequent remembrance of Christ's repeated promises that our prayers to the Father, in his name, would assuredly be heard and answered, if we asked in faith, and believed while we asked. See Matt. 7:7; Luke 11:9; John 14:13, 15, 16; James 4:2; I John 3:22, 5:14; Luke 11:10. Faith has been defined as "the substance of things hoped for, the evidence of things not seen" (Heb. 11:1); it is that operation of the soul in which we are convinced of the existence and truth of something that is not before us, or perceptible to the human senses. Every one entertains faith of some kind, which he would find it difficult if not impossible to demonstrate by visible means. It is the practice of faith—the voluntary exercise of it—which enables us to rise to the belief in those great truths which God has been pleased to reveal. Paul says that "we walk by faith, not by sight" (II Cor. 5:7). Jesus himself said (John 20:29), "Blessed are they that have not seen and yet have believed." Thus, while believing what we see and comprehend may have its merits, believing what is *not* seen and but dimly comprehended is a greater merit. There are many things in nature which we believe, yet without being able to fully grasp them with our minds; we believe because we have the evidence of others, though not of our own senses. The faith which simply believes what it can see, understand, define and demonstrate is not real faith at all. "No man hath seen God at any time," yet all men believe in a God. The things of the spiritual world cannot be demonstrated by mere material agencies, but only through spiritual agencies. The exercise of faith increases our spirituality, enables us to comprehend things which without such exercise would be incomprehensible. Paul said that to the learned Greek skeptics the Gospel was "foolishness." Pride of intellect is one of the greatest barriers to spiritual growth.

424. Is a Falsehood Ever Justifiable?

One who makes faith in God and obedience to his will the supreme rule of his life, will never find excuse or justification for a lie. Man's extremity is God's opportunity and it is in such crises, when our faith is put to the ultimate test, that the Almighty reaches out and succors our weak nature with his Divine strength and help. We are distinctly told not to do evil that good may come and that all liars "shall have their place in hell fire, which is the second death." God can deliver those who trust in him in every conflict and those who are so situated are safe according to the measure of their faith. See Is. 26:4; Psalm 3:5 and 118:8; also Psalm 15. Lying in all its forms is expressly forbidden by the Lord. (Lev. 19:11; Col. 3:9.) It is hateful to him. (Prov. 6:16-19.) It shuts out the liar from heaven (Rev. 21:27), and those who are guilty of it find their ultimate abode in hell. (Rev. 21:8.) A full faith, such as that of the glorious men and women who have illumined the world with their lives, will not hesitate to tell the truth and leave the result in God's hands, trusting to the Omnipotent arm for safety.

425. What Is the Effect of Forgiveness?

Some may ask: "Has God forgotten all about my sins now that they are forgiven, and if so why do we not forget?" God says in Is. 43:25 and Jer. 31:34 that he will not remember our transgressions. The sense of "remember" in these passages is clearly that God does not remember the sin *against* the sinner. The account is canceled; the sins are no longer imputed to him. Since the revelation of God's plan of the atonement, we see that the debt is paid. When a debt is paid it is forgotten, though the record of the transaction may remain in the memory of the people concerned. In this sense God forgets our sins, but there is no reason for supposing that he undoes or limits his omniscience by literally not knowing that certain past events have occurred. We know of them, and God cannot observe our own minds without seeing there the record of our sin. There are various passages in Scripture in which God recalls his forgiveness of the iniquities of his people, but the remembrance is not an accusation but rather a testimony of forgiveness. We cannot, by the exercise of the will, make ourselves forget anything. It would be a subtle and almost inconceivable miracle for God to disentangle from our brains the memory of our sins and yet leave there the memory of other acts and events of the same days and hours. While we know that, in every sense of debt or blame, God forgets our sins when he forgives us, it should help to restrain people from sin to recognize the fact that a sin once committed will probably never be erased from our memory, at least in this life, and that it can never be lost from the simple, truthful record of the world's events. This is good for us as a reminder and as a stimulant. Seeing the dangers we have escaped helps us against having serious lapses. Not that we are become sinless, but, thanks to the promises in I John 3:9, we are rid of the dominion of sin, and the lapses we do have are not inputed. Therefore, let none despair in the thought that anything in the past, great or small, can prevent them from having God's peace in their souls just now. Salvation is a present matter. So far as our present standing in Christ is concerned it does not make any difference whether we were converted at the time we were baptized or not. The only question is: "Will we trust Christ just now to forgive all the sins of the past and to make us truly his?" There are promises in the Bible, by the score, of forgiveness for any sinner who will ask for it. Murderers, thieves, drunkards, all sorts of sinners, have found these promises true and received God's peace in their souls. God will forgive and forget, and let you start all over again now? Cease doubting him. Begin to trust him and your trouble will disappear. Read Gal. 5:6; II Cor. 7:2; Is. 55:7; Is. 1:18; Is. 43:25.

426. Is It Right to "Fear" God?

The word "fear," as used in the Bible, has two distinct meanings—fear in the sense of dread or fright, and fear in the sense of reverence and sincere obedience. It is not easy to determine which meaning is intended for the two Hebrew words most used have both meanings. In the New Testament the Greek word used has more generally the sense of fright or dread. The whole message of the Bible is that what God most earnestly desires from mankind is their love. But sin keeps them from loving him, so he reveals to them, through conscience, and through the law, the fearful results of sin. This awakens a fear which drives them to him for pardon and safety. A man who is living in sin, when his conscience is aroused, is afraid of the power and the justice of God. After he is pardoned he feels a reverence for God and the beginnings of love for him. As he progresses in the Christian life all fear of God, in the sense of terror, is removed. John speaks of the "perfect love which casteth out fear." (I John 4:18.) Throughout the Christian life reverence abides, but love grows more and more dominant. The wonderful word is "friendship." God wants us to be friends of his, as Abraham and Moses were, to serve him because we love him, to be glad in the gifts his love bestows. Christ would like to lead us all to the place where he can say to us as he said to his disciples: "Henceforth, I call you not servants, but I have called you friend." (John 15:15.)

427. Why Was Not Foot-washing Kept Up as Well as the Lord's Supper?

Foot-washing in the early centuries and in Oriental lands stood for kindly service and for comfort and hospitality. A guest would wash the dust from his visitor's feet, after removing his sandals, just as we take a friend's coat and hat and hang them up for him. Of course, the specific acts change with changing customs and even with climatic conditions, but the spirit is the same. We want to show our friends that we are willing to serve them. Christ emphasized this by his performing this service (a universal one in the East) for the disciples, though he was recognized as their Teacher, Master and Leader. It was a concrete sign of his whole message that his followers must be humble, and quick to serve others. He did not limit this spirit and motive to one act of life, but insisted that it become the principle of action for our whole lives. The courtesies and kindnesses that hosts show to guests Christians must show to one another at all times and in all ways, and to all whom they meet.

428. Are We to Forgive the Wrongdoer if He Does Not Ask It?

Christ inculcates the forgiving spirit, the spirit which loves even an enemy. It is the spirit he displayed on the cross when he prayed to his Father for the soldiers who nailed him to the cross, though they did not pray for themselves nor express contrition. Resentment is forbidden, but on the other hand, we have a right to expect regret on the part of the wrongdoer. He has no right to assume that we shall pass over his wrong as if he had never done it. If he wants our forgiveness he should ask for it; but even before he asks we must be ready to grant it. In our hearts we may already have forgiven him, but the outward and formal reconciliation waits his contrition. In Matt. 18:15 there is an intimation that the one who has suffered the wrong should seek to bring about the contrition of the wrongdoer by going to him and telling him his fault. If after all he withholds it, we are not required to treat him as a brother, but even then we are not to cherish resentment and especially not retaliation, but rather to return good for evil. In Matt. 5:23, 24 it would seem to have been quarrels that our Lord had in mind, rather than injuries. The brother who has aught against you appears to indicate a grudge, or a debt, as the following verses suggest. In any case, there is to be no quarrel. There must be reconciliation first.

429. In What Sense Is Godliness Profitable in This Life?

Since God's Word declares that godliness is profitable for the life that now is, it must affect favorably a man's temporal affairs. The necessities of life are promised to those who seek first the kingdom of God. He who contemplates being godly for the sake of gain does not know what true godliness is (see I Tim. 6:5;

also Acts 8:19). Under the old covenant, godliness in the nation assured national prosperity. Better blessings are promised under the New Testament dispensation. Temporal prosperity is, however, still a rational sequence of godliness. The higher the tone of the mental and moral qualities the better the business qualifications. Godliness demands industry, economy, honesty, courtesy, patience, hope—all most useful in temporal affairs. "The supplication of a righteous man availeth much in its working" (James 5:16), and he is permitted to pray for prosperity in temporal affairs. We are encouraged to bring everything, by prayer, unto God (Phil. 4:6).

430. How Can We Grow in Grace?

A fair equivalent of the word "grace" is "blessing." Grace means, in the first place, the disposition which God has toward us; that is, his willingness to bless us; his love and favor. It means, also, the blessing received, the state or experience into which we are brought by God's blessing. There is always in the word "grace" the idea of something bestowed entirely without merit or payment on the part of the one who receives it. God's blessings are bestowed freely; we do not earn them; he blesses us because he loves us, because he is gracious. All he asks is that we shall be willing to receive his grace. This promise to Paul means that God will give him the necessary strength to bear the affliction, and also, as Paul implies in the remainder of the verse, that the happiness of the blessing will balance the distress of the thorn.

To grow in grace means to advance and develop in spiritual experience and power. The Christian grows in grace in the first place by growing in faith. The more we believe, the more complete we entrust our souls and all the details of our lives to God, the more we are blessed. We grow in grace by our work for God. Religious work develops spiritual muscle just as physical work develops physical muscle. The more we do the more we can do. Prayer, study of the Bible, fellowship with spiritually-minded people, attendance at divine worship and prayer services, taking part in these services, will help us to grow in grace. We should remember, however, that all grace is bestowed by God himself; as we meet the conditions and enlarge our capacity he gives us more grace, just as he gives us more physical and mental strength when we meet the conditions for physical and mental growth.

431. What Is "the Blessing of Giving"?

The generous heart is commended in many passages in the Scripture, and especially where that generosity has the poor for its object. We are told to remember the poor (see Lev. 25:35; Deu. 15:7), to be a helper to the fatherless (see Ps. 68:5; Ps. 10:14), and the widow (Is. 1:17), to visit those in affliction (James 1:27), and let them share our abundance (Deu. 14:29); and many blessings are promised to those who do these things. The bountiful are especially blessed wherever they give to any worthy cause or person (Deu. 15:10). Remember also that remarkable promise, "He that hath pity on the poor lendeth to the Lord" (see Prov. 19:17). It is a fine thing to lay up treasure in heaven, and we can do this only by doing God's work with the means at our disposal here. If we use his gifts for our own indulgence and pleasure, it will profit us nothing in the end; but if we apply them to his glory and the benefit of our fellow beings who need help more than we do, we shall then be doing his work, and shall receive his approval. In II Cor. 8:12 the apostle speaks of the cheerfulness and willingness with which believers should give to the Lord's work. He does not limit the giving to a tenth, but urges them to give freely and to spare not, that their abundance may make up for the lack in others. The widow's mite (Luke 21:3, 4) was the largest offering, in a sense, for she gave all she had, and her faith and generosity were commended above those that gave far richer gifts. There are many worthy people who practice tithing and we would not dissuade them, and there are others who do not limit their gifts to a tenth, but exceed it, and they, too, are worthy of commendation. God looks at the spirit of the gift more than at the gift itself. There are cases in which a tenth might work hardship and, on the other hand, there are many where a tenth would be a small offering.

432. What Does "Loving God" Mean?

The duty and privilege of loving God become clear and simple when we think of Christ. Aside from him, the human conceptions of God are such that it is difficult to realize just what it would mean to love him. But friendship for Christ can be very real and precious. This is a definite part of God's whole wonderful plan. He came to earth in the person of Jesus and won just a few friends. These men and women loved him ardently. They loved him as a companion and friend. When he had gone away they loved him with the same definiteness and intensity and felt that he was still with them. Paul, who had never seen him in the flesh, loved him with just the same passion and fervor as did Peter and John, who had seen him. And all these early Christians knew that in loving Jesus they were loving God. As Professor Herrmann of Marburg says: "In their minds all difference between Christ and God himself vanished." He was God; they knew it. And as they loved him and labored for him and went toward death for him, they knew that they were fulfilling the old command, that had been so strange and difficult before, to love the Lord their God with all their heart and with all their soul and with all their mind and with all their strength. This same experience is possible today for every believer. Christ can be to every one of us that ever present Friend in whose companionship we delight and for whom we live and should be willing to die.

433. How May We "Reflect" God?

The marginal reading in the Revised Version (II Cor. 3:18) gives "reflecting" instead of beholding. This makes the meaning much clearer. Christians should be mirrors, reflecting the glory of God. Visitors to the Sistine Chapel in the Vatican procure small mirrors which enable them to enjoy the great paintings of Michael Angelo on the ceiling without discomfort. Worldly people will not look at God, but they do look at us, and they should see God reflected in us, as the great master's paintings are reflected in the mirror. As we thus behold and reflect God we become constantly more like him ("are transformed into the same image") going from one glorious stage of experience to another ("from glory to glory"). "Even as from the Lord the Spirit" (R. V.) means in a manner that befits the character and manner of the Holy Spirit. He works this transformation in us in the same perfect, adequate, godlike manner in which he always works. Compare Ex. 34:29-35; Ps. 34:5; Acts 4:13. Read the whole of this chapter and the next, II Cor. 3 and 4.

434. How Is One to Know that He Is Living Close to God?

If we ask, in the name of his dear Son, for a daily infusion of strength and grace sufficient for our needs, he will grant our petition. Perhaps nowhere is the Christian life better expressed than in these lines from Professor David Smith. He is speaking of Christian duty: "The man who bravely goes his hard way by and by discovers God by his side. But there is a richer discovery—the love of God in Christ Jesus our Lord; and it is revealed through love of one's fellow creatures. Keep your heart sweet and gentle; refrain from contention; look with kindly and sympathetic eyes on your fellow creatures, men and beasts and birds; consider their griefs and sufferings, and lend them your best comfort and succor. It is only as we love like him that we know the wonder and glory of his love. There lies the twofold secret of reconciliation, of the linking of our little lives with the eternal order. Obey, and you will know; love, and the love of Christ will be shed abroad in your heart. And once the love of Christ takes possession of you, life will be more precious and wonderful in your eyes, and you will understand what St. Peter means by 'joy unspeakable and full of glory'—that deep, strong gladness which comes of the persuasion that the ultimate fact in the universe is the Love of God in Christ Jesus our Lord, the love which died on the cross for pity of the world's woe."

435. What Does Adoption by God Involve?

"And I will be a Father unto you and ye shall be my sons and daughters, saith the Lord Almighty" (II Cor. 6:18). Such adoption is according to promise, by God's grace, through Christ, and we take it by faith (Gal. 3:7, 26; Rom. 9:8; Eze. 16:3-6; Rom. 4:16, 17; Jno. 1:12). Saints are predestinated unto adoption and are gathered together in one by Christ (Rom. 8:29; Jno. 11:52), whereupon they become his brethren (Jno. 20:17). Our new birth is connected with our adoption, the Holy Spirit is a witness of it, and by leading us gives us evidence of it (Jno. 1:12, 13; Rom. 8:15, 16; Rom. 8:14). This adoption should lead to holiness and should work in us likeness to God and childlike confidence in God (Matt. 5:44, 45, 48; Matt. 6:25-34); a desire for God's glory, love of peace, spirit of prayer, forgiveness and mercy (Matt. 5:16, 7:7-11, 5:9, 6:14; Luke 6:35, 36).

436. What Is "Loving God" and What Does It Avail?

Love to God is commanded (Deu. 11:1) and is, indeed, the one great commandment (Matt. 22:38). It should be with all the heart, and is better than sacrifice (Deu. 6:5; Mark 12:33). It is produced by the Holy Ghost and engendered by God's love to us and by answers to prayer (Gal. 5:22; I Jno. 4:19; Ps. 116:1). Christ gave us an example of it, and it is a characteristic of saints (Jno. 14:31; Ps. 5:11). Those who have this love are known to God, and are preserved and delivered by him; they partake of his mercy and all things work together for their good (I Cor. 8:3; Ps. 145:20; Ps. 91:14; Ex. 20:6; Rom. 8:28). When persevering (Jude 21), and exhorting one another (Ps. 31:23), saints will have joy, they will have a hatred of sin. In their hearts will be obedience to God, and he, besides being faithful to those who love him, will fulfill in them his promises (Ps. 5:11; I Jno. 5:1; Ps. 97:10; Deu. 30:20; Deu. 7:9; Deu. 13:3; Deu. 11:13; Ps. 69:36; Jas. 1:12). This love to God naturally leads to love to Christ. Here again we have a good example set by God himself and by the saints (Matt. 17:5; Jno. 5:20; I Pet. 1:8). Such love to him should be manifested in seeking, obeying, ministering, preferring him to all others, and in taking up his cross (Jno. 14:15; Matt. 27:55; Matt. 10:37; Matt. 10:38). It is characteristic of saints and an evidence of adoption. Those who have it are loved by both God and Christ, and enjoy communion with them (Song of Sol. 1:4; Jno. 8:42; Jno. 14:21, 23; Jno. 16:27; Jno. 14:23). Such love should be sincere, ardent, supreme, unquenchable and "unto death" (Eph. 6:24; Song of Sol. 1:7; Matt. 10:37; Song of Sol. 2:5, 8:7; Acts 21:13; Rev. 12:11).

437. Why Should We Praise God and How Should We Do So?

We should praise God because he is worthy of and glorified by our praise (II Sam. 22:4; Ps. 22:23). We should praise him because it is due to his majesty, glory, excellency, greatness, holiness, wisdom, power, goodness, mercy, loving-kindness, truth and his wonderful works (Ps. 96:1, 6; Ps. 138:5; Ex. 15:7; I

Chron. 16:25; Ex. 15:11; Dan. 2:20; Ps. 21:18; Ps. 107:8; II Chron. 20:21; Ps. 138:2; Is. 25:1; Ps. 89:5). Also on account of his gifts to us as are consolations, judgment, counsel, fulfilling of his promises, pardon of sin, spiritual health, constant preservation, deliverance, protection, answering prayer, the hope of glory, and all temporal and spiritual blessings (Ps. 42:5; Ps. 101:1; Ps. 16:7; I Kin. 8:56; Ps. 103:1-3; Ps. 103:3; Ps. 71:6-8; Ps. 40;1-3 Ps. 28:7; Ps. 28:6; Ps. 118:21; I Pet. 1:3, 4; Ps. 103:2; Eph. 1:3; Ps. 104:1, 14; Ps. 136:25). Such praise of God is obligatory on angels, saints, gentiles, children, high and low, young and old, small and great, all men and all creation (Ps. 103:20; Ps. 30:4, 117:1, 8:2, 148:1, 12; Rev. 19:5; Ps. 107:8, 148:1-10). This praise is good and comely (Ps. 33:1; Ps. 147:1), and should be offered with the understanding, soul, heart, with uprightness, joy, gladness, thankfulness (Ps. 47:7, 103:1, 9:1, 119:7, 63:5; II Chron. 29:30; I Chron. 16:4). It should be offered continually, more and more, day and night, forever and forever (Ps. 35:28, 104:33, 71:14; Rev. 4:8; II Chron. 30:26; Ps. 145:1, 2). And may be expressed in psalms and hymns, accompanied with musical instruments (Ps. 105:2; I Chron. 16:41, 42) and as a part of public worship (Ps. 9:14, 100:4, 118:19, 20). In this worship we should glory, triumph, express our joy by it, declare, invite others to it, pray for ability to offer it, be embued with the spirit of praise under all circumstances, even under afflictions (I Chron. 16:35; Ps. 106:47; Jas. 5:13; Is. 42:12; Ps. 34:3, 51:15; Is. 61:3). This praise has ever been highly thought of. Thus it has been called the fruit of the lips, voice of triumph, voice of melody, voice of psalm, sacrifice of praise and of joy (Heb. 13:15; Ps. 66:8, 47:1; Is. 51:3; Ps. 98:5; Heb. 13:15; Ps. 27:6).

438. What Is God's Pardon and to What Should It Lead?

Pardon for our sins was promised to us (Is. 1:18; Jer. 31:34; Heb. 8:12). There can be none without the shedding of blood and legal sacrifices and outward purifications are ineffectual as only through the blood of Christ is it efficacious (Lev. 17:11; Heb. 9:22; Heb. 10:4; Jer. 2:22; Zec. 13:1; I Jno. 1:7). God alone can grant this pardon and does so by and through Christ and his blood (Dan. 9:9; Mark 2:7; Luke 7:48; Luke 1:69, 77; Matt. 26:28). He grants it for Christ's sake, freely, abundantly, readily to those who confess their sins, repent and believe (I Jno. 2:12; Is. 43:25; Neh. 9:17; Is. 55:7; I Jno. 1:9; Acts 2:38; Acts 10:43). By so doing God shows his compassion, grace, mercy, forbearance, loving kindness, justice and faithfulness (Mic. 7:18, 19; Rom. 5:15; Ex. 34:7; II Chron. 30:18; Rom. 3:25; Ps. 51:1; I Jno. 1:9). The result of such pardon is the forgiving, removing and blotting out of transgression, the covering of, and blotting out of sin and not mentioning or remembering transgressions any more (Ps. 32:1, 103:12; Is. 44:22; Ps. 32:1; Acts 3:19; Eze. 18:22; Heb. 10:17). This great and free gift should lead us to return to God, love him, fear and praise him (Is. 44:22; Luke 7:47; Ps. 130:4; Ps. 103:2, 3). It should also induce us to pray for it for ourselves and for others and to strive to become worthy of it as the unforgiving, unbelieving and impenitent cannot share in it (Ps. 25:11; Jas. 5:15; Mark 11:26; Jno. 8:21, 24; Luke 13:2-5).

439. What Is Meant by "Devotedness to God"?

We should be devoted to God because of his mercies (Rom. 12:1), of his goodness (I Sam. 12:24) and because of the call with which he invites us to him. The death of Christ and our redemption should be compelling forces. Our devotedness should be unreserved (Matt. 6:24), abounding (I Thess. 4:1), persevering (Luke 1:74, 75; Luke 9:62), and in life and death (Rom. 14:8). It should be with our whole being, thus, with our spirit (I Cor. 6:20), with our bodies (Rom. 12:1; I Cor. 6:20), with our members (Rom. 6:12, 13), and with our substance (Ex. 22:29; Prov. 3:9). This devotedness we should show by loving God (Deu. 6:5), serving him (I Sam. 12:24; Rom. 12:11), walking worthy of him (I Thess. 2:12), doing all to his glory (I Cor. 10:31); bearing the cross (Mark 8:34), by self-denial (Mark 8:34), and by giving up all for Christ (Matt. 19:21, 28, 29).

440. Does God Communicate His Will in Any Other Way than by His Word?

We believe that there are special cases of extreme difficulty in which, when guidance is sought, God does reveal to his children the way in which he wishes them to walk. This he does by interpositions of his providence. If we ask him for guidance in our troubles, in the name of his dear Son, he will not deny it. There are some who think they receive direction in dreams, or by casting lots, or by opening a Bible at random and noticing the first passage that catches the eye. It is unwise to give heed to intimations supposed to reach us in such ways. They are utterly untrustworthy and should be disregarded.

441. What Is Grace?

In theology, the word "grace" has been the hinge of three great historical controversies, and it is still a subject of varied interpretation. In the spiritual sense, it is divine favor or condescension to mankind individually or collectively. In the concrete Gospel sense, it is the unmerited love and favor of God in Christ, as shown in the salvation freely provided for mankind (see Eph. 2:9). It may also be described as the divine influence acting within the heart, regenerating, sanctifying and keeping it. Grace brings the peace and joy of assurance. It is "the life of the soul, as the soul is the life of the body."

442. Can the Church Heal by Faith Today?

There are several religious bodies which teach faith-healing by prayer and the laying on of hands. It is not general, however, among the denominations. But while the divine power is as great today as in the time of the early Church, and while many remarkable instances of healing through faith and prayer are adduced, the usual teaching in the regular denominations is that, in cases of sickness, we should employ the remedies at hand through medical skill or otherwise, and ask God's blessing on these means to effect a cure. There is no passage in the Scriptures, however, which indicates that Christ intended the gift of faith-healing to cease with the apostles. On the contrary, the inference is quite clear, throughout the whole

New Testament, that this gift was to remain in the Church. We have so largely lost the gift because of our lack of faith, but there are numerous incidents being reported every day of miraculous healing in answer to prayer in the name of Christ. That there are not more cases is not proof that God's power is shortened, but results are proportioned to our faith. There are many instances in the Church today of wonderful answers to the prayer of faith. It is well to remember, however, that God has placed certain means within our reach and we should employ these means and ask his blessing upon them. Jesus himself never said anything in disparagement of the profession of Luke the "beloved physician." In James 5:15 it should be noted that the writer does not say that the *oil* will save; it is merely a symbol. The healing here mentioned in the first clause of the verse is of the *body;* the second clause implies that the prayer of faith for one who has sinned will bring forgiveness. The same connection of sin and sickness is employed in Is. 33:24; Matt. 9:2-5, and John 5:14. See also Ps. 103:3. The application is found in the next verse, which speaks of repentant confession. The oldest versions of this passage read, "*Therefore,* confess your faults one to another," showing that it must be a precedent condition. This does not justify what is known as the confessional, however, in the sense in which it is employed in the Church of Rome. There, all confessions must be made to the priests. Confession, in the apostolic sense, may be made to any one who is godly and who can pray. It is to be an open confession and not one whispered into the ear of a priest.

443. How Can One Obtain a "New Heart"?

The sole resource is prayer and a constant striving against indulgence in sin. God is able to give a new heart, and when a man is sincerely desirous of obtaining that blessing there is no doubt of its being granted to him. God is more ready to bless us than we are to seek his blessing. But he does not confer his gifts unless they are sincerely sought. And there must be proof of sincerity by co-operation. If a man prayed that he might reach the top of a mountain, God would not take him bodily there, but he would give him the strength to climb. If you read the description of the condition of a man struggling against sin in Romans 7, you will see that victory is obtained through the power that Christ gives. This power is freely granted to all who seek it, and through it any one may overcome evil.

444. What Are the Consequences of Resisting the Holy Spirit?

We are warned against the danger of resisting the Holy Spirit, and Paul (Eph. 4:30) admonishes the believer not to grieve the Holy Spirit. It is possible for one to refuse to obey the call of the Spirit, yet without placing himself outside of the pale of redemption. The Bible itself furnishes several instances of this character. We should advise any one who feels that he may have refused the call at one time to take a hopeful attitude, and to seek God's mercy and forgiveness with a contrite heart, remembering that the promise of forgiveness extends to "whosoever" may come. Jesus saves to the uttermost, and has assured us that he will not reject any one who comes to him in this spirit.

We can not set limits to God's mercy, and he is at all times more ready to forgive than we are to seek his forgiveness.

445. In What Sense Is the Holy Spirit a Guide?

The Holy Spirit is certainly promised in answer to believing prayer. (See Luke 11:13.) See an account of his work in John 16:7-15. But the fact should not lead any one to be intolerant, or unreasonable. It is conceivable that a man might be so convinced that he is led of the Spirit to believe or do certain things, as to make grievous errors. He might believe himself infallible. The best and wisest men have in the past made that mistake. The humble, childlike believer seeks enlightenment and it may come to him through a preacher, or through private study, but he should keep his mind open to new light and should never assume, because he has reached a certain conclusion after prayer, that he is necessarily right. He may have been misled by ignorance or prejudice. In his talk with Nicodemus (John 3:8), Christ compared the operations of the Spirit to the movement of the wind, which could not be controlled or directed. We see this sometimes in revivals where we cannot account for one person being converted while another remains unmoved. But we may be quite sure that whenever any one sincerely desires the Holy Spirit's influence, God is more ready to bestow it than we can be to receive it.

446. Should a Christian Be Joyful?

God gives joy and Christ was appointed to give it, since the Gospels, which treat of him, are the "good tidings" (Ecc. 2:26; Is. 61:3; Luke 2:10, 11) and God's Word affords joy (Neh. 8:12; Jer. 15:16). Joy is promised to saints, prepared for them and enjoined on them (Ps. 132:16; Is. 35:10; Ps. 97:11; Ps. 32:11; Phil. 3:1). It is experienced by believers, peacemakers, the just, the wise, and discreet (Luke 24:52; Prov. 12:20; Prov. 21:15; Prov. 15:23). The joy of the saints is in God, Christ and the Holy Ghost; for their election, salvation, deliverance from bondage, manifestations of goodness, temporal blessings, supplies of grace, divine protection and support and the hope of glory (Ps. 89:16; Rom. 5:11; Luke 1:47; Rom. 14:17; Luke 10:20; Ps. 21:1; Ps. 105:43; II Chron. 7:10; Joel 2:23; Is. 12:13; Ps. 5:11; Ps. 28:7; Rom. 5:2). These being grand blessings and advantages, their joy should be great, abundant, exceeding, animated, unspeakable, full, constant (Zec. 9:9; II Cor. 8:2; Ps. 21:6; Ps. 32:11; I Pet. 1:8; II Cor. 6:10; I Thess. 5:16) and it should be manifest in every condition of life, such as in hope, sorrow, under trials and persecutions, in calamities and afflictions (Rom. 12:12; II Cor. 6:10; Jas. 1:2; I Pet. 1:6; Matt. 5:11, 12; Hab. 3:17, 18). Such joy is made complete by the favor of God, by faith in Christ, the abiding in him and his Word, and by answer to prayer (Acts 2:28; Rom. 15:13; Jno. 15:10, 11; Jno. 17:13; Jno. 16:24). When so conceived and practiced, the saints will serve God with gladness (Ps. 100:2). It will strengthen them (Neh. 8:10); they will use it in all their religious services, have it in all their undertakings, and it shall finally be their reward at the judgment day (Eze. 6:22; Deu. 12:18; Matt. 25:21).

447. Is It Wrong to Judge Others?

It is a common failing in humanity to pass judgment upon others and it is frequently attended by unfortunate results. We are expressly told in Scripture that judgment belongs to God. (See Matt. 7:1-5.) No matter what the occasion, it becomes the Christian to withhold his judgment, and particularly the open expression of it, lest he should be doing an injustice. There are cases, of course, where an act is so palpably wrong and so obviously done with wicked purpose, that we feel naturally disposed to condemn; but even here we may make a mistake, unless we are thoroughly familiar with all the antecedent circumstances. This reservation of judgment does not relate to the operation of the statute law, but to the individual. Paul tells us, in Romans 14:4, that we ought not to assume the right to condemn. Therefore, to tell a person that he is not a Christian, if he has a ring on his finger, is to assume a position to which we have no right. There may be a reason for his wearing it that we do not know; it may be the gift of some relative or friend, or a memorial. To men impressed with the urgent need there is in the world for money to use for charity and religion, it would appear a duty to give all the money available to these causes and not to spend any of it on personal adornment. Arriving at such a conclusion, let him act upon it himself, and not hastily denounce others who may have different ideas of their duty. Above all, we should refrain from censorious gossip, which is a fruitful cause of ill-founded and wicked judgment of others.

448. Why Is Liberality to Be Commended?

It is pleasing to God. He never forgets it. Christ set an example of it and it is characteristic of Saints (II Cor. 9:7; Heb. 6:10; II Cor. 8:9; Ps. 112:9). This good quality should be exercised in the service of God towards all men, such as saints, servants, the poor, strangers, and towards enemies (Ex. 35:21-29; Gal. 6:10; Rom. 12:13; Deu. 15:12-14; Lev. 25:35; Prov. 25:21). It should be demonstrated by lending to those in want, in giving alms, relieving the destitute, and in rendering personal services (Matt. 5:42; Luke 12:33; Is. 58:7; Phil. 2:30). In practice, however, we should be guided by these restrictions. We should be liberal without ostentation, with simplicity, should be willing and give abundantly (Matt. 6:1-3; Rom. 82:8; Deu. 16:10; Mat. 6:1-8; II Cor. 8:12; II Cor. 8:7). Its exercise provokes others to like goodness whereas the want of, while bringing to many a curse, is proof of not loving God, and of not having faith (II Cor. 9:2; Prov. 28:27; I Jno. 3:17; Jas. 2:14-16). Liberality is highly commended, blessings are connected with it and promises are given to those who practice it (Luke 3:11, 11:41; I Cor. 16:1; Ps. 41:1; Ps. 112:9; Prov. 11:25). God's people were always noted for having this virtue, as see Prince of Israel, Num. 7:2; Boaz, Ruth 2:16; David, II Sam. 9:7-10; Zacchaus, Luke 19:8; First Christians, Acts 2:45; Barnabas, Acts 4:36, 37; Cornelius, Acts 16:2; Lydia, Acts 16:15; Paul, Acts 20:34.

449. How Does Christ Influence the Lives of Men?

It is one of the most definitely and positively attested facts of history and of present-day life that multitudes of people have an experience of peace, power, purity and joy which grows out of their belief that God as manifested in the flesh of Jesus of Nazareth died for their sins. This experience is real, is tangible, is witnessed to; it makes the lives of those who possess it altogether different from what they were before. When we ask if such an experience was possible before Christ died, the answer is very clear—No. Many Old Testament saints had a very beautiful and exalted spiritual experience, but they could not have the experience of knowing that God in the flesh had died for their sins. The question of the relation of these facts to sin and the deliverance from it presents some philosophical difficulties, but no really practical difficulties. We can be sure that if any persons found deliverance from sin before Christ came they were comparatively few; but now the deliverance is offered to all. A few saints may have looked forward and grasped the glories of the atonement by faith; we look back upon it as a historic fact and so appropriate its benefits. Again, it is undeniably true that since the incarnation men have been able to get a totally new and infinitely clearer idea of God than if he had not manifested himself in the flesh. He has been interpreted to them in terms of human life, so it is now easy for them to comprehend how God thinks and acts and speaks. It is a higher revelation than that which came through the prophets: "God, who at sundry times and in divers manners spake in time past unto the fathers by the prophets, hath in these last days spoken to us by his Son" (Heb. 1:1, 2). It must certainly be true that the experience of loving Christ as a divine-human friend is different from the experience of loving God as he was revealed in Old Testament times. And when, as has already been suggested, there is added the knowledge that he died to save us, there is a power and depth to the love that would otherwise have been impossible. The one who fully believes in Christ receives fully the benefits of his life, death and resurrection. The one who doubts must continue to miss them.

450. Is Fasting Necessary to Christian Living?

Fasting was voluntary in the early Christian Church. It was charged by his enemies that Christ's disciples "fasted not," while those of John did fast (Matt. 11:18, 19). Our Lord did not positively enjoin religious fasting, and indeed he alluded in terms of censure to the frequent fasts of the Pharisees. His reference to the time which would come when, being deprived of the personal presence of the bridegroom, his disciples would fast, implied rather a season of general mourning than of self-denial. In the Sermon on the Mount (Matt. 6:17) he recognizes the practice, but leaves the frequency and extent to the individual judgment. Fasts were undoubtedly observed by the early Christians (see Acts 13:2, 14:23; II Cor. 6:5), but these were probably a recognition of old established usage, handed down through generations. When it is remembered that a very large portion of the Christian Church was originally Jewish, it is not surprising that fasting, which was so marked a feature under the old dispensation, should have been handed down from age to age and that it should be occasionally found to some extent in the church even at the present day. That it has merits, both spiritual and physical, may not be gainsaid. A sincere fast, which while mortifying the flesh, aided in concentrating the mind upon the things of the Spirit, is especially adapted to certain great emergencies. Our Saviour himself set us the example.

451. Should a Christian Marry a Non-Christian?

Paul gives direct teaching on the subject. He says (II Cor. 6:14), "Be ye not unequally yoked together with unbelievers," etc. In the case of the Corinthians, such a union must have been exceedingly uncongenial, as the unbeliever was usually an idolater. The disparity is not so marked in our day, but it is sufficient still to produce a lack of real harmony. Religion should be to the Christian the first and fundamental element of life. To have a partner who has no sympathy with it is to raise a barrier between the two which keeps them separate in the highest and holiest spheres of life. Generally it leads to the Christian forsaking his faith.

452. How Can the Unbelieving Husband Be Sanctified by the Believing Wife?

This probably was never designed for general application. It was meant to meet very special conditions. Paul, in I Cor. 7:14, was writing to Christians newly won from a corrupt and debasing form of heathenism. The converts were disposed to separate from their pagan partners and they wrote for Paul's approval. He told them not to do so. If the pagan husband or wife chose to leave, there was to be no restraint. The Christian must not be the one to seek separation. Rather he should remain in conjugal relations in the hope of saving his pagan wife (see verse 16). His example and tender affection and Christian kindness might win her to Christianity—might be the means of sanctifying her. So the believing wife might influence the pagan husband. Besides, there was the consideration of the children, who, if the believer remained, would be brought up under holy influences.

453. Is It Possible to Be So Trained from Childhood Up that a "New Birth" Is Unnecessary?

We believe that Christ's statement, "Ye must be born again," applies to every human being. The most carefully trained child needs it. It is true that there are many so good by nature and training, that they pass through the process almost unconsciously. They do not go through the sorrow and anxiety and distress that precede conversion in the case of people who have led openly wicked lives. They come to God as to a Father, and having learned to love him from their earliest years, they are changed imperceptibly into his image. But, none the less, the change takes place, and the child yields itself by a definite act to Christ as a Saviour. These are beautiful characters, and they have reason to thank God for giving them parents so good and wise. They are, however, very rare. The best trained child is often conscious of having lied, or committed other sins which need to be forgiven, and of having a nature that is prone to sin, which needs to be changed by the Holy Spirit.

454. Who Is My Neighbor?

The practical question, "How shall I carry out the commandment to love one's neighbor as one's self" is constantly facing the Christian. In the parable of the

Good Samaritan, Jesus taught that our neighbor is any one to whom we can be of service. There are no limits as to social standing, or creed, or race, or habitation. Any one whom we can reach has a claim upon our help, which is sanctioned by God himself. The teachings of both Jesus and Paul are plain that a man should care, with special earnestness and affection, for the members of his own household. To be sweet and kind, patient and helpful at home is the first neighborly duty of the Christian. Then the people to whom one is nearest in his daily life have the next claim upon his service. He should be on the lookout for persons and families who are in need and whom he can help. The Christian should make his influence felt for the benefit of his neighborhood, his town, and his state. Mails and express routes have knit the whole world into so compact a neighborhood that every one must feel that the needy in any corner of the world have a claim upon his charitable consideration. Needless to say the joy of such service always far outweighs whatever sacrifice may be involved. Matt. 19:19, 22:39; Luke 10:36, 37; Rom. 13:10.

455. Why and How Should We Love Our Fellow Man?

God and Christ commanded us to love man. The Saviour gave us an example in doing it (I Jno. 4:7, 21; Jno. 13:34; Jno. 15:12; I Jno. 3:23). It is taught by God and is a fruit of the Spirit (I Thes. 4:9; Gal. 5:22; Col. 1:8). Without it, gifts and sacrifices are as nothing. Love is the great commandment (I Cor. 13-1, 2, 3; Matt. 22:37-39; I Tim. 1:5). This love we should put on, follow after, abound and continue in, and, while provoking each other to it, we should be sincere, disinterested and fervent in it (Col. 3:14; I Cor. 14:1; Phil. 1:9; I Thes. 3:12; I Tim. 2:15; II Cor. 8:7; Rom. 12:9; I Cor. 10:24; I Pet. 1:22). This virtue should be connected with brotherly kindness and should be practiced with a pure heart. We should show it toward saints, ministers, our families, our fellow countrymen, strangers, enemies; yes, to all men! (I Pet. 2:17; I Thess. 5:13; Eph. 5:25; Ex. 32:32; Lev. 19:34; Ex. 23:4-5; Matt. 5:44; Rom. 12:14, 20; Gal. 6:10), and demonstrate it by ministering to the wants of others, relieving strangers, visiting the sick, clothing the needy, sympathizing with and supporting the weak, covering the faults of others, forgiving, forbearing (Matt. 25:35; Gal. 5:13; Lev. 25:35; Is. 58:7; Job 31:16; Jas. 1:27; Rom. 12:15; Gal. 6:2; Prov. 10:12; Eph. 4:32, 4:2). This love to man is evidence of our being in the light of our discipleship with Christ and of spiritual life (I Jno. 2:10; Jno. 13:35; I Jno. 3:14). It is the fulfillment of the Law, is good and pleasant, is a bond of union and perfectness and necessary to true happiness (Rom. 13:8-10; Ps. 133:1-2; Col. 2:2; Col. 3:14; Prov. 15:17).

456. In What Sense Is Our "Overcoming" Like That of Jesus?

There is more in the statement in Rev. 3:21 than a comparison of our victories with those of Christ. It is rather a statement of similarity in the whole sequence of struggle, victory, and reward in the case of the Christian and of Christ. He struggled, triumphed, and was enthroned; we, too, shall struggle, triumph, and be enthroned. This does not mean that at every step, or necessarily at any step, our experiences shall be identical with his or equal to his. His struggles, his victories, and his rewards are greater than ours can be. Nevertheless, we find it to be true, comparing this passage with others, that, whatever struggles we may meet, our victories may be as complete as his. (See I John 2:6, 4:17; II Cor. 2:14, etc.) And this is true because it is his very strength that is available for us in our times of need.

457. What Should Be the Christian's Attitude toward Pleasures?

Many Christians, especially among the young, are interested in knowing what pleasures are inconsistent with a Christian's life. What sacrifices in this respect does God ask us to make? God does not ask us to make sacrifices for its own sake. When he asks us to give anything up, it is because he knows it would be harmful to us to keep it. In all our thoughts about God we must hold with a firm grip the great fundamental truth that he loves us. We cannot think rightly or feel comfortable without starting here. Because he loves us he wants us to be happy. He does not want to take away our happiness but to give us more. And he knows that we can be happy only as we love and serve him. He really asks us to give up nothing, except to give ourselves to him. When we realize that we belong to him we also realize that certain things harm us, and that certain other things may have a harmful influence upon others. We are living for him, and for the people for whom his Son died. All these questions settle themselves quite easily then. There are many unobjectionable pleasures, but we should shun those that waste precious time; that lead to evil companionships; that involve acts and associations which interfere with our spiritual progress; that are inimical to health or reputation, and also those that, by setting a bad example, may operate as a stumbling-block to others. In this way we will find more happiness in the consciousness that we are pleasing and helping him than we could ever have found in any form of self-indulgence.

458. How May I Pray Acceptably to God?

This is a question asked by many earnest people. This is the natural state of one in whom spiritual life has not yet been fully awakened. Prayer, like belief, is not an act that can easily be made clear to the unenlightened. If you go to God as a child to its father, when you are in trouble, and ask him in simple faith to help you for Jesus' sake, you will be better able to understand why others believe in prayer and find it one of the principal mainstays of their lives. Seek the side of some aged Christian and put the question as to his belief in prayer, and you will immediately receive the answer that a large part of his life rests upon daily communion with God, and that very many of his petitions, presented in the name of Jesus, have been answered. There are tens of thousands of good Christian people throughout this land who can testify to the efficacy of prayer. Very many of these believers make it a rule to honor God by acknowledging before the world the answers to their prayers. We would advise any one who doubts and who sincerely wishes to be helped, to drop all argument and apply the test to his own case, and then give God the glory before the brethren. We would not, however, advise any one to pray for mere material blessings, or worldly honors, or wealth or luxuries, but to pray in the right spirit and to study that he does not pray amiss. Every petition should be presented in Jesus' name.

459. What Does Redemption Do for Us?

"Ye are bought with a price," says Paul (I Cor. 6:20, 7:23). This price is the blood of Christ and he was sent to effect our redemption with it (Acts 20:28; Gal. 4:4, 5). And what were we redeemed from? From the bondage and curse of the law, the power of sin and of the grave, from all troubles, iniquity, evil, enemies, death and destruction (Gal. 4:5, 3:13; Rom. 6:18; Ps. 49:15, 25:22; Tit. 2:14; Gen. 48:16; Ps. 106:10, 11; Hos. 13:14; Ps. 103:4). This redemption procures for us justification, forgiveness, purification and adoption through the precious, plenteous and eternal power and grace of God (Rom. 3:24; Eph. 1:7; Gal. 4:4, 5; Tit. 2:14). To those who partake of it there is opened up a new life and existence, for they are the property of God, a peculiar people, are first-fruits of God and are sealed unto the day of redemption. They are zealous of good works, walk safely in holiness and shall return to Zion with joy (Is. 43:1; Rev. 14:4; II Sam. 7:23; Eph. 4:30; Eph. 2:10; Is. 35:8, 9; Is. 35:10). This redemption man cannot effect, nor can corruptible things purchase it, but it is the free gift of God by Christ.

460. What Is Regeneration?

Regeneration is being born again, and is the work of the Holy Spirit, by which we experience a change of heart. It is perhaps better expressed as being "born anew from above" (John 3:7), being "awakened" (Eph. 2:1), Christ coming into the heart (Gal. 4:19), "renewing of the mind" (Rom. 12:2), the "purifying" (Titus 3:5). Man is not the author of his own regeneration. The change consists in the recovery of the moral image of God upon the heart, leading us to love him supremely and serve him as our highest end. It is wholly the work of the Holy Spirit. The change is in the heart and the will—in our moral and spiritual faculties; and the natural faculties, being dominated by the will, while they may resist for a time, ultimately follow the change. The evidences of regeneration are conviction of sin, sorrow and repentance, faith, love and devotion to God. In regeneration we *receive* from God, whereas in conversion we *turn* to God.

461. Is Regeneration Different from the Baptism of the Holy Spirit?

They are part of one process—the work of the Holy Spirit. Regeneration is the new birth by which we experience a change of heart, and it is the work of the Holy Spirit. Titus 3:5 speaks of "the washing of regeneration." We are made members of the visible Church of Christ by baptism and renewed in the Spirit by the Holy Ghost. The "higher baptism," or the bestowment of the Spirit upon faithful believers, often differs greatly in degree, but it is identical in character and is the universal privilege of all Christians.

462. Is Remorse a Discipline?

We should bear remorse until by God's grace a happier state of mind is produced. You remember that significant record (Mark 14:72) about Peter's denial of Christ: "When he thought thereon he wept." When you rejoice over sin forgiven, and are overcome with wonder and gratitude at God's magnanimity in forgiving you, it is quite natural and proper that you should grieve that you had ever offended a Being so good and kind. The forgiveness should lead you to love God more than others do, and to rejoice in his marvelous goodness and mercy. It should also lead you to be very watchful against relapsing into sin, and to make great exertions to render service to One who has forgiven you. You should also be very tender and charitable toward others. Do not let remorse incapacitate you for labor, but rather operate as an incentive to service.

463. Where Is Restitution Taught?

See Matt. 5:26; Luke 16:10-12; Luke 19:8, 9; Rom. 13:8; Philemon 18. The Roman law (in Christ's day) directed a fourfold restitution, which explains Zaccheus' statement in Luke 19:8. His generous addition of "the half of his goods," though not demanded by the law, was evidently heard with approval of the spirit which prompted it. Moralists hold that we are bound to restore the thing owed, in kind, if possible, with the natural increase added. This seems to have been the view adopted by the early Christian Church.

464. Is It Right for a Christian to Retaliate?

A Christian should never retaliate; nor should he suffer himself to be imposed upon, when possible to avoid it. Between retaliation and the suffering of imposition, he should, however, accept the latter, if retaliation implies his committing any act of vindictiveness unbecoming a Christian. Our Lord's words upon the subject are plain. Read the fifth and eighteenth chapters of Matthew. St. Paul says repeatedly, "Love is the fulfilling of the law." Retaliation is contrary to the spirit and letter of this. But while we are told to love our neighbor as ourself, we are not told to love him better; and self-protection, in a wise and proper spirit, is a duty.

465. Should the Christian Work for Reward?

The New Testament makes it very clear that the motive of our work should be love for Christ, love that springs from gratitude for his salvation. But the Christian is also reminded of the great rewards that shall come to him in the future life if he is faithful and if his work is of a high order. Study particularly I Cor. 3:11-15. The thought of these rewards helps us to be faithful, constant, and careful. The conception of what the rewards will be varies with different stages of civilization. The best idea of these rewards seems to be that every good deed done is in itself the reward. Somebody was helped, was saved, was made glad, was given power and inspiration for helping others; these facts are eternal, and will bless forever those who are responsible for them. Then, too, the reward implies power to do still greater things. If there is joy in accomplishing things for the Master now there will be greater joy when we find ourselves furnished with the new, heavenly powers for doing still greater service. But more and more the Christian should train himself to keep his eyes and his heart fixed on Christ, eager to please him. He has called us into his friendship, into his fellowship, into co-operation with him in his great tasks. We must not disappoint him.

466. Is a Saved Person Sure of His Salvation?

Many good men of whose salvation there can be no question, have at times had doubts, and have suffered acute distress. In some cases the doubts have a physical origin resulting from a gloomy disposition. In others, they arise from too much introspection. In others again, because their conscience reminds them of sins not yet overcome. You must remember that you are not saved because of your feelings, but because Christ died for you. If you have sincerely repented, and are trusting entirely in Christ to save you, and are living in his strength a godly life, you have the right to thank God for saving you, in spite of your doubts. If you cannot take his word that those who come to him through Christ have eternal life, you should ask him to forgive you for doubting him. You may be quite sure that he will keep his promise, whether you have the joy of assurance or not.

467. What Is the Christian's Duty as to Sabbath Observance?

Paul gave this advice to people who were troubled by legalists in his day: "Let no man judge you in meat or in drink or in respect of . . . the Sabbath days" (Col. 2:16). In every generation since Christ and before his time, there were people who laid more stress on days and forms and ceremonies than on essentials. The Pharisees found it much easier to give tithes of their kitchen-gardens than to do justly and refrain from robbing widows and orphans. You as a

Christian are not under the law at all. When Gentiles were first admitted to the Church it was expressly declared that they were not required to observe the Jewish code of laws. The question came up at a solemn council at which the Apostles were present and was decided once for all. You will find the result of the discussion in Acts 15. In the name of the Holy Spirit the decision was given as stated in verses 28 and 29, and it was expressly stated that no other burden was laid upon them. They naturally and properly celebrated the day on which Christ rose from the dead, not the Jewish Sabbath, with which they had nothing to do, and we follow their example.

468. What Is the True Theory as to Sunday Observance?

The Sabbath was divinely ordained as a day of cessation from labor. In the Jewish Church, the restrictions were most rigid and profanation of the day was severely punished. It was a day of rest, reconciliation, worship and religious festivity. (See Is. 58:13, 14.) Christian Sabbath observance recognizes the same general obligation to abstain from regular vocations and to devote the day largely to rest and worship. Jesus himself rebuked the slavish Sabbatic restrictions of the Scribes and Pharisees, and showed them that the Sabbath was made for man, meaning that it was designed and instituted for our common humanity, and to conduce to our highest good. He pointed out that there were various acts which in themselves were not sinful, but meritorious, and such as might be done on the Sabbath. These were the works of necessity or of mercy. This is the attitude of the Christian Church of today on Sabbath observance (Col. 2:16). It may be briefly said that no labor should be performed on that day which can be done on secular days, and that works of charity and mercy are justified on that day. We have the divine example for abstention in Gen. 2:2, 3.

469. Is It Possible to Get Beyond God's Willingness and Power to Save?

There is none who can go beyond the reach of the Divine mercy. Jesus saves "to the uttermost" (Heb. 7:25). God will always hear and answer the prayer of the earnest, penitent heart. Christ's offering of himself was once *for all* who accept him; and his intercession, which is continuous, assures us that we cannot be separated from his love if we take him into our hearts and lives.

470. What Is the Way of Salvation?

It would probably disappoint if we answered in the Scriptural way: "Believe on the Lord Jesus Christ and thou shalt be saved." Yet that is the only true answer. Stripped of theological phraseology, the way of salvation may be described as committing your case to Christ, much as you would commit your case to a physician if you were sick, or your trouble to a lawyer if you were in danger of imprisonment. "Believing on him" is the complete trust you place in him and the profound conviction that he can and will save you. This is the decisive thing, the turning point. That done, several results flow from it. One is sorrow for sin previously committed and a renunciation of it for the future. A second is the endeavor, in the strength that Christ imparts, to follow his example, to cultivate his spirit, and to live his life of purity, holiness and helpfulness. This involves prayer and submission to his will in all things. Then you should join a church to confess him openly. There are other matters that will call for your attention as you go on, but these we have mentioned are the plain, simple duties that you have to do in order to become a Christian.

471. How, if God Worketh in Us, Must We Work Out Our Own Salvation?

There is no contradiction in the passage Phil. 2:12, 19. It is very true that we must work out our own salvation; and it is equally true that it is God who worketh in us. A certain part is ours to do, which God cannot do for us; another part is God's to do which we cannot do for him. In the first place we must do the believing. Mr. Moody used to tell how he prayed for faith until he noticed the passage: "Faith cometh by hearing, and hearing by the Word of God." Rom. 10:17. God has given the Word; we must do the believing. Again, God gives us the power, but we must use it. God may give his Spirit to enable a Christian to testify or to preach, but the Christian must use his lips and tongue and voice. God dwells in us and works in us and we have his power; but by using his power and accepting his help we increase our capacity for more, we gain mental, spiritual and physical strength and skill for our work. Our bodily life bears a perfect analogy to the spiritual life in this respect; God starts our hearts beating and keeps bestowing the gift of life. In this sense he dwells and works in us. But we must work and exercise that we may grow stronger and more efficient and accomplish the work we find to do.

472. How Are We to Accept Christ as Saviour?

Though salvation by faith is such a simple thing, many souls stumble at it. It seems too simple to be true, so they go about trying to find a harder way to be saved, and of course they do not find it because there is no other way. This is what we should say to every seeking soul: The first step toward Christ is to realize what it is that keeps you away from him, that is, your sin. Christ is very near you, nearer than your closest friend; but your sin separates your soul from him. You must confess your sin, acknowledge that you have sinned; you must repent of your sin, making restitution if you have wronged any one; you must determine to forsake your sin. But these things are not faith; they are only the necessary steps to faith. Faith is the definite belief that Christ died for your sins and that he actually forgives them now. "He tasted death for every man." If that is so, then he really, literally died for you. It is very easy to believe Jesus if you will just let yourself do it. Faith is an extremely simple thing; doubt is difficult. In your brain you know that he died "for every man." How can you doubt, then, that he died for you? You know that he died for the sins of the whole world; this must include you. Nothing in the history of the world is a surer, steadier fact than that Christ was crucified to save you from sin. The moment any one will stop doubting that fact and begin to believe it he will find peace, and find Christ. "Be not afraid—only believe." "Believe in the Lord Jesus Christ, and thou shalt be saved." Have you not proved that the way of doubt is hard and sad? Will you not try now the way of trust, and find how sweet and light and glad it is?

473. How Is the Distinction to Be Made Between the False Shepherd and the True?

The test that Christ gave (Matt. 24:24) whereby we may know the false prophets, and the true as well, is practical for every age. "By their fruits ye shall know them." The Scriptures specify the characteristics of the "false shepherd" in part as follows: They serve only themselves, mind earthly things, feign piety and sanctity, fear persecution, respecters of persons, deceitful workers, prophesy false peace, wrest the Scriptures, deny the Lord that bought them, preferring questions of vain philosophy to truths of Scripture, etc. The "true shepherd" preaches the Word that is able to save and build up; he watches for souls, seeks the wandering, reclaims in love those repelled by uncharitableness, is willing to make personal sacrifice, sympathetic, faithful in warning and reproving, tender in treatment of young and burdened Christians, persevering if by any means he may save souls. Thus it is grace, producing character, and not talents, that distinguishes the true from the false.

474. Does God Allow Satan to Punish Us with Sickness?

Do not make the mistake that Job's friends made, of assuming that sickness, trouble, or bereavement may necessarily be punishment. You will find a different theory, not in John only, but in Hebrews. The writer of that epistle says (12:5-11) that chastisement is sometimes to be regarded as a proof of God's love.

He evidently regarded it as being inflicted by God, but to be in the nature of discipline and education rather than punishment. On the other hand, Paul said his "thorn in the flesh" was the messenger of Satan (II Cor. 12:7). It does not make much difference to the sufferer whether God inflicts or permits Satan or men to inflict. In either case the affliction must be endured, and if it is borne with patience and equanimity, God is pleased, because then the world sees how his children love and honor him. The statement often made that all sickness and affliction are sent as a punishment is not true, but on the contrary, is a hideous libel on God and a cruel outrage on the sufferers. Sickness is sometimes a punishment for disregarding the laws of nature, but it is not God's punishment for sin. The book of Job was written to show how false and cowardly was the theory that those worst afflicted were the worst sinners. Job insisted and God confirmed him, that we have no right to infer that the afflicted man has been a heinous sinner. Christ also indignantly repudiated the idea (see Luke 13:2-4, and again John 9:1-3). Sickness often comes as a discipline to develop spirituality, to lead to greater faith and patience and sometimes to give an example of Christ's sustaining power. People have often wondered at the patience and endurance of the afflicted Christian and have gained from the spectacle a deep impression of the power of religion.

475. "Does Falling into Sin Prove that Conversion Has Not Yet Taken Place?"

That is not a reliable test. Unhappily, even converted men fall into sin at times. There is, however, this difference, that before conversion, sin occasions little if any sorrow, whereas after conversion it is sincerely mourned and deplored and God's help is sought not only for pardon, but for strength to avoid it in the future. There are many signs of conversion. One is that just stated in the soul's attitude toward sin. Another is love for Christ, through whom all blessings come. There is, too, an intense desire to know him and be like him and a complete dependence on him, and a resolve that if his will is recognized it shall be obeyed at any cost. There is also a change of feeling toward others, especially toward all who also love Christ. The soul that has been born again is full of love to men and women and there is a desire to render them service. These are among the most conspicuous signs of conversion, but they are not always all present at the beginning of the Christian life, but develop later.

476. If Past Sins Harass the Mind Is It Evidence that God Has Not Forgiven Them?

No, it is sometimes an evidence of lack of faith. But generally it arises from a very proper sense of the heinous nature of our sin. Though God forgives, and we rejoice in the fact and adore him for his marvellous magnanimity, we cannot forgive ourselves. There is a very touching expression in Mark 14:72 which intimates that Peter's memory of his denial of Christ was life-long: "When he thought thereon, he wept." The other Evangelists speak of his weeping at the time, but Mark, who probably knew him well in his later years, phrases it differently. Yet, though Peter may have continued to weep at the thought, he could never have had any doubt as to his being forgiven.

477. Are We Punished for Sins While Yet Here on Earth?

It might be difficult to prove that there is direct punishment, but experience proves that the results of sin are often very bitter and painful. Sometimes they are felt in the body, when the sins of youth bring on disease which lasts all through life. They are often seen in the cases of Christians who set a bad example before their conversion, and they grieve when they see young people, whom they led into evil, grow worse and worse. The results of the sin of neglecting the training of children are frequently very sorrowful. The child grows up and falls into sin, and then the parent suffers remorse, as he feels that if he had only done his duty before it was too late, the child might have been saved. In many other ways, by natural law, sin works its own punishment.

478. Does Willful Sin Exclude One from Pardon?

No; we firmly believe that there is no passage that excludes him from pardon. The writer of the Epistle to the Hebrews (who, by the way, was probably not Paul), simply taught that there was no further sacrifice for sin than that which had been offered in the person of Christ. (See Heb. 10:26.) He was writing to Hebrews, who, under the old dispensation, could bring another sin-offering when they sinned again. The Christian must revert to the cross, for there remained no other atonement, and if he put that away from him, he was without resource. The backslider who sincerely repents is encouraged to return and is sure of welcome. It is the one imperative duty he is bound to perform. Peter, who denied his Lord, was tenderly welcomed. The wicked member mentioned in I Corinthians, you will see if you look to the second epistle (2:7), was to be forgiven and comforted. As a father receives a beloved child, who goes to him with confession and repentance, so God will receive the Christian who has fallen, but has renounced his sin and humbly pleads for forgiveness through Christ.

479. How Does Religion Help One to Get Over a Besetting Sin?

There is first the direct power which God promises to give through Christ to those who sincerely and earnestly seek it. Then, there is the subjective power that comes from a soul turning decisively to God. This Chalmers called "The expulsive power of a new affection." It is an over-mastering impulse which leaves no room in the mind for the old enemy. When a man falls again under the power of the sin, he need not conclude that God has not given him the aid. He has more reason to think that the aid was given, but not used. Man must work with God in such a case and must not expect to be delivered without striving, but to be delivered through striving in the new strength that God gives him. But above all there must be firm belief in Christ and his redeeming love. A mere intellectual belief is not sufficient. As James remarks, "The devils believe." Belief in the sense of trusting, confiding, is required. It is the kind of belief that a patient has in his physician when, in a critical illness, he trusts his life to a physician and calls in no other. Or, as when a man charged with murder puts all his reliance on his lawyer and believes in his power to secure his acquittal. Or it is the belief of an outlaw who trusts to a ruler who has issued a proclamation of amnesty. The man who puts himself in Christ's hands for salvation will try to resist all evil and will obey Christ's commands and will seek from Christ the help he stands ready to give to enable him to lead a holy life.

480. Are the Regenerate Sinless?

In the regenerate, the higher nature, as begotten of God, does not commit sin (I John 3:9). This principle within him is at absolute variance with sin and makes him hate all sin and desire to resist it. Luther, referring to this condition, wrote: "The child of God receives wounds daily and never throws away his arms, or makes peace with his deadly foe." His life is a continual warfare against sin, but he is kept by divine power from falling, although if he even momentarily permit his spiritual weapons to lie idle, he will feel the sharp attacks of sin. The ruling principle of his life is God's law, but the old nature may sometimes rebel. The passage from Hebrews 27 does not conflict with this. The passage in Hebrews 6 was written to urge advancement in the spiritual life and to warn them that the decline of spiritual energies would inevitably lead to a "falling away" and perhaps to ultimate apostasy. The warning was addressed not to the elect but to the lukewarm, who had shown a temporary faith, only to be followed by indifference.

481. Are Children Punished for Parents' Sin?

There is in the minds of many a misunderstanding of Scripture on this point. (Ex. 20:5.) Good authorities hold that it does not mean that God punishes a man for the wrongdoing of his parents, but that he is punished by the acts of the parents themselves. It is inevitable that we should be affected by what our parents have done. We enjoy the privileges of our free country because these privileges were won by our forefathers; we have freedom of worship because they fought and suffered and died to secure it. Having received good, do not we inherit evil the same way? The children of a spendthrift must lack the good start in life that they might have had; the son of a father who has disgraced his name is under a reproach. That the character, habits and wickedness of an evil parent must influence his progeny is generally admitted. Natural laws cannot be escaped, and the characteristics of a progenitor may be traced sometimes through several generations. The children who were born in Babylon, suffered in exile because their fathers had deserted God. It is a law of the natural life that the results that flow from a parent's wrongdoing are entailed on his children; but the children are not held morally accountable for the sins of their parents.

482. Is Sinlessness Possible?

It frequently happens that confusion arises concerning the apparent conflict of statements in the passages in I John 1:8 and 3:9. In the first of these, every one is represented as sinning, and in the latter it is clearly stated that "Whoso is born of God cannot sin." To suppose that none who sin are begotten of God would exclude every one, as John himself admits in the first passage we quote. One explanation is that the writer is speaking of the divine nature implanted in the believer. It never commits or condones sin, but always protests against it. A second explanation is that the man who is begotten of God does not continue in sin. If betrayed by his fleshly nature into sin, he repents, seeks pardon, and watches against a repetition of it. However high the Christian may set his ideal as a follower of Christ, he realizes, after all, that his efforts are sadly short of the Great Exemplar and that his imperfections are beyond dispute. At the same time, he can be said truly to be no longer under the bondage of sin, since, having laid his burden on the Great Burden-Bearer, sin is no longer imputed to him.

483. Is Every Sin Willful and Thus Every Backslider Doomed?

The subject is discussed in Heb. 6:4, 5, 6, and Heb. 10:26, 27. In one sense every sin is willful, because the sinner would not do it without the consent of his will; but the word has another meaning. It implies a deliberate and intentional act, which is different from an act to which a man is lured or deceived, or an act which he commits under some sudden and strong temptation. There was, for example, a marked difference between the sin of Judas and of Peter. The Apostle Paul, too, bade the church at Corinth restore the wrongdoer who had been expelled (II Cor. 2:6-8). Be sure of this, that any backslider repenting and turning to God for pardon, resolutely putting his sin away, will be welcomed and forgiven (See Ezek. 33:14-16, and many other passages).

484. Are All Sins Pardonable?

Divine mercy extends to the uttermost. The invitation is that "whosoever will may come." The "unpardonable sin," which was frequently spoken of in the early days of the Church, is believed to have been attributing the works of the Holy Spirit to the powers of darkness. With this exception, there is nothing in the category of human offenses that is beyond the reach of divine forgiveness. "Although your sins be like scarlet, they shall be white as snow," is the ancient promise given by God to men; "though they be like crimson, they shall be as wool." This is not to be interpreted, however, as an encouragement to sin, but rather as an inducement to repentance. If the sinner truly repents, imploring God's forgiveness for Jesus' sake; if he accepts him as Saviour and endeavors, with divine help, to live thereafter a Christian life, he will not only be forgiven, but will be kept from falling back into sin. This is the teaching of the Gospel, and it is exemplified in innumerable cases today. We have many instances everywhere of great sinners who have forsaken their evil ways and who are now living the new life, sustained by divine power.

"There's a wideness in God's mercy
Like the wideness of the sea."

We have the Saviour's distinct assurance, "Him that cometh unto me, I will in no wise cast out." There is no punishment for sins that are forgiven. "Jesus paid it all."

485. Is the Unpardonable Sin Possible Today?

In ancient times, it was generally held that the unpardonable sin (Matt. 12:32) was attributing the works of the Holy Spirit to Satanic agency. If there be a modern counterpart of the unpardonable sin, we should think it is to be found in the case of the person who uses the livery of God to serve the devil in; who enacts the role of the shepherd of the sheep, while he is nothing but a ravening wolf in disguise; who assumes the attitude, language and demeanor of a saint while his exterior covers a heart black with sin and foul with guilt; who brings to the altar of God's house hands that are stained with crime, and who keeps up this show of religion and utters the language of Christian invitation while he himself is not a Christian. It is a terrible picture and one which is almost unimaginable in the case of any sane and responsible person.

486. Is It Sinful to Do What One Considers Wrong although There Is No Wrong About It?

That is Paul's teaching, as he particularly outlines and emphasizes it in Rom. 14; I Cor. 8 and I Cor. 10:23-33. He said himself that he did not consider it wrong to eat meat which might have been offered to idols (I Cor. 8:4, 8; I Cor. 10:25, 27), but that if he knew of any one who might be offended by his doing so he would eat no meat at all (I Cor. 8:13). In Rom. 14:20 he says: "All things indeed are pure, but it is evil for that man who eateth with offense"—that is, for the man who eats, even though it troubles his conscience. The same thought is in Rom. 14:23: "Whatsoever is not of faith is sin." But our reason bears out this New Testament teaching; we know that it is wrong for a man to do something which he believes to be wrong. The whole spirit of the New Testament is away from legalism and toward a spontaneous, affectionate eagerness to please God and serve our neighbor.

Where no command or prohibition is specified, each Christian is left free to follow his own enlightened conscience. To violate this is sin.

487. Is It Natural or Unnatural to Sin?

Judging by the prevalence of sin and the early age at which children usually begin, we should say it was natural. David seemed to have that opinion (see Ps. 51:5). It was not much better before the fall. Adam and Eve do not appear, according to the account in Genesis, to have made much resistance to temptation. The fact of its being natural accounts for a new nature being necessary, as Christ explained to Nicodemus (John 3:1-21).

488. How May We Win Souls?

"How can I win souls" is a frequent question from beginners in Christian life. They remember the injunction: "He that winneth souls is wise." (Prov. 11:30.) The first impulse which comes to the newborn soul in Christ is to tell some one else of the glad experience and to bring some one else to the Saviour. The first requisite for the work of soul-winning is to have a definite experience which makes its possessor long to have others share it. The most important element of soul-winning is simple testimony to the grace of God. There must be consistent and careful living, for it is difficult or impossible to win others to Christ when one's own life does not exemplify the teachings of the Master. The Bible must be mastered by one who would be a successful soul-winner. He must have in his mind, or be able to reach quickly, passages which will meet the difficulties of those whom he tries to win.

There must be also a sympathetic study of human nature. The soul-winner must understand the workings and problems of the hearts and minds he tries to reach. Then, there must be continued activity. Mr. Moody made it a rule to speak definitely to at least one person about his soul's welfare every day. Above all, the power of the Holy Spirit must be sought and found to give wisdom and power, by which alone real success in soul-winning is to be found.

489. Is a Christian Justified in Suing to Recover a Loan?

It depends upon circumstances. If his debtor is able but refuses to pay, there is nothing in Christ's meaning to prevent the Christian from appealing to law to recover what is justly his, after all peaceable means have failed. The Revised Version of Luke 6:35 reads, "Lend, never despairing" (margin, "despairing of no man"). We are to be kind to those of whom we can expect no return in sort. God will repay us, though man does not. "It is meant of the rich lending to the poor a little money for their necessity to buy daily bread or to keep them out of prison; in such a case we must lend with the resolution not to demand interest for what we lend, as we may most justly from those that borrow money to make purchases withal or to trade with; but that is not all, we must lend though we have reason to suspect that what we lend we lose; lend to those who are so poor that it is not probable they will be able to pay us again. This precept will be best illustrated by that law of Moses (Deu. 15:7-10) which obliges them to lend to a poor brother as much as he needed, though the year of release was at hand."

This is an old commentator's explanation, but it is good and true.

490. Does Temptation Come from God?

Human nature is weak and temptations to wrongdoing are abundant. Occasionally we hear, at a church meeting, or elsewhere, some dissatisfied soul complaining that he has been tempted and he is disposed to lay the blame for his condition on the Heavenly Father. Now, God does not tempt any one. He permits us to be placed in positions where, if left to our own resources, we would fail; but he does not tempt us to evil, and if we call for his aid, we will assuredly receive it. It is the evil spirit within us and the evil influences about us that bring us into temptation. In I Cor. 10:13 and James 1:13 it is explicitly stated that while God may permit us to be tested, he is not the tempter, and that he "tempts no man." The withdrawal of the Holy Spirit exposes us to temptations by leaving the heart open to the attack of the tempter; but nothing is more erroneous than to assume that temptation, or the placing of any agent in man's spiritual path which may cause him to fall, comes from God.

491. Is It a Sin to Be Tempted?

We are not responsible for our temptations, but for yielding to and encouraging them. The sin consists in asquiescence. Christ himself was tempted. God tempts no man, but the evil spirit in our own hearts tempts us. If you will ask God, in Christ's name, to free you from these temptations and to purify your mind and heart, the temptations will have no power over you. They will come again and again, but will retire baffled and defeated. It is the only way. Christ's prayer (taught to his disciples), is better interpreted: "Abandon us not in temptation" (the power of the tempter), and not "remove us from temptation." It is a part of our earthly discipline.

492. What Are Tithes?

The question of tithing has been frequently discussed and is ever a fruitful one. A tithe is a tenth of the increase over and above all administrative expenses and not a tenth of the principal. In early days, when agriculture was the almost universal calling, it was generally a tenth part of the produce of the land or the flocks. Later it became a tenth of the profits of personal industry of any character. (See Deu. 14:22, 28, 16:12; II Chron. 31:5, etc.) There is evidence, however, that at certain times it may have meant a tenth of one's entire possessions. The modern interpretation would limit it to a tenth of the increase. There are many good people who still hold that a tenth of one's income should be set aside for the Lord's work. Under the ancient Jewish economy, tithing was regulated by a code of laws which were amplified and made still more complex by the rabbins; but under Christianity, the supreme law of love has been substituted and is applicable to the tithing problem quite as well as to others. We are to give according as God has "prospered us," and from a generous and loving heart. One who wishes to tithe his estate should reckon on the increase in value, or number, or whatever form his available assets may assume, excluding of course the necessary expenses of conducting his business. As to household expenses, these are elastic, and one's domestic and personal expenditures are liable to increase with every augmentation of income, such increase frequently being one of extravagance rather than of necessity. It is quite conceivable that the whole income might be thus swallowed up. But if we act conscientiously, we will not "rob God" by multiplying our expenditures until nothing is left for his work. "The liberal soul shall be made fat," and this especially applies to the character of our gifts to God's work. While we are not to devote to that work money which we may rightfully owe to our creditors, we can exercise self-denial in many things, so that our tithable "increase" (or, if no increase, then our surplus over and above all proper expenses) may be such as to assure a liberal gift to the cause of religion.

God is a creditor, too. A very large per cent. of the people of the United States are in debt. Surely, it would not be right for them to stop all payments to the church and to charity till they are out of debt. While they and their families are getting the benefits of the church they ought to pay their church dues just as they pay their taxes and their rent. Your creditors would not expect you to neglect to pay for the food which your body needs; they should not expect you to neglect to pay for your soul food. Remember, however, that a tithe is required not on the gross earnings or income, but on the "increase." Certain fixed charges may be deducted before the earnings are tithed. What items are to be included in this deduction, as well as all tithing, must be left to the enlightened conscience.

When Jesus stood by the treasury, he called attention to the fact that while the rich had cast in gifts of their superfluity, the poor widow had done better than they, for she had cast in "all her living" as a love offering, and it was an acceptable one. If we are to lavish all our prosperity on ourselves and our families, leaving nothing for the Lord's work, may we not be "robbing God"? Practically all of the difficulties involved in the problem would be solved if we followed the method of many Christians, who have been rich both in prosperity and good works. They gave freely from the *increase* of their wealth which remained after absolutely necessary business expenses were covered, making the Lord a partner in all that remained. They did not ask themselves how much they need give to meet the requirements, but rather how fully and generously and gratefully they could show their love in making their gift for Jesus' sake. An offering we do not feel, and which is simply of our surplus, is a gift of comparatively little worth, no matter how large the sum, while one that involves self-denial and even sacrifice, given with a cheerful heart, is rewarded with blessing. Still, the spirit in which we give is what counts. We should not plan so that our gifts to God return to ourselves or inure to our material benefit. Whatever is given to the Lord's work, whether administered personally with our own hands or through the church or its subsidiary organizations, or through any other channel, should be put wholly away from us so that we cannot derive any material benefit from the outlay. It is not giving to the Lord at all, if we attach a string to the gift.

Kindness and humanity, the voluntary outpourings of a generous heart, are always pleasing in God's sight. Zaccheus was commended by Jesus no less for his liberality in giving half his goods to the poor than for his justice and integrity. His abounding charity covered many shortcomings, and his obedience to law and his firm hold on Abraham's faith as evidenced by works were both appreciated; but it was his faith in Christ as Lord that led to his salvation (see Luke 19:9, 10). Even with the utmost liberality, we cannot buy heaven; yet no kind act, no generous gift, is unrewarded. We should give as freely as our hearts prompt and our circumstances permit. All wealth is a trust to be used for the highest purposes, and our use of our means and influence here will unquestionably have its effect in determining our reward hereafter.

493. In What Sense Are We to Understand Scriptural "Inspiration"?

In II Tim. 3:16 the statement is clear that the Scripture is given by divine inspiration—that the perceptions and work of the writers were divinely influenced. The Holy Spirit filled the hearts of those men with a message and led them to write that message for the world. This is what inspiration means. The inspired writers were holy men, prophets, evangelists and spiritual leaders who lived close to God and were in constant communication with him through prayer and meditation, and who, by their hearts and lives thus consecrated, were endowed with the power to convey to men his Word, sometimes in one form, sometimes in another. They were the chosen channels of divine communication, interpreting God's purposes in authoritative language, which could be understood by those for whom it was intended.

494. Did Jesus Baptize?

Whether our Lord personally baptized has been doubted. The only passage which may bear on the question is John 4:1, 2, the explanation of which is presumed to be that John, being a servant, baptized with his own hand, while Christ as Lord and Master "baptized with the Holy Ghost," demonstrating the outward symbols through his disciples. Whether he baptized personally or not, the fact remains that, during his earthly ministry, baptism was the accepted mode of entering his service.

496. What Is the Bible Teaching about Usury?

The most radical reference to money lending is that of Christ himself (Luke 6:35), "Do good and lend, hoping for nothing again." But it must be remembered that the words were spoken to a people very differently situated from ourselves. In our society the convenience of loans at interest is a benefit to lender and borrower alike. If the practice of taking interest were absolutely forbidden, both borrower and lender would suffer, as the capitalist would be little likely to lend money if he had no compensation, and the borrower would be unable to get the capital he needs for carrying on his business. The general tenor of Bible teaching seems to be that the lender has no right to take advantage of the borrower's necessities to exact more than a fair rate of interest. Many loans are in the nature of a limited partnership, and the borrower is simply paying the lender a share of the profit he makes out of the capital supplied by the lender, which is a legitimate transaction. References to usury in the Old Testament are found in Ps. 15:5; Nehem. 5:11; Prov. 28:8, and Leviticus 25:35-37.

497. How Can Christians Justify War?

How do you think Joshua, Gideon, David and other Old Testament saints felt about it? Do you suppose they did not know of the commandment "Thou shalt not kill"? They do not appear to have found any difficulty in reconciling their duty with it. Samuel could scarcely have been ignorant of it, yet he did not hesitate to hew a man to pieces in cold blood (I Sam. 15:33); Saul was blamed for sparing him, as Ahab afterwards was blamed (I Kings 20:42) for similar lenity. Elijah appears to have been a good man, yet he butchered 450 men (I Kings 18:40) in spite of the Commandment, "Thou shalt not kill." If you insist on literal obedience to the Commandment, we do not see how you can justify the butcher in his trade, since the Commandment (Exodus 20:13) does not limit the prohibition to human life. The ablest authorities agree that the Commandment is to be understood in its spirit. It prohibits murder, in the sense in which the word is commonly used. It does not prohibit wars of defense or war in a righteous cause. Men like Washington, Havelock and Chinese Gordon, and Stonewall Jackson, were conscientious men and eminent Christians, yet they went to war without compunction when their duty required it. On the other hand war is universally acknowledged as an evil and the logical outcome of evil conditions. It is the duty of the Christian to make war on war and to hasten to bring about peace with all men. The ideal condition is that which is pictured in Is. 2:4.

498. Why Were Women Commanded to Keep Silence in the Churches?

In I Corinthians 14:34 Paul was dealing specifically with the case of a church which he himself had founded. He had received intelligence from the household of Chloe, a pious member (see 1:11), that serious schisms had arisen and that advice was sorely needed. From other sources he had learned that the church had sunk into corruption and error. Apparently four distinct factions had sprung up, all quarreling over their respective teachers. There was much bitterness in the situation, and, besides, he had learned that immorality and disorderly practices had crept in; also that their meetings were brought into disrepute by the women appearing in them unveiled (in defiance of the common usage among decent women of that time) and that the feasts of the church were often scenes of gluttony and excess. His epistle was written to correct these disgraceful conditions, to set matters right, to rebuke the offenders and to set before them all anew the essentials of the Gospel. We can only infer, from the general contents of the entire epistle, that certain women who had been active in fomenting the trouble had merited a share of his chastening message, which doubtless produced the desired effect. Elsewhere in the Epistles we find full recognition of the character and abilities of Christian women, although it is unquestioned that they did not in those days take as prominent a part in religious affairs as they did later. Thus, for instance, there is no mention of women in Acts 2:16-18, but this does not necessarily imply their exclusion. There are many passages in the New Testament which show that godly women had a good share in the activities of the early church, but it was not customary for them to teach or preach (see Acts 16:40, 17:12, 17:34, etc.). Paul's injunction was not intended as a message to all the churches, but to the one particular church at Corinth, and it is a mistake and a grievous injustice to apply it to women in general. They have borne too noble and useful a part in the progress of the Christian religion to be subjected to any needless criticism that could only be based on a misunderstanding as to the actual conditions in the Corinthian church which rendered such a message necessary. There are many instances of godly women in both the Old Testament and the New Testament. The ministry of Jesus was to both men and women equally. Many of his most devoted followers were women. They were the last to comfort him on the way to Golgotha, the first to visit his tomb and the first to whom he appeared at his resurrection. So why should good women today be excluded from taking part in any Christian activity?

499. Is It Seemly to "Make a Gladsome Noise" in Worship?

Christianity is a religion less of the head than of the heart, and it is not surprising that the joy of the heart should find expression in songs and even at times in shouting. These are the natural, unrestrained outlets of a soul filled with deep religious fervor and spiritual gladness. Scripture literally teems with invitations to God's people to such expressions of feeling. Ezra 3:13 tells of the "noise of the shout of joy" at the laying of the foundations of the Temple. In Psalm 33:3, the congregation is urged to sing new songs and make a "loud noise," and in Is. 42:10, we read "let them shout and declare his praise"; Job 38:7 relates that the "sons of God shouted for joy," while Psalm 65:13, describing the condition of the righteous who had been blessed with prosperity, says, "they shout for joy . . . they also sing." "Let them that put their trust in thee rejoice," says the Psalmist (Ps. 5:11), "let them shout for joy." In marked contrast is the picture in Is. 16:10, of the unrighteous from whom the Lord has turned his face, "There is no singing, neither shall there be any shouting." Surely the Christian who feels his heart overflowing with joy and gratitude to God, has the best of all warrants for publishing his gladness to the world, if he be so minded. We quite understand, however, that there are many natures so quiet and reserved that they do not relish any exuberance and prefer to be moderate in their manifestations. In a majority of cases, religious enthusiasm is a matter of temperament, each kind proper in its own place.

500. What Precedent Does the Scripture Furnish for Solos, Duets and Choir Singing in Church?

In I Cor. 14:26, Paul, referring to the forms of worship of the Corinthian church, wrote: "When ye come together, every one of you hath a psalm, etc." This verse, especially when read in connection with verse 15, "I will sing with the spirit and I will sing with the understanding also," implies that certain members sang alone. Tertullian and Augustine refer to this custom: "Every one," says Tertullian, "was invited in their public worship to sing unto God according to his ability, either from the Scriptures or one indited by himself." These songs were often extemporaneous. From the time of the Song of Miriam, who either sang alone in response to the other women, or led off their singing (Ex. 15:20, 21) there have been special singers and groups of singers to lead the music in the worship of God. The organization of the ancient Hebrew choirs was very elaborate. (See II Sam. 6:5; I Chron. chapters 15, 16, 23, 25, etc.) The congregation of Israel was so enormous that it was difficult if not impossible for all the people to sing at once; and the songs were learned first by the great choirs and must have been sung first by them before the people learned them; but there is no reason for believing that all the congregation joined in all the songs. Many consecrated Gospel singers are rendering acceptable worship and service to God in solos, duets, quartets and choruses. One is undoubtedly right in holding that such music should be really spiritual, should be sung without show, simply, clearly, earnestly to the glory of God. The body of church singing should be by the congregation as a whole, but the special solos and choir numbers also have their place.

TEXTS, FAMILIAR AND OTHER

---

501. What Is Conveyed in the Statement that "God Is No Respecter of Persons"?

It may seem peculiar for Peter to have made this statement (Acts 10:34, 35) as to the vast majority of reverent minds it goes without saying. But to Peter, brought up as he had been among Pharisees and Sadducees and other religionists of the Old Dispensation, whose central belief was that God *was* a respecter of persons, the discovery of the great truth that God cares for all alike, came as a great awakening. The Pharisee who loved the uppermost seats in the synagogues and greetings in the market-places; who deliberately shunned contact with a publican, a woman or a Gentile, represented that self-righteous and exclusive Judaism in which no one else counted, but in which he was a favorite of the Most High. This exclusive Judaism Peter annihilated with the one sentence of the text, and thereby established the belief in that great, universal Fatherhood which, while it is all to all, is especially kind to the lowly and the meek; which watches even a sparrow and numbers even the hair of our heads. And because of this universal Fatherhood, everyone in every nation "that feareth him and doeth righteousness" is acceptable to him. He makes no distinctions of creeds, of theologies, of usages and customs, of observances and differences of opinions.

502. In What Sense Is It True that "The Lord Giveth and the Lord Taketh Away"?

When we use the customary phrase that God takes away any of our friends from this world, it is simply a familiar form of acknowledging submission to his will as the Disposer of all things. Life and death are in his hands. There is nothing irreverent about such an expression. All our blessings come from him and if trial and discipline also come we should accept them in the proper spirit. We should learn to bow to his will, even though it may sometimes try our hearts sorely to do so.

503. What Is Meant by the Passage "Seek Ye the Lord While He May Be Found"?

It is a wholesome warning that a probable contingency may arise when the seeker, who postpones his search, may lose his power or disposition to seek. There are many instances of men who have put off seeking until they have made a fortune, or done something else, and then the time they set, having arrived, discover that business habits and long-time associations absorb them. They are out of touch with God. Even in church their thoughts are running on worldly concerns. It is very rare for an old man who has been indifferent, or careless, or wicked, to turn to God. Not that God is unwilling to be found, but the man has become incapable of seeking him. None who really seek ever fail to find.

504. What Is the Parallel between Christ and Adam?

"As by the offense of one, judgment came upon all men to condemnation, even so by the righteousness of one the free gift came upon all men unto justification of life" (Rom. 5:18). In this passage, Paul is comparing the influence of Adam and Christ. His argument begins with verse 12: "By one man sin entered into the world, and death by sin." (Dr. Denny says: "By Adam the race was launched upon a course of sin.") Paul goes on to state that sin was in the world before the written law was given, but declares that sin is not counted as sin where there is no law. God does not condemn a man for breaking a law of which he is ignorant. But even where sin was not imputed, death reigned, because death had come into the world as the result of Adam's sin, and became a universal experience, affecting even those who broke no specific and plainly stated command, as Adam did. But the grace that comes from Christ is even greater than the doom that came through Adam. One man sinned, and many were condemned; grace, through Christ, pardons many sins. Death reigned because of one man; now abundance of life and grace reign by one, Jesus Christ (verse 17). Verse 18 (quoted above) sums up what has gone before. Adam's disobedience made many men sinners; Christ's obedience shall make many righteous (verse 19). The law was given so that sin might be revealed. Sin was in the human heart, but men did not realize what it was till the law came. The law showed them that they were disobeying God. "But where sin abounded, grace did much more abound;" there was sin for everybody, there is grace for everybody—and more grace than sin. The reign of sin brings death; the reign of grace brings eternal life.

505. What Is Meant by "As Many as Were Ordained to Eternal Life Believed"?

This passage in Acts 13:48 has been much discussed. Those Gentiles did not all become believers, but only those in whom the preaching of the apostles had awakened faith and who, being taken into the congregation, had striven earnestly to "make their calling and election sure." It forcibly reminds us that salvation is the gift of God and not in any sense something we can obtain by our own merit or acts; but at the same time, in order to attain this gift (which is divinely ordained to all those who comply with certain conditions), we must put ourselves in the attitude of faith and belief. Further, throughout the whole Scriptures, there is a pervading sense of the fact that many are specially called to be saints and to perform a certain work, who are obedient to the summons and yet who were not in such attitude before. The case of Paul is an illustration in point. He was called right out of the midst of his sinful life of persecution. Some commentators hold that in the case of these Gentiles, God had chosen for himself certain men to become witness-bearers and to be set apart for a special work. Still other translators make the passage read: "As many as disposed themselves to eternal life believed," referring to I Cor. 16:15. We may add, by way of further explanation, that while the call to salvation is a universal one, the call to *special service* is one that comes only to the few.

506. Did the Baptist Doubt Jesus' Messiahship?

John's message, asking through his disciples whom he sent to Jesus, "Art thou he that should come, or look we for another?" (Matt. 11:3), was the result of impatience, almost of desperation. It must have seemed hard to him that his Master should let him lie so long in prison, after having been honored to announce and introduce him at the beginning of his mission. He tried to get Jesus to speak out his mind, or at least to set his own mind at rest. The conclusion of the incident, however, shows that his transient doubts were set at rest by the message he received.

507. What Is Meant by "Buy the Truth and Sell It Not"?

The passage in Prov. 23:23—"buy the truth and sell it not"—is not to be interpreted as meaning that both the buying and selling must be wrong. On the contrary, the meaning is that we should get the truth, whatever it may cost us, and that we should not part with it for any consideration, money, pleasure, fame, etc., for it is more precious than all of these. (See Prov. 4:5-7.) The inspired teacher urges us to get the principal thing, the truth, wisdom, understanding; the world's motto is: "Get riches and with all thy getting get more."

508. Are Any by Nature "Children of God"?

There is a large and true sense in which all mankind are children of God. Paul could say to the idolaters at Athens, "We are also his offspring." But there is a higher, closer, nearer sense in which regenerated men only are God's children. John says: "To as many as received him, to them gave he power to become the sons of God." Speaking pointedly to believers, he says, "Beloved, now are we the sons of

God." So there is no discrepancy between Paul and John. The one is speaking of God's children in the large human sense, while the other speaks of them in the restricted, adopted sense. We have, in fact, to recognize four grades of sonship. In the lowest grade there is the whole human family. In the next higher grade we have the regenerated children, who are really children in the spirit. Then in the next grade, we have the angels, who in the Book of Job are specially designated the "Sons of God" (38:7). Then, highest of all, in a sense absolute, unapproachable, divine, we have Jesus Christ, pre-eminently God's own Son. There is no need, therefore, to stumble at the doctrine of the Fatherhood of God; only we need to distinguish between what is implied in the more outward and the more inward relationship.

509. Why Is There No Remission of Sin without the Shedding of Blood?

The thought of a sacrifice for sin underlies the whole message of the Bible. The fact that John 3:17; John 8:11, 12 and other promises do not specifically refer to this does not violate in any way the broad, general principle. The Bible as a whole states the method by which God undertakes to save people from sin. The Old Testament, in law and ceremony and prophecy, looks forward to a great sacrifice that is to be made, of which the sacrifice of animals is but a type. The Epistles of the New Testament explain how the sacrifice of Christ may be applied by faith to the human soul. The Gospels tell the story of the life of the Saviour and give with great detail and fulness the account of his sacrificial death. He himself said distinctly of his death (Matt. 26:28), "This is my blood of the new testament, which is shed for many for the remission of sins." Read with special care the 9th and 10th chapters of Hebrews, the 5th and 6th chapters of Romans; I John 1:7, and the many other passages which state clearly that salvation from sin is wrought by the sacrifice of Christ. The fact of the atonement underlies all the promises of Scripture. It seems idle, as well as dangerous, to speculate whether there may be or might have been some other way of salvation. This way fits in with our knowledge of nature and of life, and has been testified to by multitudes of redeemed souls. We *know* that through the blood of Christ salvation from sin can be found; we certainly do not know that it can be found in any other way.

510. What Is Meant by "Crucify the Son of God Afresh"?

Heb. 6:4-6 is interpreted to refer to those who having begun the spiritual life, instead of persevering toward perfection, allowed themselves to fall away or backslide. Such having already had knowledge of the word of truth and having experienced a measure of peace in the pardoning love of Christ and the bestowal of the gift of the Holy Spirit (though not in all fulness) were doubly to blame for falling away. Paul did not assert that the Hebrews themselves had yet so fallen, but he warned them that if they did not persevere in going on to perfection, they would retrograde and would need to be "renewed" over again. It is the deliberate apostate, however, who sins in the light of knowledge and crucifies Christ anew whom he holds up as an object of execration. The elect abide in Christ and do not fall away, and he who abides not is "cast forth as a withered branch." The marginal reading of verse 6 in the Revised Versions makes this passage harmonize with the whole spirit of the Bible. It is impossible to renew them to repentance *"the while* they crucify the Son of God afresh."

511. What Is Meant by "Laying Aside Every Weight"?

The passage in Heb. 12:1 means that we are to personally apply discipline, and with divine help to thrust from us all temptations to carnal and worldly indulgence, which would impede our progress in the spiritual race. These obstacles are of the character mentioned in Mark 9:42-48; Eph. 4:22; Col. 3:9, 10. In practical terms, we should include undesirable and unprofitable amusements, doubtful associates, foolish pride, habitual ill-nature or worry, planning things far ahead, striving for social show for appearance's sake, deceitfulness, gossip, profanity, exaggeration or untruth—in a word, the "familiar sins," and especially the one which does "so easily beset us," whatever it may be. All of these act as chains and drags to hold us back.

512. Why Did David Say He Had "Not Seen the Righteous Forsaken nor His Seed Begging Bread"?

The psalmist (Ps. 37:25) simply stated his own experience. He had never seen it. He did not say it never occurred. If it did not occur in his day, it does in ours. It ought not, and God never designed that it should. There is enough wealth in the world to provide food and clothing and shelter for all, but under our present system some get more than their share, and others suffer and some starve. If a good man, though he be the seed of the righteous, acts imprudently, or is wasteful, or speculates unwisely, God does not interfere to keep him from ruin.

513. Is It Possible for One to Be Over-righteous?

Commentators interpret the phrase "righteous overmuch" (Ecc. 7:16) as descriptive of religious presumption; of that self-made righteousness which would lay the greatest stress upon outward performances and would claim personal credit for results which the true believer recognizes as the gift of divine grace alone. Pharisaism, with its hypocritical assumption of superior virtue, its multitudinous observances and its devotion to form and ceremonial, forgetting the "things of the spirit," was the type of the over-righteous.

514. How Was the Term Saint First Applied to the Evangelists?

During the early days of the Christian Church, there was no authoritative use of the word "Saint" as a title. Wherever the word occurs in our New Testament, it simply means a "devout person," one who has been sanctified and specially consecrated. After the early Christian era, however, the martyrs and apostles were considered as having attained to the dignity of sainthood, although there was no formal canonization until the ninth century A. D., when the Church of Rome introduced formal canonization with special ceremonies. There is no definite rule in the Protestant Church on the use of the title "Saint." The modern Jews have their saints, as well as the Catholics, and the appellation they use is "Kadosh." Their most celebrated saint is Rabbi Judah Hak-kadosh ("Rabbi Judah the Holy"). Protestant writers are not as consistent as they ought to be in this matter, some applying the title and others not at all. The observance of saints' days applies specially to the Roman and the Oriental Catholic Churches. In the Russo-Greek Church the observance of such days has been carried to extremes and they are so numerous as to interfere seriously with business. Under the influence of the Church of Rome in America, saints' days are becoming numerous among Catholics here also.

515. What Are We to Understand by "Time and Chains Happeneth to Them All"?

You are not to take all the words of Ecclesiastes 9:11 as true and inspired because, as the writer shows, he found out that what he said at one time was disproved later on. He is relating his experience. He was seeking happiness, with everything in favor of his succeeding. At first he believed he would find it in pleasure, afterward in learning, and later in other ways. And he tells how he found again and again that he had been mistaken. In this particular passage he means that the misfortunes of life are just as likely to happen to the wise and good as to the foolish. We know it is so. In a railroad accident, for instance, a clergyman or a philanthropist does not escape simply because of his life being beneficent.

516. What Is Meant by "Cast Thy Bread Upon the Waters"?

The illustration in Ecclesiastes 11:1 is taken from the custom of sowing seed by casting it from the boats into the overflowing Nile, or in marshy ground. When the waters recede, the grain in the alluvial soil springs up. "Waters" expresses multitudes, whose seemingly hopeless character as recipients of charity may turn out better than we anticipate, so that our gift would prove at last not to have been thrown away. The day may be near when we ourselves may need the help of those whom we have bound to us by kindness.

517. What Does Paul Mean in Rom. 5:7?

"For scarcely for a righteous man will one die; yet peradventure for a good man some would even dare to die" (Rom. 5:7). The apostle is illustrating the fact of the Atonement by the facts of everyday life. He says it is hard to find one man who will die for another, even if that other be righteous; but that for a man who is really *good* (a stronger, warmer word than *righteous*) some might be found who would be willing to die. Then follows the keen application: Though we were neither good nor righteous, yet Christ died for us.

518. What Is Meant by "Where There Is No Vision the People Perish"?

"Vision" (Prov. 29:18) means communion with God and the revelation of his will. When communities or nations get out of touch with God and cease to know his will, they begin to perish. The Hebrew verb means to become "dissipated" and "unbridled" and so perish

—in a word, to lose sight of moral and spiritual ideals, as a nation or community. Individual Christians and the organized church should be constantly seeking a clearer sight of God, closer communion with him, and a more perfect understanding both of his revealed will in the Scriptures and his providential will in present-day concerns.

519. What Is Meant by "All Things Work Together for Good to Them That Love God"?

This passage (Rom. 8:28) means that the events of life, including things that we call misfortunes, will be over-ruled to spiritual advantage. The Christian is not promised immunity from trouble, but that his troubles will tend to make him a better man. He is not encouraged to seek discipline, or to act recklessly, with the idea that howsoever an enterprise turns out, it will benefit him. But if after he has sought divine guidance and if after he has carefully considered a matter, it turns out disastrously, he is not to be cast down, but to expect that in some way God will make the disaster a blessing to him.

520. How Can "One Vessel Be Chosen unto Honor and Another unto Dishonor"?

This passage (Rom. 9:21, 23) brings up the discussion of the whole subject of "election." The Jews seem to have gotten the idea, from their long habit of exclusiveness, that God had no right to offer salvation to the Gentiles. Paul is here trying to make them see that God has a right to offer salvation to any one. No one can dispute the fact that just as the potter has the right to form one vessel for high and honorable use and another for more humble service, so God has the right to create some souls for prominent and important and honorable service and others for more lowly tasks. However we may interpret the doctrine of election, we must not for an instant forget that God is just. "He is not willing that any should perish." He desires that every soul should have salvation and that every soul shall be fitted for successful service.

521. What Did Paul Mean by "Delivering" an Offender unto Satan?

As the apostle himself states explicitly it was that the offender might be saved (see I Cor. 5:5). The man, a member of the Corinthian Church, had fallen into grievous sin, and was living a vicious life. Paul, hearing of it, decides that he must be excluded from the church. He repented, as the event proved, for in his second epistle Paul directs that he shall be tenderly received, lest he be swallowed up by over-much sorrow (II Cor. 2:7). The exclusion was leaving the man without means of grace, and Paul tells the object of it, namely, that the flesh, that is, the lusts and passions of his nature, might be purged from him, so that his soul might be saved. The casting of him out of the Church meant, in Paul's mind, the giving him up to punishment and the will of the enemy, not for his eternal destruction, but for temporary chastisement. Some commentators have thought that Paul's sentence included the infliction of some malady, which he certainly did inflict in another case (Acts 13:11), but that is not directly stated. The words imply discipline that would render the man less under the influence of his fleshly appetites. The man is put out of the church, the fold of God, temporarily, on account of his wrongdoing. It was probably so persistent and inexcusable that the apostle despaired of Christian influences effecting a change. He must be made to feel how wicked he was, and by the church expelling him they practically gave him up for the time. This was probably regarded as delivering him to Satan. They ceased to bring Christian love to bear upon him. In at least one case, it is thought, the discipline had a good effect, if, as is probable, the offender is the one referred to in II Cor. 2:6-8.

522. What Is Meant by Showing "The Lord's Death till He Come"?

This passage in I Cor. 11:26 has been variously discussed. Is it the Lord's presence, the coming to take away his followers by death, or his coming to judge the world that is here meant? The best expositors hold that the apostle clearly referred to the significance of the Lord's Supper as a perpetual memorial of the Lord's death, to be observed by the Church until the end of this dispensation, or in his own words, "till he come." It could not have had reference to the Lord's spiritual presence, or to the believer's death, as Paul implied that the "coming" would terminate the observance. It must have referred to the coming he describes in I Thess. 2:1-8 and other places, when Christ will appear to call his waiting people to himself, and afterward descend to destroy his enemies and set up his millennial kingdom on the earth.

523. What Did Paul Mean by "Caught Up to the Third Heaven"?

Paul was familiar with the learning of his age, and was a "master" in literary expression. He sat as a pupil "at the feet of Gamaliel," who was celebrated in the Talmudist writings as one of the seven teachers to whom the title "rabbin" was given. In II Cor. 12 (which contains the passage in question) Paul speaks of his vision when he was "caught up to the third heaven." In the Jewish teaching of the time, the first heaven was that of the clouds or the air; the second that of the stars and the sky, and the third was the spiritual heaven, the seat of divine glory. The word "heavens" is used in the Bible in varying senses, which must be gathered from the context, the most familiar being the visible heavens, as distinguished from the earth and as a part of the whole creation. (See Gen. 1:1.) Paul's "third heaven" was thus higher than the aerial or stellar world, and cognizable not by the eye, but by the mind alone. The word "world" is generally used in Scripture in the purely material sense to refer to the habitable earth and its people. The passages in Heb. 4:3, 9:26, 9:5, 11:7, 11:38, etc., have thus material significance. In John 14:2, however, many interpreters recognize an implied recognition of other worlds, the whole universe being a "house of many mansions."

524. What Are We to Understand by "Work Out Your Own Salvation"?

Grace is inactive without our will, hence the order as to "work." "Fear and trembling" simply mean the holy reverence which accompanies obedience (see Eph.

6:5; I Cor. 2:3; II Cor. 7:15); not slavish fear, like the terror of a mind in danger of condemnation, but anxiety to do what the Lord would have us do, and the realization that our own merits are insufficient and we must trust him to give strength for our weakness. The last clause of the sentence (verse 14) confirms this interpretation.

525. What Is Meant by Being "Baptized with the Holy Spirit"?

The Holy Spirit is received at conversion, but the baptism with the Holy Spirit is a further enduement, an experience which comes usually at some time after conversion. The disciples were regenerated men when Jesus told them to tarry in the city of Jerusalem until they should be baptized with the Holy Spirit (Acts 1:4-5). This was the experience to which he had previously referred as the coming of the Comforter (John 14, 15, 16). God's Spirit is constantly trying to get into a man's heart. He speaks to him in many ways, convicting of sin, urging to repentance, etc. The impressions leading to a wise and safe course of action, which a man may receive before he is converted, are really the messages of the Holy Spirit. God is very good, and tries to help us in every way. But it is not until one has become a child of God and received the fullness of the Spirit that he can expect to have the clear guidance of the Holy Spirit.

THE HEREAFTER

---

526. Were the Jews Taught to Look Forward to a Heaven or Hell?

From the first mention of the tree of life in Paradise, the eating of which would make immortal, the idea of a continued existence has had a place in Jewish theology. Many passages might be quoted to show this belief. See the Mosaic injunctions against necromancy, or the invocation of the dead, Deu. 18:9-12; I Sam. 28; Ps. 106:28 and other passages. Moses wrote that God "took" Enoch (Gen. 5:22, 24), because he had lived a pious life. David speaks of his child in another life when he says, "I will go to him, but he shall not return to me," (see II Sam. 12:23), Job says (Job 19:26 and 27) that he "will see God for himself and not another" in the future life. Ecclesiastes, which doubtless echoed faithfully the theology of that day, shows very clearly the belief in a spiritual life (Ecc. 12:7); see also the allusions in the Psalms (the Jewish Psalter) to expectations of reward and punishment after death (Ps. 17:15, 49:15, 16, 73:24, 26, 28). These and other passages which might be quoted, make it certain that the ancient Jews did believe in a future life; but it is equally certain that they had only dim and uncertain views on the subject, and that the full knowledge was not attained by any race or nation on earth until Christ himself came to "bring life and immortality to light."

527. Did There Exist a Belief in Immortality before the Christian Era?

Although before the dawn of Christianity there were nations who undoubtedly had glimpses of immortality, it was not until Christ came, "bringing life and immortality to light" (II Tim. 1:10), that the world began to realize the glorious future which was assured to those that love God and follow obediently the teachings of his Son. The Hindus, Egyptians, Chinese, Persians, and even the American Indians, Polynesians, Australian aborigines and Greenlanders believed in a future life, but all more or less dimly. The ancient Greeks had a clearer conception of immortality, which was well defined by Socrates in his last speech. There are hints of the same belief in the Jewish teachings also, although they are indefinite (see Gen. 5:22, 24, 37:35 and other passages). Jesus lifted the veil. Some, today, deny the inherent immortality of the soul, while admitting that it is conferred as the "gift of God" upon those who are accepted. The Church of Christ today, however, teaches immortality—a future life of bliss or of woe, to be decided at the judgment. The duty of Christians is, as Paul urges, to strive to "win the prize" and so to begin to live eternally, here and now, in the realization of God's pardon and acceptance promised through his Son.

528. What Does "Damnation" Mean?

Damnation, or condemnation, does not always imply the final loss of the soul. Thus the passage in Rom. 13:2 clearly means condemnation from the rulers, "who are a terror to evil-doers." I Cor. 11:29 means that the offender would be exposed to severe temporal judgments from God and to the censure of good men. Rom. 14:23 means that such a one is condemned already by the Word and by his own conscience. The final loss of the soul of the impenitent, however, is clearly taught in many passages, including Rom. 6:23; Matt. 25:41; Jas. 1:15; Matt. 10:28; II Thess. 1:9; Matt. 25:30; Luke 16:23, 26.

529. What of One Who Lives Nobly, yet Who Is Not a Christian?

He will not be as one who lived a purely selfish life, because he will not suffer those reproaches of conscience, which may be expected to torture the selfish man. If, however, he has heard the Gospel and rejected it, we do not see how he can expect recognition of, or reward from God on account of his good deeds. Christ said emphatically, "no one cometh unto the Father but by me." If, therefore, a man rejects Christ and takes his stand on his own merits, he plainly intimates that he considers his way better than God's way. He makes Christ's life and death, so far as he is concerned, unnecessary. If a man who is bringing a suit in a court wilfully and contemptuously ignores the rules of the court, he is not likely to be heard, no matter what are the merits of his case. So a man who rejects Christ puts himself out of court. We are not to judge, however, in such cases.

530. What Is the "Second Death"?

Spiritual, or "second death," implies "everlasting punishment" (Rev. 21:8)—the utter lack of all spiritual hope of restoration or reclamation. It means entire separation from God. Death, in the destructive sense, applies to the entire man and every part of his nature. We speak even now of men as "spiritually dead" while they yet live in the body, just as we speak of men who may be already in the grave, as "spiritually alive," and who shall never die. Spiritual death may begin even in this life. Death, therefore, need not imply extinction and annihilation. One commentator writes: "The proper life of the spirit lies in the harmony and subjection of its powers and disposition to the nature and will of God; its death in contrariety and enmity to him. This involves the disruption of a holy and dutiful relation with the Father of spirits, and by inevitable consequence a deprivation of the fruits of his love and favor on which life and blessedness depend. The whole man shall go away forever from the glory and joy of God's presence."

531. What Does Death Do to the Body!

When life ceases, the body as an individual organization is said to be dead; that is to say, death is the cessation of organic life. Matter, however, is indestructible; when it loses one form it appears in another. The matter of which the body is composed does not perish on the death of an organized being; it undergoes various changes which are known by the names of decay and putrefaction and which are the preparation for its becoming subservient to new forms of life. What becomes of the mind or thinking principle in man, otherwise the soul, is altogether a matter of religious faith or philosophic conjecture on which science has been unable to throw the slightest light. But it should not be forgotten that "there is a natural body and there is a spiritual body" (I Cor. 15:44). God has revealed the truth in the Bible, and particularly in the historic fact of Christ's resurrection, that the soul which is in harmony with himself will live forever. For the Scripture teaching concerning the resurrection of the body read I Cor. 15, which has been recognized from the earliest Christian times as the expression of the Christian's faith about the future life. Note particularly verses 35-44, 50-54.

532. Will Our Resurrection Bodies Rise with Us on the Judgment Day?

See this whole subject fully set forth in I Cor. 15th chapter. A vast amount of philosophic conjecture has been expended and many books have been written about it; but the fact remains that nowhere is it more clearly and comprehensively stated than in this chapter. The belief in the resurrection of the human body has apparently been fortified by the well-known passage in Job. 19:26, which in the old version was mistranslated, but is corrected in the Revised to read "yet without my flesh shall I see God." All the evidences go to show that while the body to be raised shall be such as to preserve identity, it will be a purified, changed and spiritualized body, with the grosser material elements removed or so transformed as to render them fit for heaven and immortality. It shall become a glorified body like unto that of Christ. (See I Cor. 15:49; Rom. 6:9; Phil. 3:21.) The bodies of those who are alive at the last day will undergo a similar miraculous purifying transformation without death (see II Cor. 5:4; I Thess. 4:15; Phil. 3:21).

533. Does a Person Go Directly to Heaven or Hell after Death?

There is no passage that asserts it explicitly. There are, however, passages from which the inference is made. One of these is the assurance of Christ to the dying thief on the cross (Luke 23:43), "This day shalt thou be with me in Paradise." Another is the Parable of the rich man and Lazarus (Luke 16:19-31), in which Dives is represented as being in torment and Lazarus in Abraham's bosom, while the five brothers of Dives were still alive on the earth. A third passage is Philippians 1:23, in which Paul says he desires to depart and be with Christ, implying that his death would give him that felicity, but he prefers to abide in the flesh because he can do good in the world. From these passages and a few others the deduction is made that there is no interval between death and the eternal state; but some eminent Christians now and in past times have thought that there is an interval long or short, and some that it lasts till the resurrection. In Matt. 22:31, 32; Mark 12:26, and Luke 20:37, 38, Christ insists that the righteous who are called "dead" are still alive. The appearance of Moses and Elijah with Christ at the transfiguration was an actual demonstration of this fact. Even at the very beginning of the Bible (Gen. 5:24), there is the implication that Enoch continued in another life the walk with God which he had begun in this. And Heb. 12:1, including all the faith heroes mentioned in the eleventh chapter, states that they are alive and conscious now, witnessing the conflicts of the saints still on earth. Many books have been written concerning the state of the soul between death and the resurrection. Catholics have the doctrine of purgatory, but the early Christians held no such belief. They believed that there was a judgment immediately after death and a final judgment later, and that in the intermediate state (not "place"), every believer's soul would find a foretaste of the greater joys to come. Some non-Catholic authorities have held that the soul after leaving the body remains inert until the resurrection. The best authorities, however, hold that it retains its active powers, and is assigned to a condition which is suited to its degree of spiritual development until the final change. Dr. Tuck points out that Hades, the abode of the departed, was regarded by the Hebrews as divided into two sections: one for the good; the other for the wicked. "Both together made up the abode of the dead"; one Paradise, the other Gehenna. Paradise was to the Jewish theologians a state of future bliss with lower and higher stages; yet it is not the final stage. See also II Cor. 12:4; I Pet. 3:19; II Cor. 5:6-8. On the other hand, there are passages that are capable of a different construction. See Job 7:21; Dan. 12:2; I Cor. 15:51; I Thess. 4:14. In these passages, it is probable that "sleep" may refer to the body and not to the spirit.

534. If the Saved Go Directly to Heaven after Death, Why a Resurrection Followed by a Judgment Day?

In dealing with spiritual things, one must guard against materialistic conceptions of the after life which prevailed previous to the Messianic advent. Only as associated with the physical and material is spirit cognizant of time and place. Jesus had to use these forms of speech in order to make his teachings comprehensible to the people; but on many occasions he strove to raise and enlighten their minds to a clearer spiritual understanding. God is Spirit, incomprehensible, indescribable. God is in heaven, yet God is everywhere, hence heaven is everywhere. See Matt. 6:33; Luke 17:20, 21; Luke 23:43 and other passages. From these it must be evident that by the term "heaven" is meant a state or condition of existence. Resurrection and final judgment were taught in Egypt centuries before the days of Moses; were in a modified form incorporated in the teachings of the Hebrews, and so passed down into the doctrines of the Christian Church. They are an appanage of the belief in immortality, and mark the boundary to which the human mind can soar. But when we come to question the why and wherefore, we are seeking a deeper revelation of God's purposes than he has been pleased to give us. John 3:13 must not be separated from its preceding verse. No one can explain or throw light on spiritual conditions without having first entered into such spirituality for himself or herself, neither can such teaching or explanation be understood or accepted by any who themselves have not so entered. This is why materialistic ideas of a future state still so universally prevail. See Eph. 4:9, 10.

535. Should a Christian Dread the Thought of a Hereafter?

One who does should pray for more faith, and keep the fact constantly in mind that he who has promised cannot lie. Professor David Smith expresses this attitude very clearly and convincingly. He says: "If we were truly Christian, we would be less concerned about this question of the hereafter, for we would have a larger and braver trust in God. There is nothing more calming than recognition of the fact that it is not God that condemns, but sin. God is our Saviour, and his thoughts towards every creature of his hand are thoughts of good, and not of evil. If any perish, it is in spite of him. He is the Father of us all; and when I think what has been shown us of his heart by his eternal Son, our Brother and Lord, Jesus Christ, I am not afraid of anything that he may do, and I am well content to leave my future in his hands. He will do for every child of his undying affection the best that love can devise. Why should we fret or fear? God knows, and he is our Father."

536. Will More Souls Be Lost than Saved?

It is impossible to answer with any degree of authority. God alone knows who are lost or saved. One factor, however, that may tend to a solution of it is, that we are assured that there will come a time when the whole world will acknowledge Christ's sway. As the population of the world increases from year to year, we may assume that at that time, whenever it occurs, there will be more people on earth than at any preceding period in the world's history, which will materially add to the total number who are saved. The question is not one that is of profit. Christ did not encourage speculation on the subject. When the question was put to him he would not answer it, but gave the questioner practical advice. (See Luke 13:23.)

537. Shall We Know Each Other in the Future Life?

We find the assurance of heavenly recognition in a number of passages both in the Old Testament and New Testament. David said of his dead son: "I shall go to him, but he shall not return to me" (II Sam. 12:23). See also the parable of Dives and Lazarus, which teaches recognition. See Phil. 3:20; Heb. 12:1; Matt. 17:3; Rev. 6:9, 10; Rom. 14:12; Luke 16:23; Rev. 6:9, 10; I Thess. 4:13-18; Heb. 13:17; Matt. 8:11; Eph. 3:15. These and other passages indicate the preservation of identity. We have no reason to doubt that the redeemed will know each other, that pure friendship begun on earth will there be perfected, that we shall know the saints and our own dear ones. Heaven is the Christian's fatherland, where we shall see our friends and know them.

538. What Will Heaven Be Like?

Of heaven itself and the blessedness in the life to come, we know only what is revealed in the Scriptures, and it is not possible, from such limited knowledge, to form any adequate conception. The Bible describes the happiness of heaven in general terms. See Rom. 8:18, 22; II Cor. 4:17, 18. It is described as a kingdom (Matt. 25:1); as a place of rest; as a place where knowledge will go on to perfection, and as a state in which the saints will dwell together. It will be a place of complete felicity, where the enjoyment will be heightened by friendly intercourse. It is further described as having a city with everlasting foundations; a place of innumerable homes (see John 14:2); a place where we shall meet our loved ones and our children (see II Sam. 12:23; Luke 16:25). John in Rev. 22 tells us of the "pure river of water of life" and "the tree of life with its abundance of fruits." Beyond these little is disclosed; but we have enough to assure us that it is a place of great happiness (see I Cor. 2:9); of blessed reunions where there are eternal youth and strength and where sorrow, sighing, pain and the afflictions that wound us in this life are unknown.

539. Shall We Have Work to Do in Heaven?

A life without occupation is inconceivable. One of the great equipments for such occupation will be the enjoyment of perpetual youth—implying strength for service. Unquestionably it will be a life of intense activity—a busy place, with high avocations suited to the varied degrees of skill and to the endowments of the redeemed. Throughout the Scriptures, all evidences point to the conclusion that it is to be a life of activity, progress and spiritual development on the highest lines, when we have the assurance that God is himself a ceaseless worker (see John 5:17). Besides, in Heb. 1:14, it is clearly intimated that the redeemed will be actively engaged in carrying on the Lord's work, by a ministry to those who need help and consolation. They serve God continually (Rev. 7:15), and doubtless in a great variety of ways. "There is not the least reason to suppose," writes an able commentator, "that God will abolish this variety (of talent and abilities) in the future world; it will rather continue there, in all its extent. We must suppose that there will be, even in the heavenly world, a diversity of tastes, of labors, and of employments, and that to one person this, to another that field, in the boundless kingdom of truth and of useful occupation, will be assigned for his cultivation, according to his peculiar powers, qualifications, and tastes." This is the view now generally accepted by the Christian Church throughout the world.

540. What of Wives and Husbands in Heaven?

A similar question was put to Christ (Matt. 22:23-30). You will see how he answered it. We know very little of the conditions of life in the spirit. We cannot easily conceive of life apart from the body, yet it is obvious that there is such life. Christ's answer to his questioners appears to imply that the material relationships of life are left behind, and that while we shall recognize one another, there will be such a purification and elevation of being that all idea of marriage will be lost in the sublimity of spiritual life. In Luke 20:27-40, Jesus was questioned on a similar topic and was replying to questions about the resurrection. Marriage was ordained to perpetuate the human family; but as there will be no breaches by death in the future state, the ordinance will cease and man will be *like the angels* in his immortal nature. This immortality, however, referred only to "those who shall be counted worthy."

541. How Can One Be Happy in Heaven if He Knows His Dear Ones Are Lost?

It is difficult, in view of the very little we know about heaven and the life of those admitted there, to conceive of their feelings and condition. All that we do know indicates a condition of happiness; that is certain. It may be that in the presence of God righteousness becomes so paramount a consideration, and sin is seen to be so dreadful and heinous a thing that the redeemed and purified soul shrinks from it as utterly loathsome, even when it exists in persons he loved in his earthly life. Pure souls may seem nearer to one in heaven than impure souls, though they may have had an earthly relationship. Christ being told that his mother and brethren desired to speak to him, said (Matt. 12:50): "Whosoever shall do the will of my Father the same is my brother and sister and mother," as much as to say that spiritual likeness counted for more with him than physical relationship. Redeemed souls, in becoming like him, therefore, may not suffer such poignant sorrow as to us now seems inevitable.

542. Shall We See God in Heaven?

There are several passages in the Bible which make clear statements on this subject. See Luke 1:19; Rev. 5:8, 11; Jude 24; Matt. 5:8; Isaiah 33:17; Job 19:26, 27; I John 3:2, and others.

543. Are There Degrees in Heaven?

There are several passages that would seem to indicate the probability of degrees. Daniel's famous passage relative to the soul-winners who will "shine as the stars forever" is one; Paul implies a similar diversity when he speaks of one star differing from another in glory; so did Jesus in his reply to the two disciples for whom it was asked that they should sit at his right and left hand in his kingdom. The parable of the talents also bears a kindred interpretation.

544. Will Infants Be Saved?

In the passage in Rom. 5:18 the sin of Adam and the merits of Christ are pronounced as co-extensive;

the words in both cases are practically identical: "Judgment came upon all men" and "the free gift came upon all men." If the whole human race be included in the condemnation for original sin, then the whole race must also be included in the justification through Christ's sacrifice. Children dying in infancy, before the age of understanding or moral responsibility, are all partakers of this inclusive justification. Were it otherwise, a very large proportion of the human race would have no share in this "free gift," but would be condemned for sin which they never committed, which is contrary to the divine characteristics of love and justice, contrary to the apostolic teachings, and contrary to the spirit and language of the Master himself, who said of the innocent children: "Of such is the kingdom of heaven." This is the general attitude of theology today on this matter. Faith always presupposes knowledge and power to exercise it, and as a little child has neither, it has no moral responsibility. Even so stern a theologian as Calvin held practically this view. Any other conception of God would make him a Moloch instead of a loving Father.

545. What Will Be the Status of Infants in Heaven?

The only pertinent passage we recall is the incident of David and his infant child (II Sam. 12:23), in which he expressed the belief that he would go to him. Evidently he expected joy in meeting the child and expected recognition. Christ made an enigmatical remark about the angels of children (Matt. 18:10), as if implying that children had angels as their guardians in heaven. Then, too, he took a child and set him before his disciples with the words: "Of such is the kingdom of heaven" (Matt. 19:14). In the spiritual state, when the body is left behind, there is no question of growth. It is a matter of development. What condition then is so favorable to a beautiful development as the atmosphere of heaven? That must be a very beautiful nature, which never having sinned, has grown up in heaven in such society as exists there. There is no reason to suppose that the future life will be other than one of progress, and this would imply progress in growth in every direction. We can only conjecture, however, what that growth will mean in the spiritual world.

546. Will the Heathen Be Lost? What does Scripture teach on the Subject?

The greatest minds in religion and philosophy have discussed the fate of the unevangelized heathen. Justin Martyr and Clement held that they were called justified and saved by their philosophy and their virtuous lives under natural law. Zwingle contended that the heathen who had never been evangelized would be forgiven through the merits of Christ, although they had never heard of him. Christ himself said (Matt. 11:20-24) that the wicked but ignorant people of ancient Sodom and Gomorrah (who lived long before the Gospel age) would be more tolerantly dealt with than those who had heard the Gospel and rejected it. Paul (Rom. 2:14, 26, 27) shows that those not having either the law or the Gospel "may be a law unto themselves." We cannot therefore assert that the heathen who died in ignorance of Christ are beyond the reach of the Divine mercy, although we may not know in what form that mercy may be extended. In every age and every land God had his witnesses in the person of good men and women, whose upright lives, even under natural law, were a blessing to those around them. Who shall say that such are not acceptable to him? (See Acts 10:35.) The whole question of heathen salvation is one concerning which no one has a right to dogmatize. It should be left in God's hands. John Wesley wrote on this subject: "We have no authority from the Word of God to judge 'those that are without'," and he also wrote, toward the close of his ministry, "He that feareth God and worketh righteousness according to the light he has, is acceptable to God." (See Rom. 4:9.) God, who will judge all, will not judge unjustly. Every person will be judged according to the light he has had. There is no explicit statement as to the condition of the heathen who died without hearing the Gospel, and there was no reason why God should tell us what he does in respect to them. As, however, we are told that there is no way of attaining eternal life except through Christ, there is abundant and urgent reason for the church to make earnest effort to carry the Gospel to those who have not heard it. The heathen are in God's hand; it would be presumption on our part to say what he will do with them. It is sufficient for us to know that it is our duty to preach the word of salvation "to every creature." We can see no way in which salvation can come to those who died without the Gospel; but that does not prove that, in the infinite resources of God's compassion, there is no way.

547. Does Not the Revelation of God's Love Make the Doctrine of Hell Incredible?

Not in all its aspects. God has not revealed definitely what kind of place the abode of the lost is, but merely that it is a place of weeping, gnashing of teeth and intense suffering, typified by burning. The idea is not inconsistent with what we know of sin here. We know the kind of a life a young man will lead in his premature old age if he gives himself to vice in his youth. However loving his father may be, he cannot save the lad from physical suffering if he persists in evil courses. He can only warn him, and God does that with his children. We have no ground given us for expecting that God will give another opportunity, although he may do so, for there are no limits to his mercy; but it is an awful risk to run. Our duty is to accept the opportunity that is offered now and not to speculate on the possibility of there being another. The terms of the offer read to us like those of a final offer. We cannot conceive of God being inconsistent. The punishment of the impenitent seems to be not so much an infliction by God, as the result of choice on the part of the sufferer. You may have seen a boy at school, in spite of all warnings and all advice, neglect his lessons and give his time to play and idleness. Can he blame his teacher or his parents, if at the end of his school life he is ignorant and is unfit for a profession? If a young man voluntarily associates with men of foul life and coarse manners and acquires their habits, do you blame a refined lady if she excludes him from her home? If a child who has been warned against touching a hot stove and has had the consequences explained to him, avails himself of a brief absence of his mother to lay his hand on the glowing metal, he must not blame his mother when he suffers. If he is so badly burned that he loses his hand, he goes through life maimed because of that momentary act. We do not blame the mother, or charge her with being inconsistent. All her love cannot save him from the consequences of his own perversity. When a man deliberately chooses sin after being warned of the consequences, and refuses the offer of pardon and regeneration, what is to be expected as to his future? Still, we are not to judge others, and above all we should not attempt to set limits to the Divine mercy.

548. Is There Any Bible Warrant for Believing in Repentance after Death?

The well-known passage "That at the name of Jesus every knee should bow, of things in heaven and things in earth and things under the earth" (Phil. 2:10), has been construed by some to imply that there may be repentance after death. It rather implies a confession of Christ's supremacy and triumph. We can imagine a man dying impenitent, realizing afterwards how foolish as well as how wicked he has been. You remember that in the parable of Dives and Lazarus (Luke 16:27, 28), the rich man was so convinced of his folly that he begged for his brothers to be warned, lest they, too, should be lost. James, too (2:19), says that the devils believe and tremble. It is not so much a question of whether there is repentance after death, as whether repentance avails then. It is not for us to limit the mercy of God, but there is nothing in the Bible to encourage the hope of there being an opportunity of gaining salvation after death. Any man postponing repentance till then, runs an appalling risk against which he is emphatically warned. That there is no chance for repentance after death cannot be absolutely proved, but the trend of Bible teaching is in that direction. The passage (Ecc. 11:3), "If the tree fall toward the north," etc., is often quoted in proof, but the inference is not decisive. So also is Rev. 22:11, "He that is filthy, let him be filthy still," etc., which is more to the purpose, but not absolute proof. Another passage implying the hopelessness of the lost is Luke 16:26, "Between us and you there is a great gulf fixed, so that they which would pass from hence to you, cannot," etc. The burden of proof, however, seems to be on those who contend that there is opportunity of repentance after death. Where there are such momentous issues at stake, a man must have very positive assurance of there being the opportunity before he decides to run the risk, and he does not appear to us to have any ground at all.

549. What Is the Paradise Which Jesus Promised the Repentant Thief?

Jesus' answer to the appeal of the penitent thief on the cross "gave him what he needed most—the assurance of rest and peace. The word 'paradise' meant to him repose and shelter, the greatest contrast possible to the thirst and agony and shame of the hours upon the cross." Paul speaks of degrees of heavenly exaltation (II Cor. 12:3), and the religious teaching of the Jews of that day taught this. The promise spoken by the Saviour, however we may interpret it, conveyed to the penitent the assurance that his future place would be one best fitted for him, and beyond this it is useless to speculate.

550. Does the Soul Exist Apart from the Body after Death?

Paul evidently looked forward to such a condition when he said that he was willing to be absent from the body and present with the Lord (II Cor. 5:8). He refers to the subject again in I Thess. 4:14, when he speaks of Christ bringing with him before the resurrection them who sleep in him. John saw (Rev. 6:10) the souls of the martyrs under the altar, clearly without their bodies. The parable of Dives and Lazarus (Luke 16:19-31) implies that the resurrection had not taken place when Dives made his petition to Abraham, inasmuch as the five brothers were still living. The corrected translation of the well-known passage in Job 19:26, makes it read, "Yet *without* my flesh shall I see God." These are a few of the passages directly implying the doctrine, though there are teachers, very sincere in their belief, who put another construction on the passages, and others making them harmonize with the doctrine that the soul has no separate existence.

551. Will There Be a Millennium and What Will It Be Like?

There are some Christians who do not look for a personal reign of Christ on the earth. Those who do so, base their belief chiefly on such passages as Rev. 20:4-6: "They shall be priests of God and of Christ, and shall reign with him a thousand years." Isaiah 2:3, which describes the extent of Christ's dominion. Isaiah 11:9, which describes the change of disposition in the animal creation. Zech. 14:16-21, which predicts the supremacy and purity of his reign and Heb. 8:10, 11, promising the universal acceptance of Christianity. Besides these, there are the promises to Abraham of the possession by his descendants of an area they have never yet possessed, and those that Christ would occupy the throne of David. The Scriptures do not give clear or definite accounts of the conditions of life in the millennium, but we infer that it will be a time of extraordinary conversion, and that great multitudes will be born again in a day. (See Micah 4:2; Is. 2:2-4.) See Rev. 20:4, 5. The apostle appears to teach (I Cor. 15:35-52) that a new spiritual body will be given in place of the one that has turned to dust.

552. Have Angels Wings?

There is little positive Scriptural authority for the popular conception of the angelic form as endowed with wings. The "angels" of the Bible, who visited men, seem to have appeared in the human form, and were often accepted and entertained as men until, through the utterance of some remarkable prophecy or the manifestation of some supernatural quality, their spiritual nature was disclosed. The fact that they were "messengers" of God, may have supplied basis for the idea that they have wings as a means of swift and ethereal progression. The winged cherubim and seraphim seem to belong to a higher order of celestial beings than those designated "angels," since they are always represented as standing in the immediate presence of God in heaven or guarding his dwelling-place on earth. The golden cherubim watching over the mercy-seat in the ark of the covenant were four-winged, so were those mighty figures under whose outstretched pinions the ark was placed in Solomon's Temple. Four-winged were the "living creatures" of Ezekiel's dream, "who every one went straight forward whither the spirit was to go." Six-winged were the seraphim of Isaiah's vision, who stood above the "Throne of the Lord," crying, "Holy, holy, holy is the Lord of hosts"—almost the same song which later the four-winged "beasts" of Revelation cried day and night before the Throne.

553. What Is Meant By "a New Heaven and a New Earth"?

Rev. 21 gives a vivid description of the "new heaven and new earth." It has been a fruitful subject of comment, some holding that the earth, having been cursed by sin, will be redeemed, regenerated, purified, and transformed by the "second Adam" and made a fit dwelling-place for the righteous, where the law of love shall prevail and God shall be all in all. The "new heaven" is interpreted to mean the firmament above us. Thus the "new creation" is interpreted to mean the restoration of the physical universe as the final abode of glorified, deathless and sinless humanity. Others hold that the teaching is clear that the present earth is to be literally destroyed, and that the promise of a new heaven and a new earth will be fulfilled, as he hath said: "Behold I make all things new."

554. What Is to Be Understood by the Silence Mentioned in Rev. 8:1?

While the whole book of Revelation is of that literary character which may be described as mystical, dealing extensively in types and metaphors, there are occasional passages in which the writer descends to simpler language for the purpose of more clearly conveying his meaning. The half hour of silence in heaven at the breaking of the last seal is not to be reckoned by minutes and seconds, but is purely a figure of speech. It is meant to convey to the mind a long, solemn pause by way of introduction to the joys and activities of the eternal Sabbath rest of God's people, which begins with the reading of the sealed book. The preceding chapters have run through the course of Divine action, where everything unites in a solemn hush for the final act. In the ancient Jewish temple, the instrumental music and singing, which formed the first part of the service, were hushed immediately before the offering of the incense, so this pause immediately precedes the adoration of the blessed spirits and the angels and the imminent unfolding of God's judgment. See similar figurative expressions in Rev. 17:12, 18:10, 19.

555. What Becomes of the Soul in the Interval between Death and the Resurrection?

There are three passages from which an inference may be drawn, in the absence of an explicit statement in the Bible. The first of these is Christ's assurance to the penitent thief (Luke 23:43): "This day shalt thou be with me in Paradise." We are not sure what Paradise meant, but it was evidently a place of conscious existence, if it was not heaven itself. A second passage is contained in the parable of Dives and Lazarus (Luke 16:19-31). Some allowance must be made for the form of picture teaching Christ used, but he certainly described the rich man as being conscious and being able to see, hear, speak and feel at a time when his brothers were alive upon earth. This indicated a conscious existence for the soul prior to the resurrection. The third passage is Paul's expression of a desire for death (Phil. 1:23). He wished "to depart and to be with Christ." It is not likely that he would have had such a wish if he expected to sleep until the resurrection. So active and energetic a man would have wished to live and work for Christ rather than to lie unconscious in the grave. He clearly expected that as soon as he died he would be with Christ. These are a few of the statements from which the inference is drawn that man goes immediately after death to his reward and does not wait for the resurrection. It is not clear that Paul expected a resurrection of the body at all. He expected to receive a new body (I Cor. 15:37)—not the body that was laid in the grave.

INDEX OF CONTENTS

Index of Contents

Index of Contents

Index of Contents

Index of Contents

Index of Contents

Index of Contents

Index of Contents

Index of Contents

Index of Contents

Index of Contents